The Nature of Reality

AKASHIC GUIDANCE FOR UNDERSTANDING LIFE AND ITS PURPOSE

Aingeal Rose O'Grady

Hi Cas!
Sending you unlimited love + Blessings!
Aingeal Rose

Wild Flower Press
P.O. Box 1429
Columbus, NC 28722

Series Information
Second in the Honest-To-God Series

Library of Congress Cataloging-in-Publication Data

O'Grady, Aingeal Rose, 1953-
The nature of reality: akashic guidance for understanding life and its purpose / Aingeal Rose O'Grady.
pages cm -- (Honest-to-god; Volume II)
Includes index.
ISBN 978-0-926524-73-6 -- ISBN 978-0-926524-98-9 (e-Book
1. Akashic records. I. Title.
BF1045.A44O36 2014
133.9--dc23
2014004018

Interior Artwork: AHONU
Cover Artwork: rights received from Shutterstock.com
Manuscript Editor: Brian L. Crissey
Manuscript Designer: Pamela Meyer

Printed in the United States of America.

Address all inquiries to:
Wild Flower Press, an imprint of Granite Publishing
P.O. Box 1429
Columbus, NC 28722
http://granite-planet.net

DEDICATION

I dedicate this book to the empowering
Presence that is our God within
the ever-constant, encouraging spark of Divinity
that answers the call of
every question, every problem, every quest—
The unfailing love and wisdom that takes us eternally
higher and leads us Home.

My love—my love—to you I pledge my devotion.

ACKNOWLEDGEMENTS

Since the release of my first book, *A Time of Change*, I have had the good fortune to talk with and meet many wonderful people dedicated to the empowerment and awakening of humankind. They come in all shapes and sizes, and they are male and female, young, middle aged and old, naïve and wise, troubled and happy. They are opening their hearts and minds to Truth, willing to be participants and creators of a new world—a world that works for all of us and is based on love, cooperation, harmony and peace.

I am privileged to witness their most intimate thoughts and feelings, their fears and strengths, their humanity. I can say with certainty that they are true people, loving and wanting to be loved, caring a great deal about our world and willing to learn and change. It is because of them I have had the opportunity to write my second book, *The Nature of Reality*. Their dedication to growth has fueled many stimulating questions of Source, allowing for an incredible acceleration in wisdom and knowledge for us all.

I acknowledge them, along with my beloved AHONU, who has worked tirelessly to prepare our meetings with Source each week since 2009. He has edited and produced the recordings and the profound statements each week among other numerous tasks, and has done it with a smile and unfailing love for this work! Thank you my beloved! I also acknowledge with unending gratitude my publicist, Eileen Duhné and Pam and Brian Crissey, my publishers. Without them, you would not have seen these pages in print, nor would I have had the pleasure of sharing my experiences with Source with all of you! Unending thanks and blessings for all your work!

Aingeal Rose O'Grady
San Diego, Calif.

TABLE OF CONTENTS

Preface

We humans are an interesting species. We are a conglomeration of races, nationalities, genetics and beliefs. Some of us, it is believed, have come from other planets and solar systems, making us aliens in human bodies. Rumors suggest that our human body was genetically created or modified by others from distant stars. Surely, we are still trying to understand how we were made, how the diversity of life of which we are so intricately a part came to be. Nature itself is still a mystery—its power, intelligence and ability to continue to produce life and balance itself is quite remarkable, given the extreme attacks on it from toxins, fires, oil spills, pollutants, radiation leaks, and weather modifications. To see orchids growing out of rocks and burnt ground producing lush, tropical foliage is quite miraculous. How our bodies work is still challenging scientists. The answers to thought, healing, miracles, creation, consciousness, evolution, and the purpose of life are all still on the table for understanding.

This second volume in the Honest-to-God series continues our journey with Source by exploring questions like those above. Understanding life and its purpose is revealed among the transcripts herein. In exploring topics such as God and Original Creation, Time and Dimensions, the Brain, Kundalini, and the Chakras, we have discovered our ascent into becoming God-Man. We have understood the meaning and purpose of our lives, which encompass not only the delight of creation itself, but also the evolution of our nature into our God presence and the joyful responsibility of being co-creators with one another and the forces of Nature. We find how much we have underestimated ourselves and our potential, and we see how we have turned ourselves inside out by focusing so much outside ourselves.

Source's consistent message throughout *The Nature of Reality* is to remind us of the rich *internal* environment of our body and consciousness. We see by these discourses that we haven't even begun to touch the surface of our innate divinity. The good news is that we have been given many ways to begin the discovery of ourselves; it can be done at any age, and it is not dependent on religion, race, upbringing, or past.

It is my desire that you will find joy and encouragement in these pages and that you will embrace your True Self in all its glory. Thank you for sharing this journey with me!

Aingeal Rose
May, 2014

Explanation
of the Back Cover Image

Whenever I begin a new book, I always go into the Akashic Records and ask Source to give me the image of the cover. The image on the opposite page is the one I received for this book. When I received it, I didn't know what its meaning was, even though I trust what I receive 100%. We put the image in a folder to be reviewed later, after finishing the book. Even though we have chosen a different image for the cover of this book, we saw the amazing importance of the original image and had to include it here. It is literally, the Stairway to Heaven.

The subject matter in this second volume of the Honest-To-God series unfolded to reveal our inner journey to becoming God-Man. It explains the purpose for life and the amazing way it is constructed, ensuring that the potential for evolution and God realization is inherent in the design of every life form according to its level of evolution. We, as humans, are very fortunate to have an unlimited potential for awareness and ascension into higher realms of consciousness! We even have a quality of God within us that allows us the potential for biological transformation and ascension.

The image on the opposite page reveals this potential within us to become God realized. It shows us a pyramidal structure with steps leading upward, showing us our path into our ascended "sun" state. The stairs are pink and white, indicating that this path is one of purity of desire and intention. Indeed, purification is a major part of the success of this process. That the pyramid is gold is no accident. It suggests that we become a permanent, refined essence—as indestructible and magnificent as God Itself.

The blue color beneath the stairs shows us the Truth that what is above is also below, and also that the structure of the pyramid journey has an inner counterpart, or complement, below the surface. On the way, we encounter parts of ourselves that need to be brought to conscious awareness and refined—those parts that are hidden from our conscious awareness. The blue indicates that the achievement of inner peace is an important part of our ascent.

Finally, the gold and silver spheres at the top and bottom and sides of the pyramid show us the perfect balance that is needed between male and female, electrical and magnetic, vertical and horizontal. This image also sym-bolizes the Mer-Ka-Ba geometries of which we are composed. However, the exploration of the Mer-Ka-Ba fields is for another book!

DEFINITION OF MER-KA-BA

History has talked about the Mer-Ka-Ba mostly as the vehicle that allows a person to ascend or descend into the higher or lower worlds. But actually the Mer-Ka-Ba is much more than just a vehicle of ascension. It can be, really, anything—since it is the primal pattern that created all things and all universes, both visible and invisible (see *The Ancient Secret of the Flower of Life*, Vols. I & II).

In ancient Egypt, this primal pattern was called the Mer-Ka-Ba. It was actually three words, not one. Mer meant a kind of light that rotated within itself. Ka meant spirit, in this case referring to the human spirit. And Ba meant the human body—although it also could mean the concept of Real-ity that spirit holds. And so the entire composite word in ancient Egypt referred to a rotating light that would take the spirit and the body from one world into another.

Explanation of Terms

Within this book I refer to God as: God, God Source, Creator, Source, All That Is and Prime Creator—all refer to the Originator of love and life.

Source makes a point to describe our perception of ego as alter ego. This is because, in the discussion about consciousness, Source defines the EGO as our True Spirit Selves. EGO being capitalized emphasizes our self-realized identity. Therefore, alter ego is used to define the small self or made-up identity.

Collapse—a natural event caused by something suddenly falling down.

Gravitational collapse—the implosion of a star resulting from its own gravity resulting in a smaller and denser celestial object.

mind (small m)—describes the small self or alter ego denoting the identity we've made up to replace our true identity in God. True healing cannot occur at the mind level, as it is not the *originator* of concepts—the individuated spirit is.

mind field—a substance of creation that takes thoughts and ideas and turns them into concepts, allowing for perception to occur. Perceived as reality.

Spirit—the *essence* of which all life is created, which is perfect in its *composition or "order,"* but *not* perfect in its *individuation* into the diversity of life forms. This imperfection could be the result of the splitting off into various life forms, but it is clear that each individuated spirit is on its own journey or evolution back to God realization or "Home."

Implosion—a sudden inward collapse; "the implosion of a light bulb."

Individuated spirit—the thinker, the decider and the observer, can be injured and traumatized. Because it is individuated, it has experiences that affect how it sees and thinks of itself for good or ill. The "self concept" is made at the level of the individuated spirit.

Soul—the *accumulation* or record of an individuated spirit's journey —its successes and challenges. Inherent in this is the individuated spirit's levels of personal mastery—what it has gained—on its journey to God realization.

About the
Akashic Records

Q. WHAT IS SOURCE'S DEFINITION OF THE *AKASHIC RECORDS*?

A. It is a field of information like streams of color or spheres of light, and not necessarily language. It is similar to different frequency bands of information that vibrate as different colors or resonate as sounds. It is part of the collective unconscious where everything that ever was or ever will be resides. It is the same as saying that it is the "All That Is." Once something is added to it, it *is*—in other words—it *exists*. Once something exists, it is there in the "Field," and it registers as different colors or frequencies of information.

Q. IF ALL TIME IS SIMULTANEOUS, HOW DOES IT REGISTER SOMETHING AS HAVING "HAPPENED"?

A. Once something has happened, it is there. It doesn't have a distinction with time; it is rather part of the whole, which is timeless. It does not distinguish among past, present, or future—it just *is*.

Q. WHAT'S THE PURPOSE OF THE AKASHIC RECORDS?

A. The Akashic Records are for God's pleasure and our pleasure. It is the same as asking "What's the purpose of existence?" because they are one and the same. The Akashic Records are records of existence—of everything that exists, and existence is for God's pleasure.

Q. ARE THE RECORDS OPEN TO ANYONE ALL OF THE TIME OR ARE SOME RECORDS CLOSED OR SEALED?

A. God's information is open to everyone and is free to everyone. There are no closed Records. However, if you are not at a sufficient level of consciousness, there are Records you cannot access or read. Since they are a collection of *frequencies*, your ability to access the memory, or the "All That Is," is determined by your own state of consciousness.

Q. ARE THERE SPECIFIC "RULES" TO ACCESS THESE RECORDS?

A. There are no rules *per se*, however it is a field of *vibration,* and accessibility is a function of your own motives and levels of awareness. So the "rules" are—you can't access "the Field" unless you resonate at its frequency.

Q. ARE THERE SPECIFIC PRAYERS TO ACCESS THE RECORDS, OR WOULD AN INTENTION SUFFICE?

A. There is more than one prayer that can be said, but more than that, it is about your *intention* or your *purpose* for accessing the Records. Anyone with harmful intentions cannot access higher frequencies. The advantage of certain prayers is that they will uplift you to higher frequencies *temporarily.* Your ability to align yourself to those frequencies will determine how able you are to read the Records. Specific prayers do make a difference.

Q. ARE CERTAIN PEOPLE BETTER ABLE TO ACCESS THE RECORDS THAN OTHERS, AND IF SO, HOW DOES THIS AFFECT THE INFORMATION COMING THROUGH?

A. Yes, certain people are able to access the Records better than others, which affects the *translation* coming through in the down-stepping process. It depends on an individual's own filters of consciousness—*i.e.* their opinions and belief systems may taint the purity of what they can receive.

You can teach a prayer to anyone, and that prayer can help them reach a certain frequency level, but how *able* that person is to *match* that frequency or down-step the information is a function of their own abilities. The exception to this would be to go into a hypnotic state similar to Edgar Cayce, where the perceptual filters are bypassed and would not be interfering. Keep in mind, however, that with the hypnotic process, the translator could be susceptible to wear and tear on his mind and body if he or she is not *naturally* attuned to certain higher frequencies.

Q. CAN YOU PREDICT THE FUTURE IN THE RECORDS?

A. In the Akashic Records you can see probable futures. By this is meant that there are an infinite number of possibilities or "time lines" that offer future potentials. When we see a "probable future" in the Records, it is showing a possible future outcome if no change is made. However, a "probable future" is not etched in stone—it is only a *potential* based on consciousness at the time the question is being asked.

Q. CAN THE RECORDS BE CHANGED?

A. No, they can only be *added* to. For example, let's say science/technology has discovered a way to go back into the past and change an event. The original event is still recorded as it happened. You can't go back and take something out of existence once it has existed. What you *can* do is create a *new* event in a certain time period, but you are not taking away the old event. You are *adding* to the existing event or time period. This can be done because thought is creative, and in the realm of thought, time, space and distance do not exist.

It is easy to go to an event and create a new scenario with your mind. Because you are thinking and visualizing it, it is added to the Field. You have now created another possible time line with a different outcome in a certain time period. In the thought field, your visualization is being registered in the "place" or "time" of your intention.

Q. CAN YOU ERASE YOUR OWN RECORDS?

A. No, you can't erase your own Records. Nothing is ever lost, but what you can erase is any *attachment* you may have to an event, time period, experience, person, *etc.* When we talk about erasing the Records, we are talking about erasing the "charge" that's attached to them. It is a way of reconciling your past. Think of it as psychic energy or cords that you may have to certain aspects of your personal history—some might call it "karma."

It is desirable to go back into your own past and make peace with it. It is still recorded as memory, but there are no longer any cords or unforgiven issues. You don't really erase it out of the "Library," but you do erase the *attachment* or anything left undone or not forgiven. By forgiving you add another timeline and another time period to the event.

We were talking about the Records being frequencies. Any frequencies that lock parts of you "in place" or anchor you to a certain event or time period need to be reconciled. That way your "time stream" is clean—it becomes frequencies of beautiful, ribbons of harmonious colors, as opposed to frequencies that would keep you locked in a place or time and cause you to reincarnate.

For example, you really wouldn't want a prior lifetime still affecting you today, keeping you from being free. This is what is interesting about reading your own Records or your own "Book"—you can see where you still have things to resolve. You can also see what you've *gained*—you can get a good measure of yourself.

Q. WHERE ARE THE RECORDS LOCATED?

A. Everywhere, throughout all existence. Even though the word *Akasha* implies a plane of Spirit, the truth is that the living field of information is recorded throughout all of existence, even in the cells of your body.

Q. ARE THE RECORDS IN DIFFERENT LOCATIONS FOR DIFFERENT UNIVERSES, OR ARE THEY ALL IN THE SAME PLACE?

A. Again, it is about frequency. In one sense you could say that everything exists simultaneously, but you would not necessarily have *access* to every universe if you are not vibrationally compatible to it. Each person's Records are contained within the fields where they resonate and have had experiences.

Q. CAN ANYBODY GET INTO YOUR PERSONAL RECORDS?

A. Yes, if they can access your frequency,. No, if their intention is not honorable or if there are lessons personal to you that need self-discovery. In those cases a blank wall of energy will appear, preventing them from reading.

The Records have their own safeguard against persons whose intentions are not honorable, in that such people's frequencies will not be high enough to access the Records. Anyone trying to read another's Records without their permission is not acting honorably. In principle, the Records are open books, but not in application. It's a perfect system.

Q. WHO ARE THE "LORDS" OF THE RECORDS?

A. They are beings whose job is to "guard" the Records, meaning that they make sure that each person's Records do not get mixed vibrationally with another's. They are *not* beings who demand any kind of permission. The Records have their own safeguards against impure intent.

Q. HOW DOES THAT MAKE SENSE IF WE'RE ALL THE SAME—IF AT A SPIRITUAL LEVEL WE'RE ALL ONE? WHY WOULD THERE BE BEINGS TO KEEP US SEPARATE IF WE ARE MEANT TO BE UNIFIED?

A. Each individual spirit is on its own journey to self-realization. You are misunderstanding "unified" or "one." Unity does not mean everyone dissolves into one thing. Unified means "in harmony with." It means that you understand that everything is in relationship with everything else—we all affect each other—it's a unified field in that way—but it doesn't mean that you don't have individuality. It is like the definition of love—love is the field of all that is—it doesn't mean that it is one big identity in which you lose yours.

Q. IS THE NAME "LORDS" AN APPROPRIATE NAME FOR THEM?

A. Yes—the name "lord" in this case means "overseer" or guardian. It does not refer to any kind of adoration or hierarchy.

Q. DO YOU NEED TO ASK THESE LORDS FOR PERMISSION TO ACCESS THESE RECORDS?

A. No. Their job to keep the Records in order. The permission to gain access is asked of the *person being read*, and it is they and their own higher aspects that agree to this.

Q. ARE THERE DIFFERENT LEVELS OF RECORDS, AND IF SO, WHERE ARE THEY AND WHAT DO THEY PERTAIN TO?

A. There are different levels of Records in that there are different universes and differing frequency ranges in those universes. The levels pertain to the experiences of those universes wherever they are, but the information is accessible by anyone, anywhere.

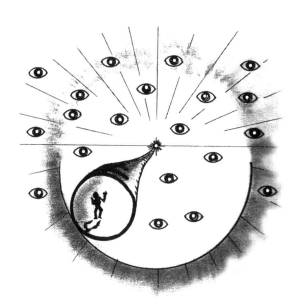

Chapter 1

God & Original Creation

As I'm saying the opening prayer, I'm being transported upward into a vast field of crystal-clear light, which is appearing as crystalline, undulating waves of light. I have a very ethereal and lofty sensation going all through my body.

Q. HOW DID *CREATION* BEGIN, AND WILL IT EVER END?

A. I am being immersed in an incredible sea of life-force energy and vibration, and I am being raised up higher and higher. I feel much love—so much love—and I am moving into a massive place of love. I'm feeling deep desire and love. Creation has a lot to do with love and desire.

Maybe you can all imagine this with me. Imagine yourself floating in a sea of beautiful colors and waveforms. They are undulating, and they are everywhere—beautiful undulating waves of light and color; and as I'm moving into that, I'm feeling incredible love and desire. That's all I'm surrounded by.

Creation first came into being by Creator's love and desire. This feeling is so very powerful, and I don't see that it will ever end. Once the desire for creation was, it became a permanent intention and function. It will never end, and I just keep seeing more and more desire and more and more love. This is intense love; it is just so incredible! I'm going to use the word creation simultaneously with the word life. I am feeling the desire for life to be expressed, which is what creation is.

Q. WHO OR WHAT IS *GOD SOURCE*?

A. Please bear with me, because I am being transported to a very different frequency. I am moving into a gigantic white sun. This sun is pure white light. There is no yellow or red in it. It's white and it's not solid. I'm entering into this beautiful, huge, radiating sphere of white light, and now I'm entering a tunnel or hallway. I'm now in it, and I'm walking down a hallway with rounded walls.

I can hear sound tones as I walk, and the frequency here is making me shake a little. The intense feeling of love is bringing tears to my eyes. I'm hearing incredible sounds that are echoing in my head and even in my ears and in my breathing. There's a breath in this hallway as I'm walking, like a soft and peaceful rhythm. I am still in the tunnel in this hallway, surrounded by this breathing rhythm that I'm feeling through every cell of my body. I'm also aware of a reflective quality here almost as if I'm surrounded by mirrors, but I'm not surrounded by mirrors. I'm aware that the sides of this hallway all feel reflective. I'm emerging now out into vast fields of beautiful, bright white light. It's alive, and I'm engulfed in millions and billions of eyes!

These eyes are dynamically alive and filled with awareness and presence. Every cell of my body is being penetrated by this. When we ask what God or the Creator is, this is what it is. It's this incredible brilliant white light that is filled with billions of eyes that are alive. It's not that these eyes are each separate beings—these eyes are one Creator. I feel such incredible love for everybody—incredible, never-ending love.

God is a being, but not limited as a being. God is dynamically aware and alive, pulsating, breathing and loving. It's everywhere, and I see a smile now from this Presence as if to say there's nothing to worry about, everything is love, the intention is for bliss and enjoyment. Life and love are the most important things. There is no judgment whatsoever. This Presence is not using languages. As It desires, It vibrates Its intention into being—into new creations.

Q. WHERE OR HOW DID GOD BEGIN?

A. God is laughing at me when I asked the question!

God just says, "I AM" and laughs uproariously. "I exist because I AM! How do you (meaning us) know you exist? You know because you are. No other explanation is needed." It began with Consciousness, or the awareness of the I AM.

Q. DOES GOD HAVE A GENDER?

A. What I hear Source saying is that there are billions of elements that make up creation—much more than if you are masculine or feminine. Source encompasses masculine and feminine and much more. In this dimension we are used to dividing things up into masculine and feminine, but that is so very limited compared to what I am seeing. I'm actually in the cells of God, in these billions of eyes, and I can see and feel these billions of elements.

So, Source is saying, "I am masculine and feminine and much more, and then I'm none of it." What It is imparting to me is that the diversities we call life are filled with a myriad of colors and elements we've never seen before. It is definitely not identifying Itself with a particular gender, yet it does encompass all of that.

Q. IS THERE MORE THAN ONE GOD? I THINK THIS QUESTION COMES FROM OUR SMALL IDEA THAT THERE IS A GOD OF EACH RELIGION, AND IT IS PUZZLING THAT ONE RELIGION HAS ONE GOD AND ANOTHER RELIGION HAS A DIFFERENT GOD.

A. I want everyone to keep in mind that I am in a very different place/ frequency here today—I am not answering these questions from an Earthly frequency. I am not answering this question from any perception of an Earthly God—not Jehovah, not Allah, not Jesus, nor any of those beings—because those are all Earth beings.

So, in answering this question I find I'm in this place that is far beyond Earthly identifications. There is this singular Presence that I am seeing and feeling, and this Presence has billions of eyes and It's calling every one of those eyes God. Those eyes that encompass God are not separate gods, but are part of this one huge Presence—this incredibly vast awareness. The gods of religions are not Gods, nor are they what I am seeing as God.

Q. IS THE GOD YOU'RE SEEING AND THE PRIME CREATOR ONE AND THE SAME?

A. Yes, It would accept being called Prime Creator in the context of what we've been seeing.

Q. DID GOD CREATE HUMAN LIFE?

A. Keep in mind again, everyone, that I am answering these questions from this place of God's Presence. This Presence has all these striations of what we call light coming out of It as I answer this question. Source is saying, "You are all a part of me." Imagine a vast Presence that has all these striations of light coming from It and every one of those striations or creations is one of us. Source is gathering all of us unto Itself saying, "You are all part of Me," and every single pinpoint of light coming out of Its Presence is a different aspect of It's creation. In other words, God's very being comprises us as well as everything else in creation.

I'll go now to the human-form question. It feels as if all creation has come out of God's *heart*, and I'm only using that word to describe the love that I'm feeling. Love is why we're here; love is the reason we are all created, and why all life has been created.

What I'm feeling about the human form and all the different forms of life everywhere (not just us or our planet, but the diversity of life forms throughout creation) is that they come into being through various combinations of elements, not specifically formed by God. There are many expressions of creation that don't have physical forms like those in which we find ourselves. Many expressions are color or sound or geometry. There are so many different parts of God, but what I feel Source saying is that form itself could never come into being if the underlying elements of God's intention were not in place.

All forms, shapes, geometries, light beings, etc., come from the elements, or substance, of God, but God doesn't individually create forms. God is saying it doesn't matter if It deliberately created our human form or not, the fact is that all life forms are still composed of the elements of God from the simplest life form to the most complex. We are all gathered unto It, and It delights in all of it.

Did God deliberately create our human form? It's saying, "In the bigger picture, yes, I did because you're composed of Me, but I did not directly mold you in your particular human form."

I hope you can all grasp what I'm trying to say here. Source does not want us to focus so much on how our human form came to be, but more on the fact that we wouldn't exist at all if we were not made of God's Presence, which is love. We humans have awareness, and we have an ability to partake in creation with God. It is all about expressing love and love's desire, and that is what It wants us to understand and realize.

Q. IS LIFE ITSELF INTENTIONAL OR ACCIDENTAL?

A. Are you asking about life as we know it here on Earth?

In the big picture, life is definitely intentional, as we already expressed. God's desire for life and its expression is definitely intentional.

Life on Earth is also intentional because Source's intention is for love to have unlimited expression and for creation to be. This intention extends to every single place in the universe. This intention is the life-force energy that allows life to come into being everywhere. It is the template behind everything. This loving intention manifests itself in a myriad of diverse, unlimited expressions. Every expression of life has behind it God's intention for life, otherwise it could never come into being.

Q. DOES GOD INTEND EVIL?

A. No, God views evil as a distortion of Its intention. Its intention is clearly unlimited heartfelt love and desire for the pleasure, enjoyment and delight of creation. The fact that people can take the elements and rearrange them, isolate them and use them to produce distorted things has nothing to do with Source. Source does not have a desire for that.

Source sees it as unfortunate that there are life forms that do not understand what the I AM is. I just got this flash of the most beautiful colors and patterns you could ever imagine. If we and other life forms understood the elements of God/love of which we are composed, we would never be manipulating those elements in such a way as to create anything destructive. There is confusion about what God is, and it's harder to remember what we're made of once we start rearranging elements in a destructive way. This applies to our thoughts as well.

Q. IS THERE LIFE ON OTHER PLANETS?

A. Of course. Life is throughout the entire Universe. Regarding life forms on other planets, some planets are teeming with life forms and other planets are not. There are planets that once teemed with life forms, but their inhabitants destroyed their environment, making them inhospitable. Some places once supported life forms and don't anymore, but they will again someday.

What looks like a barren planet that once had life is really a planet that is in an internal process of regenerating itself. This process can take millions of years, but those planets will have life again at some point.

I'm seeing how cosmoses change, different universes change—they may take billions of years, but they do change, because the elements that compose the universe rearrange themselves constantly. This process eventually develops new life forms. It could take billions of years for some, but rest assured that everything will have life again, even in places that have been barren for long periods of time. There are other planets in other universes with civilizations on them that are similar to ours, while others are different, so there is a wide array of life everywhere.

Q. IS THE SUN A GOD?

A. No, only God is a God. The sun is a magnificent being that is also made up of the elements of God and I feel incredible love from it also. The sun has self-awareness, and it desires to contribute to the life forms in our solar system. It is composed of elements that make it possible for other life forms to come into existence. It's a presence that is extremely loving and happy. It is a source of light, warmth, stimulation, and regeneration. It would not want to be called a God because God is a word reserved for the Prime Creator. It's not appropriate to call anything else God, not even a highly advanced being. The word God with a small "g" is silly, really, because it reinforces separatist ideas.

The sun has no problem being called a magnificent being of its own design or being appreciated for what its donation is, but in terms of being a God to worship, it's saying, "No, no, no!" It has consciousness just as much as a human life form does, except its shape is round and it is glowing. It is comprised of different elements, but it is alive and aware. We can certainly have appreciation for the sun and what it gives us- it would enjoy that.

Q. WHAT IS THE HOLY SPIRIT?

A. The Holy Spirit is the presence of God within us, and, more importantly than that, it is the awareness of God within us. It is contained inside every one of us and is the remembrance of where we came from, what we're all about, what we're doing here, and how to be in this world.

Q. WHEN WE PRAY, DOES GOD HEAR OUR PRAYERS, OR ARE WE PRAYING TO OUR HIGHER SELVES OR ANOTHER GOD OR ASSIGNED ENTITY?

A. That's a great question! God definitely hears every prayer, and, more than that, everything is felt by God. Once again, I'm in the upper levels speaking with this God Presence as I am answering this question. Every form of expression is a cell in Its body, therefore It feels every-thing—every aspect of everything, every aspect of us. It feels every experience, every thought, every emotion, every plea.

Source is composed of such intense love, desire and peace that every prayer is answered with this same love, desire and peace. I feel it pouring unconditionally out of God's very being. God does *not* respond to prayers by telling us what to do or by rearranging our lives for us. Rather, It sends intense pulses of love, desire, peace and comfort to us, which, when felt by us, increases our inner knowing and strength and puts us back in alignment with Truth, which then rearranges our lives. God answers us with a greater awareness of Its Presence. This translates down into the lower dimensions and causes the rearrangement of elements in our dimension. You could say it causes a change that we term a miracle. (See Chapter 6.)

Each pulse from God will manifest itself in a way that has to do with our particular combination of elements. Two people could be making the same prayer to God for a job, let's say. God's answer will manifest down through the levels and the form of expression it takes has everything to do with the individual persons' combinations of elements, their consciousness, how they perceive and believe, and what they can accept. What means love to one person may be totally different for another. For one, it could be a new job, for another it could be a relationship or a healing of some kind. This is where the love of God will come down and manifest the best it can, according to the makeup of the individual.

God's answer is always to send out stronger and stronger pulses of incredibly powerful love, comfort and peace.

Q. IS THE REASON WHY SOME PEOPLE SEEM TO GET ANSWERED IMMEDIATELY AND OTHER PEOPLE DON'T BECAUSE OF THE WAY GOD'S LOVE GETS FILTERED DOWN THROUGH AN INDIVIDUAL'S CONSCIOUSNESS?

A. Yes. When we come down into the lower/denser levels, we begin perceiving ourselves as separate and finite with our own personalities and beliefs. The form a manifestation takes as it comes down through the levels will be according to our beliefs and what we can accept into our perceived reality.

Q. HOW CAN WE BE SURE THAT WE ARE COMMUNICATING WITH SOURCE WHEN WE PRAY AND NOT SOME OTHER ENTITY? ALSO, WHEN SOMEBODY PRAYS TO THE LIKES OF JEHOVAH OR BUDDHA OR A SAINT, WHOM THEY MIGHT REGARD AS GOD, DOES THAT PRAYER HAVE THE SAME IMPACT AS ONE SENT DIRECTLY TO GOD?

A. Let's go to part one first. God is aware of every prayer and answers them all the same way. There's nothing God misses—that's how you can be sure. Answers that come from God are always loving answers. They are always based in love, and with them is a feeling of deep knowing and peace. All fear disappears immediately. You will feel there was never anything to worry about. You will feel love and peace throughout your entire body and may even feel transported to a higher place in your consciousness.

For part two of this question, when people pray deliberately to a perceived god or saint or holy person, they will receive an answer based on the quality of the one they are seeking. In other words, you may feel peace from Buddha, Judgment or command from Jehovah, love from Jesus, Mercy from Allah, and so on, whereas God's answer is always the same for everyone.

There are no gods with a small 'g' at all. They could be more advanced spirits, but they would still not be called gods.

Q. YOU MENTIONED IN A FORMER SESSION THAT JEHOVAH IS NOT THE TRUE GOD OR GOD/SOURCE. WHEN SOMEONE PRAYS TO THEIR PERCEIVED GOD, DOES THE I AM PRESENCE HEAR THOSE PRAYERS AND RESPOND?

A. Yes, your own I AM Presence and the I AM God always hears and answers every prayer. If you are praying to a perceived god such as Allah or Jehovah or any other entity, Archangel or Ascended Master and you direct your prayers to those beings, you will receive an answer that reflects the likeness of that being. God Source does hear those prayers as well, and will respond by sending Its pulse of love to you, but if you're focusing on an answer from another being, you may only be receptive to an answer from the being of your focus. The quality of that being could be quite magnificent and its answer might serve you or help you. If you wait for an answer from Jehovah, for example, its answer may or may not be loving.

We need to understand that when beings come into form, they all have particular qualities based on what they are and who they are. It's the same for us as well. Your own beliefs about gods or higher beings will determine the answers you receive.

Q. WHY DOESN'T GOD JUST FIX THE EARTH AND THE WAY THINGS CURRENTLY ARE?

A. God's first reply is why would It fix what we're creating? It sounds like a simple answer, but it's really not. Source has just told us that It continually sends Its love and it's such an incredible love! Its desire is always for love to be expressed. When we have our own self-awareness we choose and create all sorts of scenarios. The fact that we see a world that needs fixing shows us that we have errors in our perception because there's so much else going on. When God looks down at the Earth, It sees a lot of love happening everywhere. God sees everything, as all is well.

Imagine there are billions of different thought waves going on around us with an infinite diversity of different ideas and perceptions floating around. We are all doing this all the time—thinking, imagining, perceiving, judging, loving, denying, sharing, restoring life, killing, giving birth, dying, etc. All these things coalesce into unique forms of expression on a wide variety of levels. These forms may unravel at some point, or they may stay in their form of expression by the focus of consciousness. There's a huge diversity of things going on constantly—it's a constant movement. Source is not interested in coming down and rearranging our creations or making them appear all nice and neat for us. Our world and our experiences are our creations of consciousness. We were given life to be able to express as we wish. We are free in that way. If we don't like what we have formed as a result of our consciousness, we are the ones to unravel it and make it different.

Life forms develop different degrees of consciousness and awareness, and they play with creation and mold it with their thoughts, desires and perceptions. Each aware being has the responsibility for the quality of what it manifests with its thoughts and desires. We each are in charge of our lives because we have the self-awareness to do so. We can think, decide, observe, feel, invent, inspire, change our minds, and connect with Source. We are blessed!

God plays Its part by reminding us that at the core of everything love is all there is and love is what's most important to uphold. It is a *standard* to live by—a quality to uphold—the Truth and the answer to every question. If we want to use our thoughts to create other than that or to judge or condemn other people or find God or people guilty, or make a mess of the environment, we are free to do so. It will not be God's fault, nor is it God's responsibility to fix it. It is ours. We can turn it all around and have it be a blissful existence whenever we are ready. It could be an instantaneous shift.

It's easy to focus on what's wrong or look at things and not see love. What we see out there is a decision we each make with our perceptions.

In God's Presence, love is still in existence, and it will always be constant, sure, patient and accepting. love is never going to be affected by anything we do with our consciousness. We can destroy a planet and put ourselves through all manner of suffering for as long as we want. God knows that at some point in our existence we will change our minds and be tired of our foolish use of our consciousness. We have the awareness and freedom to create and choose.

So, you can see why God is not interested in coming in and taking away our beautiful creative powers or freedom to express and experience, which It would be doing if It suddenly rearranged our world. It would be taking away our power of creating it all! We can understand how free we really are—we are free to rearrange the elements of our physical world with our own consciousness and change what we experience. It's the delight of creation to create. If we understood this, we would not be interested in creating destruction or wasting our thoughts and desires on negativity.

Q. ARE WE HERE TO LEARN LESSONS?

A. Many people believe that, but Source says, "No, we are here to experience bliss and joy." It may seem we are here to learn lessons because we are on a path of awakening to our true presence, which might also be considered an evolution. That evolution will eventually result in the realization of Source's intention- to experience bliss and joy, which is really to be the love that we are, to understand what *we as God* means. To be in love, to be love itself with no fear. What appears as lessons is really a gradual path of awakening from the dream of the necessity for suffering and hardship. We create our own hardships by the content of our beliefs. If there is a lesson to be learned it is that "Like attracts like". We will experience what we believe. God does not give us lessons- God gives us more and more love until we get it that its all that's going on.

Q. I PRAY FAITHFULLY FOR THOSE I LOVE AND FOR THOSE WHO HAVE PASSED ON. IS THERE MORE I CAN DO TO ASSIST THOSE WHO HAVE PASSED ON?

A. It's a really good question, because *some* people who cross over do not go to the light right away and experience the love we've been talking about. Some are stuck in spirit out of fear of Gods judgment or an inability to accept they have died, so any prayer you send is helpful. It provides momentum for them to be able to move on. When it is really an intention of love that you send towards someone, it always helps.

Part of the problem is that we have forgotten the love that is God that we are composed of. We've really confused things here, but sending someone heart-felt love or a blessing is opening the door for a miracle for everyone. When someone gives and receives love, it opens the potential for a miraculous shift and a miraculous rearrangement of elements.

Q. DO WE HAVE THE ABILITY TO CREATE OUR OWN SURROUNDINGS AND MANIFEST OUR OWN DESIRES? CAN WE FEEL CONNECTED TO SOURCE ALL THE TIME?

A. You can create anything because perception and desire rearranges the elements of creation. When you have a desire and you apply deliberate and focused intentions for manifesting, the elements of creation start to rearrange themselves into the form of your desire. So, you do have the ability to change your environment. The success or failure of your manifestations or lack of them is determined by how clear you are at the level of your subconscious, your soul contract and your motivation for your intention. In other words, why do you really want it?

Feeling your connection to Source is really dependent on how willing you are to see only love everywhere. Since God is made of only love, making that your only intention and purpose brings you closer and closer to that experience. Yes, it is possible to feel God's love everywhere and to see God's love in everything, but it is a choice. It is where we decide to put our attention in every moment.

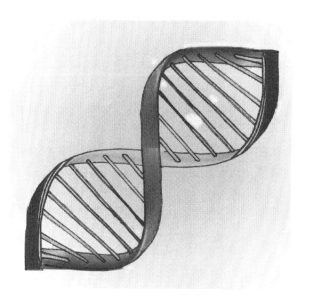

Chapter 2

Exploring DNA

Our discussion today focuses on DNA and the multitude of questions regarding it in today's world.

Q. WHAT IS SOURCE'S DEFINITION OF DNA?

A. I am looking at little squares of white light, and I am seeing that the DNA is the building block of creation. It follows a sequence or a pattern. One block seems to build upon the next and the next, like a chain. We've seen this in the images of DNA that science has shown us. Source is saying that it is literally "the chain of events." It is formed and unfolds in its diversity of forms by the sequence of events that have taken place in particular areas of the universe. DNA strands are woven patterns of light with varying informational sequences in them, occurring through the process of adaptation and experimentation. Contained within it is a record of a life form's history and evolution.

Our own individual DNA is based on historical events encoded throughout time. It comes into being or "builds itself" by what's coded within it and has an evolutionary process to it. As I go back further toward Source, DNA itself seems to reflect an original pattern of creation built upon different molecules.

Q. WHAT IS THE POTENTIAL AND PURPOSE OF *DNA*?

A. It has unlimited potential for expansion and change because it is built upon sequences of events that can change and alter its chemical composition. I am watching a collection of ribbons of light that intertwine and carry specific information. Its purpose is that it establishes patterns for life forms to be. In its history is its evolution, and, without that information, a life form wouldn't know what to be or how to form. In its codex of information and history are contained the intelligence to unfold a particular life form. I'm seeing light, colors, chemicals, hormones, and other aspects of cells that are all coded inside DNA with quite complex information. As I'm looking at it, I see a glistening white crystalline and liquid-gel-like structure that has a reflective quality to it, but it also feels moist. This makes me feel that it's alive, with living and breathing life-force energy.

Q. How many strands make up the DNA?

A. Since the DNA is a latticework of information, the number of strands contained within a particular life form corresponds to the evolution and type of the life form. The number of strands is different for each particular life form. For a human being, we've been at a particular 2- or 3-strand activation of DNA for a very long time. Activation determines the amount of strands that are actually alive and functioning. Even so, our specific coding can be altered and changed. Source says that we currently have a 12-strand potential, with the 13th potential also encoded. Potential implies evolvement capability, meaning we can activate and "turn on" 12 strands of DNA within our biology. We are meant to evolve and actualize up the 12-strand ladder, and then, once that happens, we have the potential to activate a 13th strand. At that point, this will make us a very different biological life form. We do not have 12 strands activated at this time. It will actually be a long while before we do!

Currently we have the potential to turn on our fourth, fifth and sixth strands. We've been at three-strand activation for many millions of years, and now many people are having their fourth strands turned on. With the cosmic awakening process we are now in, some people will activate their fifth and six strands. If we can do that, we will be able to retrieve our higher gifts and abilities such as telepathic awareness and communication, past-life recall, perceiving subtler energies, having X-ray vision, the ability to move between some dimensions, the potential to understand consciousness at a much more expanded level, telekinesis, teleportation and bi-location, and the heightened expansion of all our senses.

This is a great answer to get from Source, because it puts a lot of other things in perspective. If we were to activate our seventh and eight strands, for example, which we aren't doing right now, we'd be moving into higher aspects of our own Godlike nature. In the session on the Kundalini, which is in a later chapter in this book, we saw that this activation process is also a purification process up the chakra system. The potential is there within us to become a God-man, and this has to do with the activation of our 12-strand potential. Once this is achieved, we now have the potential to activate the 13th strand, at which point we'd become an entirely new type of being. As you can see from where we are currently, we still have a long way to go. We will be waiting for another stellar-activation cycle to occur after this one, which will afford us the opportunity to activate strands 7 through 12. The potential for the activation of the 13th strand will occur after that.

Each stellar-activation cycle allows for an increase of light and activation, which provides the potential for awakening and quickened evolution or adaptation.

We can see this happening in our world today. Much darkness is being exposed, and people are waking up all over the world, but this process also involves the conflict between the old order and the new. Think of all the things we are trying to change. We need to respect Nature and all life, we need to stop suppressing the rights of the individual; we need to uproot dogmas that enslave the human being. We need to stop wanting to condemn criminals to death. We need to stop killing our environment and our food. We have a lot to do, and we can see how this change will still take many years and dark forces along the way will challenge us. The old paradigm-the reptilian part of our own anatomy-has to be purified, and this has to occur at the level of consciousness and DNA.

We're talking about activating the DNA and our six strands within our current lifetime. When the spirit leaves the body, it will eventually decide what it wants to be when it comes into incarnation again. It may decide to not be a human. It could choose to be another species entirely for specific reasons. It could choose to be a human but have a different gender. Each time it comes in it will obviously have a different DNA, depending upon the life form that it chooses to be. Only when the spirit enters the body will it also bring with it its own soul history, and this will be added to the DNA content.

It is true that individually, in between stellar-activation cycles, we can still do a lot to activate our own DNA by doing our own purification process. This process can take many lifetimes, however, stellar-activation cycles provide us opportunities for accelerated activation and growth.

Q. WHAT ACTUALLY HAPPENS TO THE STRANDS WHEN THEY ARE ACTIVATED?

A. There is a chemical change that occurs, because the DNA is about information and in activation the DNA spiral itself gets new information. You can say that the DNA strands receive new light codes, if you want to, but what they really are is new messages and new information, like a new set of instructions. Once the DNA receives the new information, it starts to change the chemicals and hormones in different functions, according to those activations, and, because the message has changed, the evolution of the species changes.

Q. WE HEAR OF PEOPLE WHO ARE OFFERING 22-STRAND DNA ACTIVATION THROUGH THE USE OF CRYSTALS AND SPECIFIC

CEREMONIES. IS THIS FOR REAL? WHAT IS ACTUALLY HAPPENING IN
THESE CEREMONIES?

A. The first thing Source is saying is that we do not have a 22-strand
DNA potential in our current human form. A 22-strand being is a very
huge presence that is very much out of our solar system. Even though
our DNA potential is unlimited, in our current biological state we have
a 12-strand potential, which in and of itself is still quite huge when you
consider the gifts and abilities that go with it. There is no fast track to
that type of evolution. Anyone who promises to activate 22 strands of
DNA has been misinformed. If this was available to us, we would all be
turning into light bodies.

The ceremonies performed, however, can do a degree of DNA activation by bringing in higher light codes, which begin to restructure specific geometries in the body and cause subtle changes in the light body.
In any activation, the people being activated still have to be able to
maintain and integrate those frequencies within their bodies and con-
sciousnesses. It is one thing to have something catalyze a change in yourself and quite another to integrate that change into your biology. We
need to keep in mind what this particular stellar-activation cycle affords
us, and that is the activation of our fourth, fifth and sixth strands of
DNA.

Q. IN OUR CURRENT HUMAN FORM, ARE OUR GENETICS FIXED?

A. No, it's not fixed based on what we've been shown. We have to go
back to explaining how the DNA is formed and how it changes through
history. Without this history and without the information in the history,
the life form would not take its shape and form. The genetics we inherit
from our parents are the building blocks for our particular life form or
body. That contains a certain pattern of information that determines
what gets passed down from parent to parent, person-to-person. But
here's where I want to put things in perspective, because the DNA is
alterable. It is not fixed in the sense of the DNA you were born with.

Once you have your own life form, you don't have to accept that there's nothing you can do with your DNA for the rest of your life. We just explained how the DNA could evolve by activations, but it also evolves by consciousness and emotional changes.

If no changes are ever made in consciousness or emotions, there will be nothing to catalyze your genetic pattern, and it may stay in place for the duration of your life. But if you become more conscious or are being activated by the current stellar-activation cycle, the potential for the evolution of your DNA, and therefore your individual genetics, is very strong. It's an evolution going on now. It's easy to see the effects of this process in the new children that are being born nowadays. They are coming in with more strands turned on. Most of them have 4.5 strands activated with their added abilities, to put all this in context. So, your genetics are fixed while your biological form is being created, but once you start working with your DNA, it can be altered by shifting emotions and consciousness. You're creating a new DNA structure, which is unique to yourself and that will be passed on generationally or genetically if you have children. Whenever we evolve to a higher level, that potential can be passed genetically.

Q. I HAVE BEEN DOING ANCESTRAL DNA RESEARCH ON MY FAMILY AND I WAS TOLD BY SOMEONE I RESPECT THAT DOING THIS KIND OF WORK CLEARS SEVEN GENERATIONS BACK AND SEVEN FORWARD. COULD SOURCE PLEASE EXPLAIN THIS?

A. What Source is saying to me is that the DNA changes by us purifying negativity and our lower nature thoughts, beliefs and emotions. Our diet contributes on a very small scale, but we're really talking about a purification process in consciousness. Source is saying that we cannot really clear things for our relatives backwards and forwards, because we do have to take into account individual soul journeys. In other words, when you think of all your ancestors going backwards who are all having their own relationship with their own soul and spirit, the work of mastery is personal. Another person can't magically clear others' karma for them.

We can be a force that catalyzes and purifies ancestral patterns in ourselves and thus affect future generations. Each spirit has its own challenges and its own things to become victorious over so that it can become more masterful. What we do when we shift our own DNA is we offer higher energy and higher consciousness to our ancestors and to the world. If I were to research the patterns that show up in my own family's DNA over centuries, I might be able to notice recurring patterns and thus be able to see how those patterns are evidencing in my life today, and, with that information, I would know better what my choices need to be around those patterns. In this way, I have the potential to alter a pattern that's been in my family historically for generations.

When we think about the past and about ancestors and relatives who have passed on, we're not really altering their DNA because DNA is a physical thing in the body and these people are no longer here. What you are doing is ending particular patterns and providing new potentials for future generations. A person will still inherit things from their parents. Let's say you know you've got somebody in your family who is still making choices that are not the healthiest, or there may be a particular aspect of the DNA that's not so great causing issues. You may be offering some higher coding for them so that they can receive more light, which has the potential to awaken them, but you don't necessarily correct the issue for everybody in your family line.

However, here's the exception: It all goes back to the story of Jesus. The Christian belief is that Jesus died for our sins on the cross. The implication is that he wiped out the sins of humanity. In essence, he purified the human race through the forgiveness of sins. There is a fundamental truth in the story, even though there are some who claim that Jesus never really existed. It doesn't really matter if he lived or didn't live, because the principle of forgiveness is the point. It's a principle that says that it only takes one person who truly realizes the love of God and the innocence of all brothers and sisters to completely purify the human race. The idea of Jesus shedding blood is the symbolic idea of releasing an old DNA program and replacing it with a "resurrected" program.

The resurrected program is that everyone is forgiven and deserves love and is continually given this love by Source without fail or end. Only the actualized realization of this purifies the old genetic code of guilt and punishment. So, if Jesus did exist, he could have completely forgiven the world. This would mean that all effects of karma are forgiven and that all bloodlines have been purified. So, we look around and see that there is still suffering going on, people are still struggling, people are still behaving in ways that are criminal, our own thought processes are still both positive and negative. It doesn't look as if all has been forgiven because, we still "sin," and we are still punished in this world.

But here's the point—each person has to choose to acknowledge that they've never been guilty. Each person has to come to the awareness of his or her own innocence and that love is the truth of God. Each person has to become completely harmless within themselves to the point that they have no desire to judge another and wish only love to everyone equally. It's easy to see that this is the work we all need to be doing. Only when this happens will we have completely changed the patterns of our ancestors and those to come. This is why those who believe in this story of Jesus can say he is their savior. This kind of love is what releases everyone from the bondage of guilt and judgment, which releases karma. Has everything already been forgiven? Does our DNA hold this truth? Yes, it does and we have only to accept it. Until we do, we won't see it evidenced in our outer world. You don't have to believe in Jesus for this to be true. It is true because this is what Source is and does.

Q. IS THERE A RELATIONSHIP BETWEEN DNA AND KARMA?

A. Yes. Remembering that DNA is a chain of events, the DNA will hold the karmic imprints from the past. Karma is the set of imprints that are being transferred from generation to generation or lifetime to lifetime. It carries not only parental information, but also the information of our other lives, once our spirits enter the body vehicles formed by our parents. "Karma" is our spirit imprints being transferred into the DNA coding when we incarnate. As long as we believe in karma as a balancer of evil or good, we will not understand forgiveness and the love of God. You will see these patterns repeat themselves through generations until we understand that love and innocence are the same thing. We can now also understand why it takes many thousands of years for anything to change at the DNA level. Evolution has occurred slowly because consciousness hasn't changed throughout the centuries. There is also a strong ancestral loyalty pattern, which follows through generations. This loyalty, whether healthy or distorted, is one of the blockages to work through in evolving centuries old ancestry.

Q. DOES HUMAN DNA CONTAIN ALIEN OR EXTRATERRESTRIAL DNA?

A. That question is taking me into a totally new place, so hang on. I'm feeling an opening into a bright light that I feel like I'm breathing in. Source is telling me that our DNA originally was a pure blue white spiral flame. It feels extremely clean, pure and powerful. Our original template came down from Source. I'm being taken way back to the beginning-to the original template for all life forms, which came from the spiral of Source. What It wants us to know is that the original life-force template has been very much "nullified." I find that an interesting word, because it implies that our DNA has been altered to such a point that some of the original power and force we carried is no longer present. Source wants to make it clear that originally our DNA spiral was modeled after something very divine, but it has digressed since then.

Up to now in our discussion we've been talking about our particular human form, which has a 12-strand potential contained within it. At this time we have to climb back up the ladder to activate our 12 strands through the purification of our lower nature. Activation needs to be integrated now in steps. In other words, when we re-activate certain strands, we will then have the potential to re-activate more and then more. However, Source wants to be clear that this process of ascent is still a very down-stepped conversion of our current human DNA, compared to the potential that we had originally. Things have become so far down-stepped that our process of bringing our DNA back online has been a very slow process of evolution with some help from the various stellar-activation cycles. Even when these cycles come along, we have still only made slow progress, as the dark forces have succeeded in keeping us enslaved. Hopefully, we will make much more progress this time.

Q. REGARDING HUMAN DNA CONTAINING ALIEN DNA?

A. Yes, we are a combination of many ET races. Our DNA is encoded with this historical information. The alien mix has resulted in the chemical compositions of our bodies. This DNA chemical composition is weak compared to the eventual potential of Source within us. Even though we've been altered by having our higher-center DNA strands shut off, our potential to evolve into a God-man is still very real. Our cross-breeding with other life forms and animals long ago has left us with a lower, animal nature mixed with a higher, God-like nature which is why we have the task of purifying our lower nature so we can recover our higher nature. The original imprint of Source is still biologically within us, because, if it weren't, you wouldn't have any possibility for life at all. This original imprint is still much stronger than any impurities of cross-breeding that happened long ago, but the job confronting us now is the transformation of our lower nature.

Here's a small example of what part of this process looks like biologically. We have a lower portion of the brain that is considered the reptilian brain, which is also called the "pons." Currently, it has too much influence within our brain. It carries a type of dominance that makes us aggressive, reactive and warlike. Yet, there are certain brain exercises you can do that will develop higher brain pathways and reduce the reptilian portion of the brain, so that the evolution of our DNA can occur. The higher brain is what bridges the gap between God realization and us. I am describing God in this example as higher intelligence, genius mind, inspiration, clarity, energy, and solutions to all problems. This is only one small example of the task at hand. The good news is that new brain pathways can be developed at any age.

Q. WITH REGARD TO REINCARNATION, COULD WE HAVE BEEN OUR OWN ANCESTORS IN ANOTHER LIFE?

A. Yes, it's definitely possible that you could be an incarnation of someone who was your relative in the past. I wouldn't say, however, that your entire past life history is necessarily connected to your current family lineage. Your DNA research into your family ancestry could be a very interesting project. If you could trace that back and discover that the person you remember yourself to be in a past life was actually a relative of yours somewhere back in time that would be quite fascinating!

Q. IF I SEE A SPINNING BLUE DNA STRAND IN MY MIND'S EYE DURING MEDITATION, AM I ON THE RIGHT TRACK?

A. I would say so, based on the fact that DNA does contain information. It sounds to me as if you are in a relationship with your DNA now, and it is able to present its information to you. I would definitely say that's wonderful!

Q. IS THE DNA OF OUR TWIN FLAME[1] THE SAME OR VERY SIMILAR TO OUR OWN?

A. Yes, and no. Your DNA is not the same because biologically, as physical persons, each one of you comes from different parents, making your

---

1. See O'Grady, Aingeal Rose. *A Time of Change: Akashic Guidance for Spiritual Transformation* Wild Flower Press 2012. On Amazon.com.

physical bodies unique. However, once your spirit selves enter the body and your soul history becomes encoded in your DNA, you will find similarities there. To help with this process, each of you would have chosen, as part of your soul contracts, to be born into the physical family that would best serve your relationship and soul evolution.

Twin Flames are truly connected because they are the same spirit, and this is what really needs to be understood. At this level, you're not a body at all; rather you are one spirit flame. You don't have DNA-you are pure spirit twins who are the same spirit. Once this original flame splits and each part begins incarnating into different life forms, each will take on a different pattern and a different history. Still, when they meet one another in particular lifetimes and they remember that they are each other, they may find that they have had very similar experiences in their individual sojourns through time and space, because twins are always connected energetically. Because they're the same Spirit, what one experiences in a lifetime, oftentimes the other will also have experienced something similar in their lifetime. This doesn't mean that they'll necessarily remember each other's past lifetimes, for example, but they may! They could very well remember incarnations that they spent together.

Many times Twin Flames have the same unhealed wounds and some of the same spiritual experiences. Whatever they experience in their "separate" incarnations, the other is affected by, and vice versa. The exception to this answer is if the Twin Flames were born into the same family as siblings in the same lifetime, then they would share the same biological DNA.

Q. IS IT POSSIBLE TO CHANGE OUR DNA IF IT IS CODED FOR POVERTY CONSCIOUSNESS FROM OUR ANCESTORS? CAN WE CHANGE THIS INTO ABUNDANCE CONSCIOUSNESS, AND IF SO, HOW

DO WE DO THIS? IS THE POTENTIAL THERE TO ACHIEVE FIFTH-DIMENSIONAL DNA ACTIVATION?

A. It's possible to achieve up to sixth-strand activation in this particular time cycle. The success of that depends upon each person's evolution. Part of what we're doing in this cycle is also purifying mass consciousness beliefs. It isn't just about ourselves-we are also looking around the entire world, and we're watching the patterns that are occurring now and have been evidenced historically.

AHONU and I were talking about what the martyr complex really means within mass consciousness and in us as individuals. We all still very much believe in victims and victimizers, which equates to beliefs in guilt and punishment. If someone commits a crime or behaves badly, the victimizer is to be punished and the victim is innocent. This thinking is very pervasive. We aren't only clearing our family patterns, we're also clearing centuries of old paradigms. We're all a part of that, and we've all agreed to it. Poverty consciousness is one level of mass-consciousness beliefs. It goes along with the victim-victimizer mentality and the beliefs in guilt and punishment. It is very possible for you to clear those beliefs in yourself.

All changes require decisions and choices. It's all a decision about what you want to believe is true for you. Poverty is the belief in victim-victimizer, because God's will is abundance and is everywhere. It's in the life principle, and we see it everywhere in Nature. Every spring you see the evidence of abundance. We see the billions of seeds that get blown around each year by trees and plants of all varieties. Hundreds of pine-cones are created and fall to the ground each year from one tree alone. Look at all the new buds and blades of grass. This is the natural state of God's will. When we're experiencing something other than abundance, it is because we still have beliefs within us that make us think that we deserve less, or that the supply is limited. If you had parents brought up during the depression, you may have inherited their fear that there isn't enough. It is still possible to shift these ideas, even if they've been handed down generationally. It's a choice but it's a diligent choice. In other words, you really have to watch yourself and look at where you're going with your thoughts and the experiences in your life. Your experiences are symbolic representations of your thoughts. We would really like to get across that the foundation of life is love and love is abundance, happiness and expansion. It's unlimited potential. You can clear all that when you take a look at your beliefs and experiences that are contrary to love. Take a look also at your desires and intentions towards yourself and others. Ultimately, everything comes down to the perceptions you have of yourself, others and life.

Source has said that it really doesn't matter about your history, because you don't necessarily have to go back and remember other lifetimes. Sometimes you are shown them for informational purposes, but you don't have to know them all. All you have to do is look at your present life and see what's occurring in your present day-to-day life. Those are your own patterns and limitations and it doesn't really matter where they came from. You can still undo them in the present. Make a different decision, and redefine your ideas about what things mean to you. Turn them into associations that are positive. This is easy to do in concept, but it's not necessarily easy to do in practice, because it requires constant awareness of your thoughts and re-choosing in the moment. It is well worth the practice, however!

Q. DID WE EMERGE FROM SEA CREATURES THAT LATER EVOLVED TO BECOME CREATURES THAT WALKED THE FACE OF THE EARTH?

A. Let me put this in context. There is a part of the human being that did evolve from other species, but that's not all that happened, because we were also genetically changed at different time periods. Some of the species that evolved to be our particular type of form were implanted with higher-potential DNA codes from other advanced races, causing a quantum jump in evolution. Others came later and altered the DNA in such a way as to regress our potential, as mentioned earlier.

Some of us have spent time in the sea, and some of us may have a memory of being in the sea as a particular creature. Others of us could remember the sea but may not have been sea creatures. This is because our DNA has cellular memory and is composed of our history. Life in the sea is part of our DNA history. This is why some of us can also remember being from another dimension or planet. Some of us belong to those advanced races that came here very long ago and put their DNA into the animal-like creatures here to evolve them. We are talking about a wide expanse of evolutionary history covering billions of years. Some of us have been those original beings who upgraded our DNA, or we could have been those who came later and down-stepped our biology, making a portion of our DNA dormant. This is why it is now necessary for us to "resurrect" ourselves as a species.

Q. HOW CAN WE TAP INTO OUR DNA POTENTIAL IN THIS LIFETIME MORE QUICKLY?

A. You can meditate with it as the other participant mentioned earlier in this session. You can see it in your mind's eye and talk to it. Practice asking it questions and waiting for an answer. Source is saying, however, that the highest way to change your potential is to change your purpose into becoming only love. It's literally talking about desiring to be only love, compassion, understanding and harmlessness. It's choosing that state of consciousness and being so that your higher gifts will naturally appear, which is the evidence of your evolving DNA.

Q. HOW DO WE CLEAR A MARKER FOR DISEASE IN OUR LIVES THAT MAY BE REFLECTING OUR ANCESTRY?

A. Those that get handed down as potential diseases aren't necessarily absolutes. The likelihood doesn't necessarily equal the destiny. A person in a family who may have had more emotional trauma or stress or who may not be eating really well may manifest the illness, while everyone else in the family might not. The exception to this is if there is a person in the family who is the one to manifest the illness with the job of curing it in his/herself, thereby changing the repetitive pattern and what it symbolizes historically in the family line.

I wouldn't focus on worrying about disease markers. Instead, I would make sure that I'm eating the best that I know how and that I am emotionally taking care of myself, being positive and doing my clearing work. Taking care of yourself means that if you're stressed, then work with that, find out what's underneath it, and make some changes. If you need massages or acupuncture or organic food, start choosing it. Care for your emotions and look at what motivates your desires. Examine your fears honestly. All of those things have a factor in what happens to you.

We know of a woman that had a family marker for ovarian cancer. She had a complete hysterectomy out of fear of getting cancer. It hadn't manifested in her, but she was afraid that it might. Another example is women who have double mastectomies because they find that they have a predisposition to breast cancer. We all have cancer cells in our bodies and our immune system handles millions of pathogens daily. When we have family predispositions to specific diseases, we also need to look at what these diseases symbolize. They usually show the history of particular patterns or belief systems in families or even in mass consciousness. It's a valuable exercise to take the time to look into what these patterns are and what these diseases may symbolize. It is easy to do. Just sit down with a notebook and pen and write the disease name and ask yourself what it means to you. Then take a look at the people in your family and see if you can apply what you wrote to particular patterns that may be unhealed in your family lineage. After you identify these, rewrite these patterns into something new. Create an entirely new scenario for the family line with your imagination. In other words, make a new story for your family that reverses or disempowers the old pattern.

Q. DO THE FOODS WE EAT SUPPRESS OR POTENTIALLY ACTIVATE OUR DNA ABILITIES? IF SO, WHAT KIND OF FOOD SHOULD WE EAT OR NOT EAT?

A. What I hear Source saying is that food does not directly change our DNA. The DNA changes by evolution/adaptation. It needs to evolve to a different frequency entirely. Think about food in terms of providing nutritional building blocks to the body. Food can contribute life-force energy to the body, which gives it the ability to process life and keep the immune system strong. Food does provide light and energy, but it doesn't directly change our DNA. Source has talked to us many times about food, and we all have to find out which foods are right for our particular body. Whatever type you are, stay away from GMO foods and processed foods. Buy organic vegetables, grass-fed beef and butter, free-range chicken and good quality oils. The brain needs fats to think, so avoid foods that are low fat. Eat good-quality oils from coconut or nuts. Always reading labels on food products is a very good idea.

Q. IS IT POSSIBLE FOR HEALERS TO CHANGE A PERSON'S DNA?

A. What healers or energy workers do is to bring more light into the body of a person. This can activate some DNA changes by bringing in more light, depending upon the quality of it. However, the only way that's going to become a permanent change in a person is when the person can hold the activation. The person must maintain this shift in frequency in order to have a permanent DNA activation.

In the story of my own spiritual evolution, I had both things happen. I meditated every day and I was taken into many different worlds, which raised my frequency. These worlds held different paradigms, which were more loving and cooperative. I had to incorporate these paradigms within myself in order to maintain the higher frequency. I was taught a lot about inner purification, and I had to do much inner work to examine myself.

As you can well imagine, this is an ongoing process to this very day. I was also activated by beings that appeared in a dream. I was given a golden-orange liquid to drink that activated my healing abilities and opened up my X-ray vision. In my case, I was given a mini quantum jump in DNA evolution, but I also did my own study to keep pace with that change.

Q. HOW SIMILAR IS THE DNA OF HUMANS TO SASQUATCH AND MERMAIDS?

A. Sasquatch is definitely a genetically altered creature. It has similar DNA to us, but is also a combination of animal and ET experimentation. Some of us do carry that genome within us, but not all. Some of us have angelic coding or other ET coding. There are angelic beings who took on human form early on before it was modified that did not go through the experimentation process mentioned above.

In terms of mermaids, there would be some humans who would have once lived in the sea as those creatures, but again, not everyone would have. Those that were mermaids would most likely remember that they were or would have a strange longing for them. Even though we could say that we are all of the ocean, we didn't all live in the ocean or emerge from the ocean. Our biology contains the elements of the ocean—we all have a history of the ocean in our DNA. Remember that each diverse life form has its unique DNA, which has brought about its particular form. There may be many species that have DNA similar to humans, but with unique characteristics, which make them very different from humans.

Q. COULD A SPIRITUAL EVENT OR SEVERE CHANGES IN
ENVIRONMENTAL CONDITIONS CAUSE A CHANGE IN DNA?

A. Yes, it is possible when different qualities of light come from the cosmos, which contain elements that are released throughout the universe. This could affect life everywhere and cause many changes in activation and adaptation. It doesn't look like we're all going to achieve mastery from such an occurrence, however. Some of us could die from those types of changes because we wouldn't be able to handle the difference in frequency, while others will be able to shift and change in their consciousness. Remember a shift in consciousness has to come first, and the biology follows.

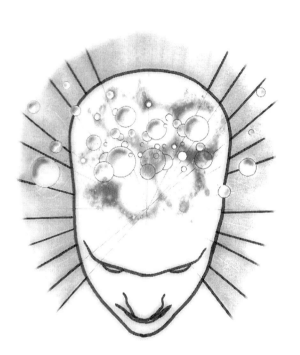

Chapter 3

Consciousness

In saying the opening prayer, a beautiful white pillar of light appears in the room. It feels very illumined and bright.

Q. WHAT IS SOURCE'S DEFINITION OF *CONSCIOUSNESS*?

A. "It is the ability to know yourself and to know Me." Inherent in this answer is an ability that is embedded in us in a foundational way. The ability to become conscious or to have consciousness has been gifted from the Creator to every life form. This does not mean that every life form has the same degree of consciousness, but the ability to have consciousness is built into every living thing. Consciousness implies the ability to know ourselves and knowing ourselves implies purpose. In other words, the purpose of consciousness is to know yourself and to know Source. Consciousness is also the ability to be alive and awake, to be aware of surroundings and to perceive definition, form, structure, and order. It is also the ability to perceive knowledge, to love and to extend love.

Q. WHERE OR HOW DID CONSCIOUSNESS ORIGINATE?

A. Source says that consciousness originated from It, the original I AM. The I AM is Source's definition of Itself. Consciousness originated in the I AM and is inherent in the I AM.

Q. DOES ALL MATTER HAVE CONSCIOUSNESS? EVEN ROCKS AND NON-ORGANIC MATTER?

A. Yes, everything has consciousness, but consciousness is at varying degrees of self awareness.

Q. HOW DO WE THINK?

A. We think from our I AM Presence. Thinking is also inherent in the I AM Presence. You think by God-awareness. We organically have within us an awareness of God-Source. If this were not so, we would not be able to think.

Q. ARE THE MIND AND CONSCIOUSNESS ONE AND THE SAME?

A. No. The mind is the alter ego that came into being through varying degrees of awareness. Varying degrees of awareness make perceptions, which make a view of reality that is different for each person. Even though everything has consciousness inherent within it, not everything is awake to consciousness. There are varying levels of consciousness inside all life everywhere.

Source is distinguishing mind and consciousness from each other in the sense that mind is something that was invented by perceiving; particularly, perceiving outside ourselves. By perceiving outside ourselves, we build up a false self that Source is calling the alter ego. This is the mind that Source is talking about. Our view of reality is determined by each of us, by how and what we perceive, and this is determined by our own unique level of awareness.

Q. WHAT'S THE DIFFERENCE BETWEEN THE EGO AND THE ALTER EGO?

A. The true EGO is the I AM Self that Source created, the original beingness coming from Source. It is the Truth that is inherent within each of us that we do not realize or remember. We need awareness to become self-realized. Because we are all at different levels of awareness, our perceptions of ourselves are limited. Therefore, we define ourselves based on our perceptions or level of awareness at the time. The alter ego is the self that gets made up through limited awareness and perception.

Coming into God realization or remembering our True EGO Self may take many lifetimes or may happen in an instant, if one is ready for it. Another name for our True EGO Self is our I AM Presence. It is also called our True Organic Self (see Book I, A Time of Change). In the process of remembering our true selves, we first have to undo the alter ego self we have constructed through many lifetimes.

Q. HOW DOES INDIVIDUAL CONSCIOUSNESS COMPARE WITH GROUP CONSCIOUSNESS? HOW DO WE RESOLVE OUR PERSONAL CONSCIOUSNESS? WHAT IS THE RELATIONSHIP BETWEEN PERSONAL AND GROUP CONSCIOUSNESS?

A. Individual consciousness has to do with your own perceptions of reality. It is the collection of your own thoughts, beliefs and associations through your various experiences in life. It extends into your past lives and includes your collective soul impressions. Throughout your many and various lifetimes and sojourns into other dimensions and planets, you create your own karmic imprints based on your experiences and your choices. This includes positive as well as negative karma. Anything we have not forgiven holds us back and keeps karma in place. When we address the issue of forgiveness, we really address everything that has happened in our soul stream. Where there has been a lack of forgiveness or a lack of love, there is still unresolved karma. We create karma when we judge another person or when we judge ourselves. This is because we create separation by our judgments. When we create separation, it builds up in our soul stream, and, sooner or later, we will have to resolve it. You can't go into unity consciousness with judgment. Unity consciousness implies there is no separation between yourself and anything else.

Group consciousness is the collective set of beliefs of everyone in the group. In other words, it is the agreement of beliefs and concepts of reality within a group. These group agreements create a physics for a given dimensional space or planet. As long as the group agrees to these beliefs and concepts of reality, this will create the laws that they operate under, as well as the forms that species take. If the group mind were to collectively change its concepts or beliefs about reality or about what is possible within their given dimension, it would alter the physics or laws of that dimension.

The relationship between personal and group consciousness is that there is a common agreement beneath the surface about the reality that they are in. They agree to the limitations and boundaries of their dimension. Still, it is possible for an individual to go beyond the beliefs of the group mind in their individual spiritual journey.

Q. WHAT IS *TRUE REALITY?*

A. True reality is the I AM Self that is pure Love. Nothing else is actually real. Our limited perceptions and ideas about what we can be aware of at any given moment of time makes up pseudo realities, dimensions, and planes of existence. It also makes up the planes of existence after death. It's the alter ego self that does this, because it does not have full God realization of its Self. When we finally arrive back at our I AM Presence, we are back in true reality. In true reality, you are in all knowledge, and you know yourself as true reality.

Our limits in perception and awareness "create" false realities because all thought is creative at its own level.

Q. WHAT IS *ACTUALITY?*

A. Actuality is what you create through your experiences, ideas and perceptions. We all have the ability to be creative. You could say that actuality is what you actualize, or what you manifest. It is something that we do ourselves.

Q. HOW DO REALITY AND ACTUALITY RELATE TO CONSCIOUSNESS?

A. They relate in the process of becoming self-aware. We are all on this journey to more and more awareness of our I AM Presence. Reality and actuality relate to consciousness in the sense that they are helping us become more self-aware. The process of becoming self-aware is where they relate. Since we are talking about actuality in the sense of what we

manifest, playing with manifestation, coming to the place were you realize you can manifest, and you do create experiences—all this is part of
the process on the way to becoming God Realized. There will be a time
after you play with manifesting when you will naturally seek for things
that are more real. The satisfaction that you think you will get from
manifesting things externally will be temporary. This doesn't make it
wrong, because it is part of the waking-up process. However, because the
satisfaction is temporary, it will make you inquire more and more deeply
into what is true and lasting satisfaction. Therefore, reality and actuality
are both stepping-stones on the way to deeper and deeper self-realization, which is true consciousness.

Q. WHAT IS THE *SUBCONSCIOUS*?

A. The subconscious is what you decided and continue to decide is true
but are not consciously aware of. Throughout our life experiences we
make conclusions. We make associations about life based on what we
experience, how those experiences affect us, and what we decide is true
about reality. These conclusions are stored in our subconscious as we
continue moving through each day and have new experiences. We forget
the conclusions we have come to about reality, yet they are still very alive
and active, but at a level that we are no longer aware of. This would be
termed the subconscious.

Q. WHAT IS THE *UNCONSCIOUS*?

A. The unconscious is that which denies that it is. Deciding to be
unconscious is deciding to be in denial of yourself, or what is. The "what
is" can be on many levels. It can be a part of us that denies God within
us, or it can be the parts of us that deny what's true in our lives on a
daily basis, for example, denying the truth of how you feel, denying
what's really going on in your relationships, or your career, *etc.* It can be
the parts of us that actively decide that they don't want to know the
truth.

Q. WHAT DETERMINES WHAT WE THINK ABOUT?

A. Your individual perceptions and also divine inspiration. Our own perceptions formulate what we think about or what we focus on. There is also a mechanism inherent in us that allows us to receive thoughts directly from the Mind of God, or divine inspiration. This mechanism is called the Holy Spirit. Thoughts and ideas do come to us from higher places or higher levels of awareness or knowledge through the Holy Spirit of God within us. Both of these things determine what comes into our awareness or what we think about. We also have the ability to tune into the thoughts around us in our environment. These could be the thoughts of others or Nature. We can also be influenced by negative entities who send us negative thoughts.

Q. HOW DOES THINKING WORK?

A. It works by awakening to consciousness. Thinking is the result of the ability to be aware of thoughts, which is consciousness dependent. Even though consciousness is embedded within us, it still needs to be awakened. Once this happens, thinking is a natural result. It is easy to see then that not all life forms have the ability to think in the same way.

Q. I'VE ALWAYS WANTED TO KNOW THE ANSWER TO THAT! SO, WHAT GENERATES THINKING?

A. Consciousness, light and sound.

Q. DO ANIMALS THINK?

A. Yes, most animals do think, but they are not aware of formulating thought. For example, humans have the ability to formulate thoughts and actively decide, whereas this process does not go that far with animals. Animals do have the ability to think and receive thoughts, but they don't seem to be generating them actively and deliberately the way humans do. They definitely observe and feel certain ways about things.

The process of thinking at the level of awareness where they are is limited for them, which goes back to what we've been talking about, where life forms are each at varying levels of awareness and consciousness. The ability to think and reason is dependent upon a particular life form's level of awareness. You can see this evidence even in humans. Not every human is at the same level of awareness or consciousness, therefore the ability to reason, think and decide is not the same in every human.

Q. DO PLANTS THINK?

A. Some do and some don't, based on the same information we've been discussing. What's missing here is the ability to reason, as with animals. Having said that, plants have the ability to be aware at the level of the group consciousness, or Nature. This is not an awareness of the I AM Presence, but rather an awareness of the field of all Nature at this 3-D level. Animals and plants do not receive divine inspiration. Their thinking processes are not to that level.

Q. DOES EVERYTHING HAVE CONSCIOUSNESS?

A. Source is saying no, but let me explain. Some things have *history*, but not consciousness. Some things are inert and have not gained consciousness. Even though Source is saying that all things have consciousness embedded within them, not all things have the same potential for self-realization. A rock, for example, would have come into being by things acting upon it from outside of itself. Some things come into being by other elements being pulled to them or their being pulled to other things. This process causes a level of form that Source is calling *inert*. These types of forms come into being as a collection of history or a collection of a series of events. These types of things are too compact or dense to have consciousness activated from within their forms. They have no self ability to awaken. These types of forms usually have to implode or explode and go back to light before they would have the potential to begin a journey of consciousness awakening. Forms that are a collection of history, such as rocks and crystals, will carry the data of their journey, but will not become God-realized at the level of density they are. In other words, they have not developed the consciousness to be aware enough to make decisions or manifest.

Q. WHAT DOES IT MEAN TO "KNOW YOURSELF"?

A. "Knowing yourself" is coming to the awareness of your I AM self. This is logical, based on what we've been discussing so far. It is all a journey of awakening to the true self, or the I AM Presence. When we look at the fact that there are many life forms that cannot take on a journey of self-awareness, it makes our present state of consciousness so much more sacred. What's different in people, for example, is that humans have evolved in consciousness to have the ability to become self-actualized. Humans have the ability to reason, to receive divine inspiration and higher knowledge, and to transform themselves through their ability to choose and reason.

We also get acted upon by things around us or outside of us. For example, as we are having this conversation today, our consciousness is being acted upon by something higher than itself at its present state of awareness. We are interacting with one another by these questions and Source Itself is answering us. This is stimulating more awakening within us and helping us to evolve and expand into more God realization. This could happen also by reading a good book or watching a movie, going to a seminar, or experiencing a tragedy or miracle. Everything in the universe is being catalyzed constantly by various forces. This affirms that we are in relationship with everything, and in this relationship we progress or regress each other.

This is where the alter ego comes in and has the potential to mess things up for us. We all have made an alter ego sense of self. We have created a sense of identity based on perceptions, dogmas, beliefs and associations with our experiences. We have fallen into a false persona different from the I AM Presence that is our natural true self. There will be a point, however, where we will begin to awaken to this realization and understand that we have to undo this false perception of ourselves. This is where many people are on their path—they are disassembling their preconceived ideas about who they think they are and beginning to understand that they have to go within to discover their true selves. This realization is something you come upon of your own accord. No dogma or teaching can do this for you. It's not anything someone or something else can give you. When this happens, we are at a decision point as to whether we want to continue to live as our false selves or awaken to our true selves. There is no judgment by Source about any decision we make. It is entirely up to us whether we progress and expand in our consciousness to God realization or stay around and play with the alter ego. Every aspect of life is valid, but we will come to a point where we will want true happiness, and this can only be achieved by what is permanent. Our I AM Self is the only permanence.

Q. WHAT IS THE *I AM PRESENCE*?

A. The I AM Presence is God. It is the flame of Source individuating and having consciousness. When you know yourself as God incarnate, you know the I AM Presence. Incarnate doesn't mean as a physical body. That is only one tiny aspect of it. Incarnate means as God.

Q. HOW CAN WE COME CLOSER TO OUR I AM SELF?

A. Our decisions bring us closer to God realization or take us farther away. Our spirits naturally prompt us to awaken to more of ourselves. This prompting can be felt as a gnawing or questioning that occurs from within to know more about life and truth. That is, we will have a need to discover, or a restlessness that doesn't go away. We'll have the feeling that where we are isn't enough, or that we're missing something. It can also manifest as a feeling of being stuck, when we know we need to move forward or move on, but we're confused about what to do or where to go. Unfortunately, the alter ego will have us go searching externally for more gratification, while the real gratification can only come from knowing who we truly are.

So you can see that there are many aspects to this journey. We build up a false sense of self, we play with experiences, we play with manifesting abilities, and we search for truth. Ultimately, when we find that none of these things fulfill us, we begin a real search for our true nature, which requires that we undo our false personas and achieve virtues upon our path. We will be tested and tried to see if our resolve is sincere, and if we have the willingness to continue. We will have to become very self-honest and examine our motivations for everything. We begin to realize how important our choices and decisions are in their effect upon our goal. We become disinterested in mind games and manipulations and focus our attention on being more sincere, real and loving.

When we finally begin to realize and actualize our true self, we will only be interested in being love and extending love. Until we get to this place, we will continue to play in false realities. We will continue to reincarnate and have lifetimes in other dimensions and on other planets, which I mention because I want us to realize how big this journey is and how much of the alter ego is in existence and to what extent it continues. We only end up Home, back in our true selves, when we naturally arrive at the place where it is all we desire. This has to be a natural process—it cannot be forced, otherwise it is not authentic. It needs to be said again that there is no judgment in this journey with all its ups and downs, false personas, learning and experiences. It is all part of the process of becoming and awakening to consciousness.

Some people have no interest in finding out that they have made a false persona. They are not at a consciousness level that would naturally push them to seek higher. They may be at the level of consciousness where they only desire to experience mundane or material, outward things. If this is what their consciousness can hold, this is where they will be, and there is no judgment in it. So you see, that even the desire to know will be something that occurs from within, as a restlessness or a questioning of one's existing reality. The search will have begun at this point. This is when one will desire to meditate, go within, or read and learn about esoteric knowledge.

This search will also allow you to see the relationship between your outer and your inner worlds. You will begin to see your outer world as a mirror, or reflection, of your own consciousness. You will begin to see your beliefs and opinions playing themselves out in your everyday experiences through your relationships and situations. You could ask a question of a higher part of yourself and see the answer being played out in your 3-D world. Before this, you may not have seen this relationship or noticed answers coming to you from a variety of sources. You may not have been paying attention in this way, but now you see it. It was there all the time.

This is evidence as to how consciousness is inherent in all life, but is not actualized in all life.

Q. DO OUR GUIDES AND TEACHERS USE THE DREAM STATE TO COMMUNICATE WITH US?

A. Yes, they do. Let me tell you a story. A few years back I lost my sister. She came down with this strange illness and, within six months, she was gone. We had a phone conversation a few weeks before she died, when she was feeling better. She told me that she had two dreams of my brother Chris, who had died when he was 22, many years earlier. I thought this was very strange, as none of us had dreamt about him all that time. I actually had a fearful feeling when she told me this, that this somehow meant he was coming for her from the other side. She too thought it was very curious that she was dreaming of him. She told me that while in the dream she said to him, "Why haven't you come to me before now?" He said, "Because you've always been so busy."

This answer makes the point that when we are in our 3-D lives, we are so busy thinking and working and focusing our attention on other things that we're not aware of things going on in the spirit state or on other levels. Our guides and teachers sometimes can't get their messages through to us because our attention is focused elsewhere, so they use the dream state to attempt to get their messages through.

If you keep a dream journal and record your dreams upon awakening, and then take the time to realize that everyone in the dream is some aspect of yourself, you can find out a lot about what you're being shown, which can really improve your life and make you much more aware. It is a wonderful way to get to know yourself on other levels, since dreams will often bring forward activities that are going on in the subconscious mind. They can also be higher messages from your higher aspects.

In my sister's case, it can be seen that spirits coming from the other side can also be bringing forth messages. In her case, seeing my brother was letting her know on a level that she was preparing to leave this world. I didn't want to believe it at the time, but she did pass three weeks later.

In most cases, dreams are a symbolic language that we can interpret when we begin to ask what is being symbolically represented by the sequence of events in a dream or by who is appearing in our dreams. Since we all make associations with people and events, in the sense that we give them all the meaning they hold for us, we can inquire into our own symbolic associations with the 'players' in our dreams and recognize it as our own internal language to ourselves. If you take the time to do this process, dreams that may seem to mean one thing when you awake oftentimes turn out to mean something very different upon reflection. This can especially be true if you have a bad dream and wake up in fear about it. However, if you take the time to go back and look at the series of events in the dream and ask yourself what all those events and actors mean to you, oftentimes you will see that you're being given a very positive message—possibly one of a transformation, or of a situation that you need to resolve, or a decision that needs to be made. In these cases, the bad dream can be a wonderful tool to change your life in a positive way.

There are actually many levels of dreams and many things that can be going on in the dream state. I won't go into all of them now, because Chapter Seven deals entirely with dreams.

Q. DOES GRAVITY HAVE ANY EFFECT ON OUR CONSCIOUSNESS?

A. What I am hearing is that gravity is the result of our consciousness. Gravity changes according to the consciousness of the masses. In other words, our collective beliefs and levels of consciousness dictate how much gravity is in a particular place or reality system. Gravity doesn't affect our consciousness; our consciousness affects gravity.

Here's an example: when people have images of ascending, it is always that we are ascending out of gravity or out of time-space. We become so light that we move beyond the effects of gravity and the limitations it seems to impose. In actuality, we become free of it. We each have the ability to get beyond the gravitational field of time and space by shifting our own consciousness to a different state of being. Our consciousness keeps gravity in place for us until we change it. When your consciousness becomes in alignment with more and more truth, it will hold more and more light within it. The more light we each can hold, the less gravity plays upon your bodies. This does mean that if the mass consciousness of the planet continues to awaken further, gravity will also shift in its properties. Have you ever noticed that people who are highly evolved in their consciousness don't seem to age as rapidly? This shows us that the effect of gravity on their bodies has been lessened.

If the collective consciousness of a planet or solar system has a very limited perceptual range about its reality, its process of manifestation will be very slow. What we have witnessed recently in contrast to that, however, is that when people's consciousness shifts, their ability to bring manifestations into our material plane speeds up. This is a very good example of how the shift in consciousness is affecting the gravitational field. When the gravitational field is very dense and slow, it takes longer to see the effects of our consciousness materialize. But when our consciousness shifts and we awaken to more and more Truth, gravity changes and becomes less dense, and we see our manifestations materialize at a faster rate.

Q. HOW CAN WE BUILD WEALTH WITH OUR CONSCIOUSNESS?

A. Source is saying that there are several levels to this answer. First of all, it is really the alter ego self we have created that wants wealth. We can manifest wealth by our thoughts, by our imagination and powers of visualization, and by looking at the limiting beliefs we have that may be interfering with wealth, and then reprogramming ourselves. Our powers of visualization are incredible. We underestimate the power of our imagination to bring things to us, and we underestimate the power in the imagery that we create with our thoughts.

Wealth can be very easy, and we have a tendency to make it too important. Putting it in perspective, the material wealth that most people desire is a desire of the false self. Having said that, there is still nothing wrong with it, no judgment around it. Having it or not having it can be part of your awakening journey. There are so many stigmas and fears around having wealth that we really have to look into ourselves and make the necessary changes so that our subconscious gets a positive message about having it. Asking yourself what you want wealth for will determine what happens to you in relation to it. When you use your imagination to manifest wealth, you also must manifest keeping yourself in balance with it, otherwise you will lose it all. Another point is to acknowledge money as having a consciousness and asking yourself these things:

1. Do you have a conscious relationship with money?
2. What is the quality of your relationship with money?
3. Do you express gratitude, respect and appreciation to money?
4. Do you consider it a friend or an enemy?

Answering these questions will help you become more aware of the consciousness that is money.

Balance is very important in any process of manifesting. You need to know what your motivations are and what the purposes for your desires are, in order to hold the balance of having what you desire as well as the responsibilities connected to it. Anything you can imagine can come into manifestation. The truth is that Source doesn't care if you have wealth or you don't. If you want it, Source says have it! We are speaking of the material level of wealth.

The higher form of wealth has to do with your ability to love everything. Being in love with everything is also the ability to be in communication with everything and see the interrelationship of all life everywhere. True prosperity (see Book I, A Time of Change) is when you're in communication with all life everywhere. You become part of the abundance all around you by being in harmony with it and by accepting everything as yourself. You become sensitive to life on very intimate levels, and your intention is completely harmless. This results in feeling complete love and peace with everyone and everything. In this state prosperity happens naturally and flows through all levels.

It is important to be honest with yourself and to acknowledge what level of wealth consciousness you are at. If you're in the consciousness of the alter ego, which believes that if it acquires more wealth it somehow becomes bigger and has more important status in the world, you can manifest that for yourself. If you desire wealth for security purposes, that's alright too. Let's not deceive ourselves into thinking material wealth is our ultimate key to happiness. We understand it can make life easier on some levels. Just be aware however, that the world of the alter ego is a temporary world that holds no permanent happiness or peace of mind. There are responsibilities that go with every state of being.

If you are moving toward the true EGO and are headed toward understanding your I AM Self, you will arrive at a different type of wealth in which abundance on all levels flows naturally and easily. It is called love. This path has purification of the alter ego as its directive.

Q. DO WE INTERACT WITH OTHERS WHEN WE ARE ASLEEP, UNCONSCIOUS, OR DREAMING?

A. Let's clear up the language first. When we are dreaming we are not unconscious—not in the way that Source defined unconsciousness earlier. Unconsciousness is us denying who we are or not wanting to know something. So, we are not unconscious when we are sleeping. We are just sleeping. Certain parts of the brain shut down and other parts turn on while we're sleeping or dreaming, so it is very possible to interact with others while in these states. You can communicate with people who have crossed over, or with people who are here in 3-D, if you are mutually having an experiment to see if you can meet in another dimension in the dream state. You can also meet other aspects of yourself in other dimensions while you're in the dream state.

Q. TELL US ABOUT THE PROCESS OF MEDITATING AND WHY WE SHOULD DO IT. HOW DOES IT WORK?

A. Meditation, according to Source, is really the decision to know yourself. There are many types of meditation, and people have different purposes for meditating, making the result dependent upon what your motivations are. For instance, AHONU learned Transcendental Meditation™ many years ago. He was looking for inner peace after the death of his first-born son. His meditation was focused on going to a place of peace and solitude within. When I meditated, I would call on my own higher self and ask to be taught. I was looking for knowledge and truth. I would lie on my bed at the same time every day while my children were taking naps and call on my higher self to teach me. Then I would wait. For the first two weeks I didn't receive much, only some dabs of color. Eventually those colors turned to symbols, which turned to telepathy, which turned to journeys into other dimensions. My meditations became an entire mystical path in which I was taught about developing virtues and overcoming my alter ego. In one of my journeys I went to a dimension where I saw a higher aspect of myself teaching a classroom filled with students. I realized that each one of those students was another aspect of myself. There were males and females of differing ages and many nationalities represented. The progress I made was due to my practice of making time every day to be taught by my higher self.

Meditation is a decision to set time aside to go within and discover your inner world, whether that is a more peaceful centered state or a rich landscape of knowledge of other dimensions. If you are practicing meditation daily or even twice a week, you will eventually come to the place where there is no separation between your inner world and your outer world. All life becomes a meditation. Meditation is not complicated, but it is a practice of putting yourself in a quiet receptive place. Many feel meditation is difficult because they cannot stop the thoughts that come in, so allow the thoughts to come in and then leave, and eventually there will be no more thoughts coming in.

> AHONU offers these thoughts: I myself have done over 20 years of meditating of several different types. Two of these types are concentration and contemplation. The contemplation type is where someone is contemplating Scripture, for example, or contemplating the Sacred Heart of Jesus or other various types of sacred literature or objects. Concentration is another method where you concentrate on your breathing or on a candle flame or some other object. Transcendental Meditation is different from these two types in that it doesn't concentrate or contemplate. It attempts to make the mind blank by focusing on a mantra in the short term until the mind arrives at a state of nothingness. So there are differences in all these ways, and, as Aingeal Rose said, there is no right way or wrong way. Just be clear about your purpose for meditating, because that does determine the result.

Q. WHAT ACTIONS WILL BUILD A LIFE OF FULFILLMENT AND JOY WHILE WE ARE HERE IN 3-D?

A. Actions is an interesting word, because I'm not actually seeing that we have to do anything. A life of fulfillment and joy only happens when you can truly love yourself. This is not airy-fairy, because Source is saying that you will not be able to have a life of joy and fulfillment until you do love yourself. When you don't love yourself or you make choices that are self-destructive or not in your highest good, there will always be guilt and fear attached on a subconscious level. There are small things we all do every day that we know are not in our highest good. These could be on any level of your life.

Loving yourself is a huge piece of the puzzle on the way to becoming harmless in your intent toward all life. Harmlessness is what gives us a life of fulfillment, because we become in love with everything and that is what joy is—being in love with everything. You look out and you see beauty and love everywhere. You don't get upset over the many little things that occur during the day that perhaps aren't perfect. You know that all is well and your intention toward all life is innocent and benevolent. You have no more desire to harm or judge anyone or anything. Especially yourself. Your internal guidance is in harmony with your 3-D life at this stage and you know what to 'do' clearly and easily.

Therefore, the action to take for this is the willingness to look at the alter ego, because it's inevitable that it is going to die. It has to at some point. The pretend self, the self we make up, the self that we measure, will disappear. The alter ego tells us that we will be happy and fulfilled when such and such happens, or if this person does this for me, or if I attain measurable successes or have that perfect relationship or wealth or security. Joy and fulfillment to the alter ego are all dependent upon outer experiences, successes or accumulations. Of course you can enjoy life and have all of those things, but remember the journey of consciousness. Challenging yourself in the outer world to demonstrate accomplishments can be an important part of you becoming self-aware. The balance comes in when you understand that the outer world is not you-it is merely a stage where you get to act out your desires. There will always be a point when the inner gnawing or restlessness to know yourself will return. This restlessness is inherent inside of you because it desires to take you into the knowledge of your true EGO. It wants to return you Home to real love.

On the journey of life you will find that all the material things in the world still do not bring you a sense of fulfillment and joy for lasting happiness. You will begin to desire things that are more permanent, such as inner peace, love and giving, and deep connection to all life. You come to the place where you realize that the outer world is a dream where your thoughts and beliefs play themselves out. It has no permanence of its own and fluctuates, depending upon your beliefs and feelings. This realization can relieve a lot of unhappiness if it helps you to stop searching for happiness outside yourself. This does not deny that things happen in the dream, but it will put it into perspective as we see that we are making up our perceptions as we go along. They rise and fall and rise and fall, over and over again, proving that there is no lasting permanence to them This is why the foundation of the alter-ego self doesn't last, because it fluctuates and changes on a whim. If a person bases their identity on the alter ego, they will be very vulnerable indeed to anything that destroys their idea of who they think they are or disrupts their 3-D reality. There is no lasting happiness in the alter ego with all of its accomplishments and losses. The only thing we are all really looking for is love that is everlasting. I'm not talking about love as in relationships, but love as the only true reality of which we are all made.

Q. WHAT IS THE *HIGHER SELF*?

A. The Higher Self is the same as the Holy Spirit inside your mind that bridges the gap between your alter ego and your true self. The Higher Self or the Holy Spirit is the memory of Source within you. There is a point in your conscious evolution where you will actually become your own Higher Self. When this happens, the need for the bridge disappears, and you will be in direct cognition with Source itself.

Q. WOULD SOURCE'S CONSCIOUSNESS EXIST WITHOUT OUR
CONSCIOUSNESS?

A. Source is amused by this question. Yes, Source's consciousness would
exist without our consciousness. It was there before we were created.

Q. WHAT GIVES US THE ABILITY TO COMMUNICATE WITH TREES?

A. The trees are saying that they want to communicate with us! This
implies that communication is a two-way street. We all have the ability
to communicate with everything. We could see the whole history of the
universe by picking up a stone and communicating with it. The ability
to communicate with everything is built into us. Not everything wants
to have a conversation with us, but there are plenty of things that do. So,
the ability to communicate with trees happens because the trees want to
converse with us. Conversations imply giver and receiver and without
one or the other, the conversation will not happen.

Let's distinguish between communion with all life and conversations
with other life forms. Communion with all life is the recognition and
experience of being all that is, while conversations with other life forms
involves a separatist perception where there is a giver and receiver
exchanging thoughts or feelings.

Q. WHAT ARE SOME PRACTICAL THINGS WE CAN DO TO GROW IN
AWARENESS AND BECOME MORE CONSCIOUS?

A. Source is saying that the very first thing to do is to have the desire to
know yourself. This may not sound like a practical application, but we
have to remember what comes to us in our perceptual field is a result of
our desires and thoughts.

> For myself, I learned a lot through my meditations, but I also
> kept a daily journal, and I inquired deeply and honestly into my
> own associations and beliefs. I was so interested in how my
> thoughts created my experiences and how they played out in my
> relationships for positive and negative that I wanted to

understand how my thinking and believing were the causative elements of the experiences in my life. I needed to confirm that my associations did have a manifestation in the outer world.

As I journaled, I found many thoughts and associations that were causes, and I also had memories of past lives surface that were affecting my perceptions in the present. Once I saw this, it gave me the opportunity to redefine and change my subconscious programming, and then I saw the reflection of the change also appear in my outer world. This led me to teach a weekly program on Transformational Writing. I will have a workbook published for this process in 2015.

So, begin to inquire about everything in your life. If you wake up in a bad mood, sit down for five minutes with a pen and paper and describe your mood. Ask yourself what this mood represents or means to you. Every emotion and mood has an inner association within us. We give things all the meaning they have for us. If we find we've made a negative association with something, we can change the definition into something positive that serves us. This is all done by journaling. It is one of the most powerful things you can do and one of the least expensive. It will transform your life by leaps and bounds in just minutes. Self-honesty is crucial to this process. We all have a dark side that is not nice and can be very judgmental. Being honest about this in our learning process helps us move out of it and realize that we're no better than anyone else. Seeing this and being honest about this leads to compassion and understanding for ourselves and others. It helps us undo our judgment of ourselves and others. All this is a necessary process in clearing the way to the love that has always been within us.

If you really want to shift your consciousness, the first and most important step is to have the desire and the willingness to inquire or meditate. You can also partake in release work or energy work that is designed to help shift your energy and awaken your higher centers.

Chapter 4

Angels, Archangels
& Ascended Masters

As I was saying the opening prayer, the room filled with many tiny little flames of fire. They belong to each one of you, and they're suspended in the air above your heads. They are teardrop in shape. They may have something to do with our topic tonight.

Q. WHAT ARE *ANGELS*?

A. Angels are emanations and expressions of the Rays of Source.

Q. WHAT ARE *ARCHANGELS*?

A. Archangels are masterful angels who have been appointed by Source for specific functions. Angels and archangels differ in that angels are rays of light that are very soft, loving and gentle in their nature and are an extension of God's rays. They do have various personalities or aspects to them that can be quite varied. Archangels are beings that are very masterful in certain arts, and they have divine appointments, or missions, usually to uphold God's Plan for creation in some way. You could say they are adept in the arts of the Creator. They are appearing very tall and huge and more defined in density than what I am seeing as angels, which have more of an emanation of light in their make up.

Q. WHAT ARE *ASCENDED MASTERS*?

A. Ascended masters are beings who have evolved in their spirit/soul consciousness and have achieved varying levels of mastery. They have had many lifetimes on many dimensions and planets, including Earth. They have developed skills in manifesting, healing, transmutation, de-materialization, physical immortality, higher sciences and the arts, to name a few. They have achieved individuated mastery in these ways but would still be evolving in their spirit selves.

Q. IS THERE A HIERARCHY OF ANGELS?

A. They wouldn't use the word "hierarchy." Rather, they'd say that they have different purposes. There's not a hierarchy in terms that one is better or higher than another. However, there is a difference in terms of their individuated vibration, mastery and purpose. Some would have achieved more knowledge and expertise than others, but they do not consider themselves unequal to other angels in any way.

Q. DO ANGELS FIGHT?

A. They are smiling at this question, saying, "We don't fight, we have discussions!" So, no, they don't fight in terms of what we would imagine as emotions of anger and the like, but they do have lively conversations. I feel no anger from them.

Q. ARE THERE ANGELS ON EARTH?

A. Yes, millions and billions, perhaps even more! They aren't exclusive to Earth, however. There are some that are here in physical bodies and some that are not, and they can be in many other dimensions at once We all have a guardian angel so there is at least 7+ billion angels, however our guardian angel would not be taking on a physical form unless it was for a particular temporary purpose.

Q. CAN AND DO ANGELS INTERCEDE FOR US?

A. Yes, guardian angels can and do intercede for us as often as they can. They always show up for babies. Every time a child is born, there is an angel who is appointed to look over them and help them fulfill their soul purpose. We would recognize this angel as the guardian angel, and it accompanies the individual throughout his/her entire lifetime.

Q. DO DIFFERENT ANGELS HAVE DIFFERENT RELATIONSHIPS WITH HUMANS, OR CAN ONE ANGEL BE ALL THINGS FOR ONE PERSON? DO WE HAVE WEALTH, CAREER, HEALTH AND PROTECTOR ANGELS?

A. When you ask, "Are there specific angels for specific purposes?" what I'm hearing from your own guardian angel is that It would like you to have a better relationship with it. This one angel has been assigned specifically to you to help you fulfill your own unique soul purpose. This would cover all the various aspects of your soul journey—protection from things that would take you off your path, guidance into the correct career path, *etc*. Your angel can't do everything for you, however, it can and does help you with the things you need to fulfill your soul contract. Many aspects of the fulfillment of your contract have to do with the decisions you make along the way. Some guardian angels appear as warrior types, some as loving and gentle and others as wise guardians. The type of guardian angel chosen is because of what the person's individual soul requires. Your guardian angel will carry the tools, qualities and attributes needed to help you fulfill your contract. Of course, their guidance can be thwarted by the free-will choices that you make in your life.

Q. ARE THERE ANGELS OF KARMA?

A. Yes, there are angels of karma, but let me explain. There are angels that you encounter after you cross over from this life who help you with your life review. You could call them "angels of karma" in this sense because they help you evaluate the life you lived when you leave this Earth. I do not see angels that are judges or that keep a record of your transgressions, however.

Q. DO ANGELS TAKE ON FORM?

A. Angels can and do take on physical form in certain cases for specific reasons. In these cases, the purpose for taking on a physical form determines how long they stay in form. It could be for a few moments, or it could be a lifetime. Angels are mainly spirit beings. They sometimes make themselves known to people as rays of varying colors, depending on their specific qualities or attributes.

Q. IS THERE A DIFFERENCE BETWEEN GUIDES, MENTORS AND ANGELS?

A. Yes, there is. True guides are most often people who have lived other lives on Earth or other planets and are now in spirit form. They have gained various degrees of knowledge and experience and have been given the assignment or opportunity to be guides for people on Earth or on other spiritual planes. Many relatives can become guides once they cross over, once they have grown in their soul experience enough to be allowed to be guides, when that is their wish.

You can have lower-astral beings pretending to be guides for people when they really aren't, so discernment is necessary. These spirits can fool those who have limited skills of discernment or who haven't cleared their distorted beliefs and judgments. False guides tell people what to do, and they pretend to be saints, Jesus or other famous people. They will use people who are naïve, need their ego bolstered, or are insecure. True guides will never tell you what to do, but they will always lead you to the greater truths of self-mastery, love, and healing. They help you face yourself and strengthen your ability to discern and choose. They may even leave you for a period of time if you are meant to become more mature or masterful of your own accord. These times may feel as if you have been abandoned, but they are still very much aware of you.

Mentors don't ever incarnate on Earth, as they are higher-dimensional beings. They could be angels, or beings from other dimensions, or a being from a person's galactic soul family who is appointed to be a mentor, like a wise parent watching you grow, experience or learn or help you fulfill a planetary mission. They influence you with thoughts and telepathically give you information. Their purpose is to watch and support your personal mastery and mission, while stepping back and allowing you to make your own choices. They, as well as your guardian angel, will be present at your life review when you cross over. They also help you decide what your next incarnation will be about when the time comes for you to come into another lifetime. They may also encourage you to go on other missions not on Earth. They are very masterful and appear as very powerful beings.

Angels are extensions of the Rays of Source as mentioned previously. They may be appointed to be guardian angels for the sole purpose of helping a person fulfill their soul contract. They would protect as much as they are able, deter negative influences, keep you away from as many wrong paths as possible, and thwart relationships or situations that would hinder or set you back on your soul's journey. I say they do this as much as they are able, because they have to allow for your own free-will choices. If you have to go through certain experiences to achieve mastery on some level, they will not interfere with those experiences. They will, however, protect you as much as possible throughout those experiences.

Other angels who are not guardian angels have other duties and purposes throughout the many dimensions between here and Source. There are angels of healing, angels of teaching and learning, angels of music and the arts, angels of science and geometries and on it goes!

Q. ARE THERE DARK ANGELS OR FALLEN ANGELS?

A. Yes, there can be angels who have descended and gotten caught in lower densities. If an angel keeps descending to lower densities, Source no longer calls them angels, but calls them demons. Angels that have fallen too far from Source no longer retain their angelic frequency.

When I tune into fallen angels, I feel hot from the inside out, and I see that demons are in a process of disintegration. By the time something falls to the level of a demon, even though they wreak havoc, they are disintegrating from the inside. Because of this, they are limited in their effect. They have a limited lifespan. Source wants everyone to be aware of this, so that when demons put on their big shows to make people fearful, you will remember where they are on the scale of things.

Source is saying that a demon's biggest ability is manipulation and lies. "Deceit" seems to be a big word for them. Their game is to deceive predominately on mental and emotional levels. They work on people's mental and emotional bodies by putting untrue ideas or feelings in people to cause divisions. So remember that they have a limited lifespan and need to take power from others to continue to be.

Q. ARE THERE OTHER WAYS THEY INFLUENCE US?

A. They influence us through chaos and division. They like to cause and produce insanity and separation in people and situations. If a demon can give us negative thoughts or feelings and make us angry, make us crazy, they can then feed off of these emotional energies in us. We then contribute to creating chaos in our lives and in our world, which causes accidents, sickness, death and violence—more fuel or food for demonic forces. Still, we have to be really clear. Demons don't carry much power of their own. Their influence is limited. They have to use our energy fields to accomplish havoc. They use our emotional and mental bodies to cause problems by instilling fear or confusion within us.

Here's an example: Let's say someone's just come off of a broken relationship and they're devastated by it. A demon will use that opportunity to put all kinds of ideas in the person's head to make them suspicious, or make them go one step further into despondency so they're not in control of their emotions. I see these little spheres of thought being created when we think. In actuality, we're sending out negative chaos balls. Anyone else who is vulnerable to the same thing is now influenced or affected by these balls. This is how war, divisions, murders, suicides and all sorts of catastrophes are caused. It is done through the implantation of negativity in vulnerable people.

I also see demons gathering around soldiers in battlefields. I see hordes of them over soldiers who are fighting wars. This is a major way in which chaotic forces are kept in place, by allowing them to feed off humans. However, Source is being really clear that demons, of their own accord, are very limited in power. So much of what they do is based on deception. They will hover over one soldier and then hover over another one, to create a mass energy of chaos through the collective group of soldiers. Demons themselves are not an army en masse—they use the group of human soldiers to achieve negative power and force.

Q. DO RELIGIONS USE ANGELS AND ARCHANGELS IN RITUALS?

A. Yes, the invoking of angels and archangels has been and still is commonly used in rituals by religions as well as those who are performing white- and black-magic ceremonies.

Earlier we said that archangels have specific assignments given to them by Source because of the specific qualities and powers each one has. Those that use ritual have found out about those qualities and powers and know how to invoke them for their own desired result. It is not the angel or archangel itself that comes to the ritual, rather it is the manifestation of the qualities and powers that occurs through the medium of words, elements and geometric arrangements. When you perform a certain ritual, the ritual will generate its own power. The angel or archangel itself does not come down to accommodate those rituals.

Specific angels or archangels called by people do not individually come down to them. What a person is really tapping into is the angel's particular frequency, which can be brought into a desire, to help it manifest. An angel's mission is not to come and visit a person's personal ego, but a guardian angel is appointed to the individual at birth and stays with them throughout their life. Our own guardian angel is our gift from Source—even so, it's job is not to grant us wishes.

Q. WHAT IS THE PROPORTION OF GOOD ANGELS VERSUS DEMONS?

A. There are many more good angels. Let me explain it to you vibrationally. There are billions of good angels, and you could equally have billions of demons. However, their power does not compare. Angels have much more power than demons. A billion demons is much weaker vibrationally than a billion angels. There's a huge difference here in terms of what each is capable of doing.

Q. DO DEMONS CAUSE A PERSON TO THINK NEGATIVELY?

A. Yes, but you can offset this by remembering that any unloving thought directed at others or yourself is not coming from Source or from any true guide or higher being. You can ask Source for help in reversing any negative thought so you can choose peace instead.

Q. ARE ANGEL CARDS HELPFUL?

A. Anything that helps someone shift into a positive place is helpful. If the association a person is making with the information on the card helps them move positively forward in their lives, then it's helpful. Once again, it is good to remember that the angels that are printed on cards do not specifically come to people. It is the qualities and attributes assigned to the angel that bring upliftment and shifts. It's not that they wouldn't come to someone, but not in the majority of cases. When using angel cards, you're calling on a certain image energy or quality that you may need to help move you forward in your life. This can and often does, produce positive results. Most likely it is your own guardian angel who helps you choose the card that helps you the most.

Q. IF PEOPLE ARE NOT CHANNELING ANGELS OR ARCHANGELS, ARE THEY CONNECTING WITH THAT ANGEL'S FREQUENCY?

A. Angels and archangels don't channel through anyone. That's part of the deception that's going on. They have qualities and are given assignments by Source. Part of their assignment or mission could be to hover over Earth to hold a certain energy or impart particular light rays that allow certain things to unfold. Only in rare cases do they deliberately come into the particular affairs of men. I am not talking about your own guardian angel here—that angel is very much a part of your personal affairs.

Q. IF A PERSON CLAIMS TO BE CHANNELING AN ANGEL OR AN ARCHANGEL, ARE THEY REALLY CHANNELING A DEMON ENERGY?

A. There are demons that would take advantage of that opportunity, but I wouldn't say that all the messages that people seem to get from angels are from demons. Sometimes a person could be tuning into their own angelic nature or higher aspects, or their own guardian angel. This is when discernment becomes very important.

Q. SOMETIMES PEOPLE BUY LITTLE ANGEL PINS THAT THEY WEAR FOR PROTECTION. DO THEY REALLY PROTECT?

A. Yes, they can help protect because of the intention around them. It is the intention that offers the protection, not the pin itself.

Q. DO WE SEE ANGELS WHEN WE DIE?

A. Your own angel most definitely will be there! It's being really clear that it has never left your side and never will leave your side until the end, when its assignment is finished. Sometimes there are groups of angels who come to attend to someone who has crossed, but this is not the case for everyone. It can be the case for those who are angels themselves returning home to their angel family, or for someone who needs to go to a certain or specific "healing plane." All people will, however, meet their own guardian angels.

Q. WHEN YOU COME BACK IN DIFFERENT LIVES, WILL YOU HAVE THE SAME GUARDIAN ANGEL?

A. Not necessarily. It depends on what your soul contract is. Earlier we mentioned that angels have their own personalities and qualities—different wavelengths is really what it is. You may have the same angel or not, depending on what your soul desires to accomplish in a particular life. Remember that the angel assigned to you at birth is chosen because it carries the frequencies or qualities that will help you fulfill your soul contract. This could change with each life. It is good to know that your guardian angel also progresses through the victories you make in your life and by its own efforts in its assignment with you.

Q. IS THE ANGEL GABRIEL MALE OR FEMALE?

A. Predominately female, but all angels carry both essences within.

Q. HOW CAN MY GUARDIAN ANGEL ASSIST ME IN A POSITIVE WAY?

A. Once you know your own angel and establish your connection with it, it can do a lot to help you. It acts as a liaison between you and Source. It's interested in helping you establish a direct relationship with Source so that you're always able to move forward and receive clear information in any situation. It guides you in that direction by sending you thoughts that you receive as inspiration or new ideas; they prevent and deter harm; they soothe and comfort and remind you that you are loved and are important. You can begin a journal with your angel and write it letters or pour out your thoughts and feelings to it. Ask it for what you need and pay attention to the little, or big, signs that show up in your life that let you know it has heard you. This works!

Q. CAN MY GUARDIAN ANGEL INFLUENCE ME NEGATIVELY?

A. No, your guardian angel wouldn't do that. Demons could, but we've already talked about that and the type of influence they could have.

Q. CAN THE INFILTRATION OF NEGATIVE INFLUENCES OVERRIDE THE POSITIVE ASSISTANCE OF MY GUARDIAN ANGEL, IF IT IS THERE TO PROTECT ME?

A. Good question! Everyone has their own vulnerabilities. Negative influences come in when and where you are vulnerable or weakened. They use what you haven't healed in yourself to influence you. It reminds me of the old cartoons, where the good angel is on one shoulder and the devil is on the other shoulder. Both are trying to influence the person, and the choice of which voice the person will listen to is up to that person. If they choose to listen to the negative voice, they will fall into negativity. If they choose to listen to their angel voice, they will have help in overcoming their vulnerabilities. Everyone has their own power of decision. Indeed, we are choosing all the time which voice to listen to. The power of our own decision is very important here. Many people pick the weaker position. They'll say, "I'm a victim in this situation. I'm down and out. I can't get out of this." There's a point of intersection here between the two voices where your own voice has to make a choice. When do negative forces get in? When we give up. Even then, you can still make another choice. Even if the negative gets in, and you're down in the depths of despair and feel immobilized, you can still make another choice, even if it is only to say, "Source, help me!" This is also the perfect time to ask your own guardian angel to intervene for you and protect you. You can also call on your own I AM Presence and surrender the situation to It.

> I've been in situations when I have felt so horribly in despair that I felt paralyzed with no willpower left. I couldn't make a thought to save myself. In those dark nights of my soul, the only thing I could do was say, "God, help me. Just help me." I would always be answered. Sometimes it was a ray of light in my feeling, or a new and brighter thought. Sometimes all anxiety left and I'd feel immediate peace. Other times, I'd be reminded of my power to create my own reality, so I'd leave my victim perception. Still, other times some one would call me or stop by, or offer me some healing assistance.

> Help can take many forms, so pay attention. It took me asking and making the sincere choice to be helped and just surrendering, in other words. I always surrender to God when I feel I'm in a situation I can't get out of myself. I have no problem admitting I can't figure something out. It really is all about our decision. Even if you say, "I don't think I'm consciously choosing the negative..." ask your angel to show

you the many times when you could have made a different choice and you wanted to wallow a little bit longer in the negative. You will be shown how much you participate in staying in negativity. We do receive much protection from our guardian angel all the time. Most likely, we are not aware of just how much we have been protected!

In relation to the influence of negative forces, I'm also hearing that we need to watch what food we eat. We do absorb the vibration of whatever it is that we're eating. Your angel will help you get sensitive to the vibrations of foods. We'll use meat as a good example. We know that animals are killed for our consumption. I've been around cattle, and I have seen them interact with their families. They know when something's wrong with a family member. They go through a trauma just as we would. It wouldn't be any different than us knowing that we're all in a line to be killed. Cows know. Think of the trauma and fear that is in an animal when it is being killed.

The other thing to be aware of and sensitive to is how foods are grown and treated. We spoke about this in great length in *A Time of Change*. Shifting into eating foods that won't leave negative imprints in your energy field is a good practice. If you are a person who needs animal protein, try to buy meat that is humanely treated and killed as well as grass fed with no hormones or other chemicals in their diet. Remember to always bless your food with gratitude, no matter if you're a vegetarian or a meat eater. Try to choose only 'happy foods' – this is an intuitive exercise. Without any preconceived ideas about food, try to go into a food store and ask to be led to the 'happy foods' for you or your family and see what you gravitate towards. *Don't analyze what food you're drawn to – just allow.* It could be different each time you shop. This exercise requires you to trust your instincts.

Q. HOW CAN MY ARCHANGEL ASSIST ME?

A. You don't have your own personal archangel. What you do have is a part of you that's an archangel self in a higher dimension; it's a part of your own higher aspects on your way to God realization. We do not have an archangel assigned to us other than this.

Your own archangel self can assist in the sense that it can provide you qualities or virtues like strength and courage, the impetus to pick yourself up, or the ability to discern greater truths. This part of us offers strength, courage, determination, perseverance, knowledge and Truth. I'm seeing steps to an actual ladder of ascent between the you here and that part of you that's more ascended up the ladder. It's just an image they're giving me. If you put yourself on a rung of the ladder and climb up to it, you can actually put yourself in your own archangel energy and feel it. It does not come down to you; you go up to it. You can do this through meditation also. Eventually, the you that is physically here now will incorporate the frequency of your archangel self into your life here, if you are doing the inner transformation required.

Q. WHAT IS THE PURPOSE OF LITTLE CHERUB ANGELS?

A. Cherubs are very close to what we consider elementals, forests and Nature. They work more with Nature than with people. They could be considered part of the elemental kingdom or the in-between worlds. They can perform specific functions for us, however, when necessary.

Q. WHAT ARE ELEMENTALS?

A. The spirits of Nature—fairies, sprites, Nature and tree spirits, and gnomes, to name a few. They are also earth, air, water, and fire as living elements.

Q. SO THEIR PURPOSE IS TO DEVELOP NATURE?

A. Anything to do with Nature is their job. Interestingly, "cherub" angel forms look very different than Nature spirits, but they are very similar vibrationally to that kingdom. They would have a different job to do than, let's say, a fairy would. They unify kingdoms in that they bridge the Nature Kingdom to the angelic world. They're not Nature spirits, but they work with Nature. They are a connection between worlds. They oversee and work with the Kingdom of Nature, but their light is different. Nature needs angel light as well as sunlight to function properly.

Q. ARE THEY PROTECTING THE EARTH?

A. They do whatever job needs to be done that helps keep the kingdoms of Nature in order. They could be in the forest with the trees or in the water. They could help fish or work closely with amphibians or water creatures or birds, but I don't see them working very much with humans in this way. There are many factors that go into keeping the Earth is order—cherubs play one part in this process.

Q. ARE THE ANGELS GETTING READY FOR SOMETHING BIG?

A. There is a war going on here now between good and evil, and it feels like it's getting more intense and is coming to a head. This war between dark and light has been going on for some time now. There have been many wars in many dimensions, as well as here on Earth.

Many demons in this dimension are about to be banished. It's the final fight before they have to leave. They've been given a certain time to wreak their havoc, and that time is closing. They're going to be sent elsewhere. They're trying to see how many souls they can take with them before then. So you are right—it is intensifying.

Q. WHY CAN'T WE SEE MORE ANGELS?

A. You would be able to, if you would meditate on them. I feel it right in the solar plexus for me, and I smell flowers, lilies specifically.

Q. WHY ARE MAINSTREAM RELIGIONS AFRAID OF US CALLING IN ANGELS?

A. They are very aware of demons, and they are generally concerned that people will leave an opening through which they could be possessed. They are concerned about people opening themselves up to realms about which they don't know enough about.

Q. WHAT DO ANGELS WANT FROM US?

A. They want us to pay attention. "Pay attention!" That's what I heard. They want us to establish a relationship with them. Everyone's own angel has incredible powers of discernment. If you could get close to your own angel, you'd know your own powers of discernment, which seem vitally important right now. If there's anything that people lack, it's that they don't know how to discern who's talking to them, and they can't discern negative energies from positive ones. Therefore, I'm hearing words like, "You could avoid tripping yourself up," if you had greater powers of personal discernment.

They also want us to fulfill our contracts. They feel we waste time, that we entertain too many negative thoughts, and that we don't perform to the best of our abilities because we have vulnerable parts of us, and we're listening to the wrong side. So, I feel frustration from our angels in the sense that they want us to accomplish; they don't like us being lazy and wasting time and wasting our lives.

Q. SAY YOU'RE CONSTANTLY NEGATIVE ALL THE TIME. WHERE IS YOUR GUARDIAN ANGEL THEN, IF THE DEMONS ARE WINNING?

A. In terms of the type of power demons have, it's an illusion that they are winning. They can make somebody feel lost; or cause insanity, which leaves you unable to make good choices. So yes, they can wreak havoc in your life, and they can actually ruin your life, but only because you've chosen at some point to listen more to the negative than the positive. That's why your angels are saying, "Look. We're your strength. If you're down in the depths of despair, you need to call on us for strength." If you can't think of a positive thought, just say. "I need strength. Help." Meet yourself where you are. Don't give yourself some lofty goal, if you know you're in a black hole and you just need to be able to have some peace of mind. You say, "I need peace of mind right now."

Demons play with your mind, but ultimately, you're the one who has to choose to heal whatever is underneath your mind or emotions. You still have free will to ask for help. Source is saying that the direction of your life is up to you. There are many times when you have to fight. I can remember one of my dark nights—I've had so many—when I felt that none of my guidance was there. I kept saying, "Where are you?" No answer. This went on for a couple years. I felt nothing—no help, to the point where I thought I must be really bad, because I felt so abandoned, or I must have really gone off my path, because none of my guides were showing up. They weren't helping me. It actually took me two and a half years before I actually got an answer, which was that they left because it was time for me to be more masterful. This meant that they wanted me to be more of my own self-sovereign being, because ultimately, we all need to master ourselves. They will assist you along the way and help you with choices and give you a sense of direction, but there's a point when Source says, "Okay, it's time to grow up. You need to become a more conscious, discerning being who can self-create."

Q. DO WE EVER OUT-GROW OUR GUIDES?

A. Yes, but this doesn't mean that you won't have another type of guide come in and take you to a higher level. When people get through some of their hardest challenges by sheer perseverance of their own, their lives can change drastically. Think of it in terms of maturity. Every one of us is being asked to become our own creator. This implies that the dependency we have on higher beings to look out for us and save us will have to go as we become more self-realized. When your spirit is ready, you will be guided to grow up and become a more conscious manifester.

We are all given powers of manifestation. There comes a point when you have to examine your own consciousness, look into your own issues, and see how your perceptions and beliefs are creating your experiences. You have to undo your own belief structures and build new ones that are positive and beneficial to yourself and to all humankind. Ultimately, as a sovereign spirit, you're the one who's responsible for yourself. Guides will help you, and then the time comes when they'll say, "Okay. You've come to this place. Now the next step is to grow further." They will step aside and be silent so you can grow on your own, much as parents who step back to allow their children to grow. We may perceive this as abandonment, but it isn't really. These times are called dark nights of the soul because you feel as if you've been left in a pit with nobody to help. You're being asked to stand up by yourself and walk up the mountain.

Even so, there is always help on every level to God realization. Even though there are times when your guides step back, you can still ask for peace instead of conflict and you will receive it. But this is precisely the point - as we go through dark nights of the soul, part of our maturing process may be to practice choosing peace over believing in conflict. We may be being asked to decide which side of the fence we're going to energize and make real for ourselves. Deciding for peace when you're filled with inner conflict or fear is a huge victory for the soul. When I say there is always help, I mean encouragement and love is always sent to us while we are going through a dark night. Where the drawing back from our guides happens is that you will hear no message from them during this time because it is a time of choosing in our soul growth. The choices we make determine the growth

Q. I WAS WITH A FRIEND WHO CLAIMS TO CHANNEL THE PLEIADIANS. I DON'T KNOW WHO HE'S REALLY CHANNELING. I FIND WHAT HE SAYS VERY VALUABLE. I KNOW THAT ULTIMATELY WE HAVE TO STAND IN OUR OWN POWER, BUT IS THERE A PLACE FOR CHANNELED INFORMATION AS WELL, IN TERMS OF GUIDANCE?

A. Source is saying that higher beings do not channel through anyone. By channeling I mean when a spirit talks *through* a person, as in a trance state, or when the spirit uses the channel's body and voice to deliver messages. I am distinguishing this from telepathic communication in which the "channel" is receiving messages telepathically, which is the appropriate form of channeling. Source has always said that a higher being has no need to use another person's body to speak. Why would it need it to get a message across? In fact, a higher being would be very careful about *not* using a person's body.

The Pleiadian world is very scientific and they have given brilliant technological advancements and healing methods, but we've also had some negative technology come from there too. Positive Pleiadians may spend time talking to (not through) people who are going to promote the evolution of the Earth and its species in some way. If this is the case with your friend, that's great. It could also be that he was once a Pleiadian, and it is his own Pleiadian self coming through.

> A higher being has no need to channel. When I personally bring forth this information, my communication is telepathic—no other being is altering my voice or inhabiting my body. I am having a telepathic conversation with Source.

Higher beings give inspiration or genius—something on a much higher level. They're very clear in that they never need to channel *through* a body. High frequency information comes through telepathically or through direct knowing.

Participant: I like that we are here asking questions about angels and archangels, which heretofore would have been very entrenched in our religious upbringing. We're asking, "Is it valid to believe in this?" The very fact that we're asking these questions at all is making us choose, which is where, if I understand correctly, Source wants us to go. It wants us to make our own choices based on our knowledge, our information, our growth, our level of maturity.

Yes, that's it. What I'm hearing about self-mastery, isn't that your life is always rosy. It's about how we respond to life. Can you respond without freaking out? Can you not be paralyzed with fear if something happens? Are you connected enough to receive an inspiring answer? Let's say something totally out of the blue happens, something you've never had to deal with before, something you have no training in. When you're connected to your inner self you'll receive information on how to solve any problem. You'll get that solution because you've asked for it. You'll be able to respond to any situation without feeling powerless.

Achieving higher levels of self-mastery doesn't mean that you'll never go through a hard time, or that you'll never be tested, because you will. In fact, sometimes, the next level could require something difficult for you to go through. Even if you think you've grown past something, you'll be presented with it again in the future to make sure you've healed what you think you've healed. It isn't because anyone's attacking you—it's because this is how you measure your true progress. This is the tempering process that you go through on your ascent.

Q. I'VE HEARD IF YOU HAVEN'T OVERCOME SOMETHING IN YOUR PREVIOUS LIVES, IT'LL HAUNT YOU IN THIS LIFETIME. HOW DO WE KNOW, IF WE CAN'T REMEMBER OUR PAST LIVES?

A. You really don't have to know what's happened in past lives. All you have to know is what's happening in your life now. If a situation in your life now is similar to a situation in a past-life experience, you're still in the same place. What are you going to do with it? It's always about "What are you going to do with it?" What do you need to choose, release, forgive, learn, or overcome? There are times when you'll be "shown" one of your other lives if there is something in it you need to know. It can be a spontaneous remembering in a flash. But if that isn't happening, carry on with the task at hand.

The reality that you're experiencing now will tell you what your issues are. Do you like what you're experiencing? Do the same things show up over and over again? It doesn't matter where they came from. It only matters what you do with them and how you can grow from them. Can you transform a pattern if it's something that you don't like? Will it take courage, change, forgiveness, purification or releasing?

At other times, you will get help from your own inner guidance if it will benefit you to know where the pattern came from that you keep repeating, or the decision that you keep making that is counterproductive to your well being.

It might be tempting to associate transforming patterns with 'learning lessons', but the energy behind them is very different. 'Lessons' imply something that is given you from an outside source- a test in which you can pass or fail. Lessons imply a training, or going through a challenge or hardship in order to learn something.

'Patterns' are things inside us that are there because they're passed down or the result of our own chronic choices and decisions. We can keep repeating the same thing forever if we want to and no one will be there to tell us we can't. There is no authority telling us we have to learn something. We ourselves will eventually want to change because we will get tired of the same experience. In this way we cause our own awakening. A guide would be there to help you see what the pattern is.

We have also mentioned that the spirit/soul complex wants to achieve *victories*. Victories are defined as the making of a higher choice when presented with a lesser one. It is when a challenge is met with courage and the choosing of a higher virtue. These are victories in that they are evidence the person is becoming more aware of God consciousness. They are understanding that what they choose and decide makes a big impact on themselves and the world.

My last partner, before AHONU, committed suicide. I didn't see it coming, and yet I knew he was depressed. I knew him for eight years as a friend, and he had been suicidal many times, but I didn't see this time coming. Because I never saw his suicide coming, I went back to our cabin six months later because I wanted to know, "What did I miss? I must have missed something." And sure enough, because I asked to see what I had missed, I was put in touch with his emotions so I could feel and think what he was feeling and thinking at the time. I felt the degree of his pain, his inner torment, his thoughts, his horrible sadness. I don't want to miss something like that again. If I ever come across anybody who is like that in my future, I want to be able to know, so I could possibly do something different. I am saying this with the awareness that each person has the right to their choices, but presenting other options to them might be helpful.

Although the entire event was devastating for me and for everyone who knew and loved him, I was able understand it in a way that was much more mature and centered than I would have been able to do even ten years prior. I could see it spiritually, and I could look at it from different angles. I wanted more awareness about the entire thing and went back to the cabin two more times to gather anything more I could realize from that time in my life. Each visit back gave me more awareness, which helped me with my own healing of it, but also in understanding others who feel this way. I had dreams about him for a long time afterwards, seeing the different stages he was going through in spirit and the progress he was making. There was no 'punishment' of his suicide by God, no abandonment or being cast out. He had his life review just as we all will and it was himself that chose to contemplate his choices and decisions. When a person is in spirit, they are still presented with choices and decisions which affect their own further awakening to God realization.

Let me tell you another couple of stories. Last week there was a woman at our meeting who had to take her mother into the emergency room at a hospital in Dublin. Apparently the negativity in this particular hospital is horrendous, from what people say. The woman was affected by this negativity the minute that she walked into the emergency room. There was a man in the waiting room who was staring at her with what she felt was evil intent. She felt she was being totally disarmed by this man's negativity. Severe panic and fear went through her. She did everything that she knew for protection and felt that none of it was working. Then, thankfully, another man started a conversation with her which broke the negative energy. That could have been her guardian angel's way of helping her in that moment. Even when telling us the story, she was still affected by it and was crying.

In a situation like this, watch your own fear in the moment. Try to become an observer. Take stock in the moment and observe yourself feeling fear, terror and panic. Watch the scene, watch your fear. Ask yourself, "What is the fear really about?" Feel it as deeply as you can, and you will locate what is being triggered in you. This way, you do not run from the fear, but instead receive information from it, understand it, and allow it. This process alone will cause the fear to move through you and dissolve. You can also make a different choice in those moments such as saying, "I choose peace instead of this." (from the Course In Miracles)

There is evil floating around, and it's obvious that there are entities afoot. Is this the collective dark history and shadows of ourselves coming out to be purified as greater light comes in?

I had a series of dreams when I was in my thirties and forties in which I would be confronted by evil energies—as well as invisible or dark energies. I consider those confrontations spiritual challenges for awakening.

I'll tell you one dream I had, because it was so bizarre. In the dream, I was in an older house in which we had lived some years back. I was going up the stairs to the attic. Stairs are usually a symbol of ascent in a dream where you're going to a higher level. As I climbed these stairs, three evil beings suddenly appeared to block my way. I knew they were called "The Bishops of Evil." They were tall, and they were an ugly, putrid, green color. The energy coming from them was menacing. I was paralyzed with fear. They were very threatening as I looked up at them, and I felt very little and powerless in comparison. I heard the same voice I had heard in another dream say, "There's only one God." As soon as I heard it, the evil beings vanished. What I awakened to from that experience is that Source is the only real Truth, and anything else that appears to be different, or unloving is an illusion. I had to learn that over and over throughout my spiritual journey.

In conclusion, the important thing to realize is that we have so much help and protection from so many things. We are not alone. We can become much more conscious of our own guardian angel, and our own higher aspects. As much as we are given guides, mentors, and a guardian angel, it is still Sources's intention that we rise up into our own magic presence and be a force for good. We are not meant to stay dependent like children, but become our God Self incarnate. This goal is what all true guidance is all about.

Chapter 5

Love

This session is an exploration of love as Source sees it.

Q. WHAT IS SOURCES'S DEFINITION OF *LOVE*?

A. Love is the field of all expression where everything is, and is allowed to be expressed. It is a dynamic, alive field where anything is possible. It is the desire and intention of Source that allows life to be, and it is the relationship of all life to life. It accepts what is expressed within it, whether that expression is for good or ill. It upholds the highest creative possibility and integrity and can't be destroyed. It says "yes" to whatever you desire, in the sense that it is a dynamic, creative field. Love holds all things in high esteem and promotes expression in greater and greater measures. It does not measure or judge. It is forever responsive to our thoughts and desires.

Q. WHAT ARE LOVE'S QUALITIES?

A. Love is free because there is no judgment within it. It is a dynamic field in the sense that it responds to everything, even though it doesn't judge what it's responding to. Its response is to allow. Love is innocent in its allowance, meaning it is completely harmless in its intent. It's the field where all possibilities exist and can be expressed and actualized. It is a dynamic and creative field. Love never ends. Love never dies. It's not an energy—rather, it is the creative life force itself and everything in existence is composed of its essence. It is the will and intention of God Source, which is that life exist and express itself.

Imagine looking up into the universe and watching the field of all possibilities, knowing that everything and anything is possible, accepted and allowed. Imagine that there are no limits to this creation. Imagine yourself as a life form that is formed from love's essence, completely loved and accepted, who has permission to express itself as it desires without limitations. Imagine that there are no boundaries to life. Imagine a quality of life that upholds your highest possible expressions and also allows your lowest. Imagine a presence that is ever patient because it allows, until you decide differently. Imagine never being judged; imagine only being welcomed.

Q. IS THERE AN OPPOSITE TO LOVE?

A. No. Within this field of love, you can express however you wish. Some people express in an unloving way, but yet, in the field of love, all is allowed. Unloving expressions are not loves opposite, because the field of love cannot be damaged in any way. I know many of us have experienced very tragic things, but love is still intact, and its benign presence can be felt through any adversity. Love is not the cause of tragedy or suffering—it is our choices that cause suffering. Still, love allows all our choices until we are ready to make higher ones. In this regard, how much of love we can feel or experience is determined by the quality of our choices. As our choices become more and more loving in their nature, we can then feel more love, because like attracts like.

There is no opposite to love because love is all encompassing. It is the original template from God Source, and it is the Truth that never changes. It is an absolute Truth—a constant, the blueprint behind all life. Without it, life would not be. Choices that are unloving in their motive have their consequences as a result of the Law of Cause and Effect. Love is a field that allows for all expressions and choices—it doesn't judge them and cannot be destroyed by them. This is why it has no opposite.

Q. HOW PRESENT IS LOVE IN OUR WORLD?

A. Love is completely present in our world, but the ability to feel and actualize itspresence and experience itspower is determined by our own choices and beliefs. The proportion of love in our world is unlimited, but the experiencing of It in our world is determined by the quality of our decisions and beliefs.

Q. WHAT'S THE RELATIONSHIP BETWEEN LOVE AND HATE?

A. I don't see that they have a relationship. Love *is*. It didn't say that love is the expression of everything. It said that love allows the expression of everything. There is no relationship between love and hate.

Q. ARE THEY OPPOSITES?

A. No, they are not opposites because love has no opposite. To think that it does is part of the illusion we're all under. We think, because of the limits of our polarity perception, that if you have love, it has to have an opposite. This is not so.

We try to down-step the different experiences we have and put them in certain categories so we can make sense of them in our world. Source is saying that evil, or hatred can't come close to what love is. Evil and hatred are the formations that result from choices that are made and beliefs that we have. Love allows for those expressions, but it clearly does not create them. They have no comparison to love. There are no similarities, because evil and hatred's perceived power and reality are based on illusions held in the mind. It's the difference between real and unreal. Love is real—meaning it is forever and unlimited in its qualities and power—but evil or hatred is finite and limited in its power. This is because love is the life force of creation and just is, whereas negative expressions come from beliefs, which are illusory and have no life force of their own, save what an individual gives them. They can seem to take on very potent and powerful expressions, as indeed the mind is very powerful, but negative expressions do not carry true life-force energy, therefore they are finite in their expressions.

Beneath all expressions of hatred or evil is a fear of being unloved, or an unawareness of love's presence. Because of this underlying fear, it appears that we must take or conquer what we need from life. We all have varying degrees of this fear within us. It is always the fear of not being loved or sustained by love or of being unworthy that lies beneath all expressions of hatred or evil.

Still, in this field of love that I'm seeing, there is no judgment around unloving expressions, even though we judge them here on Earth. The field of love doesn't put them in any category whatsoever, which is very interesting. You see, the problem with judging things and putting them into categories is that we just make more of them. The minute we label something or make a judgment about its being bad or good, or right or wrong, we make more of whatever we're judging. Source's intention is love, bliss and ecstasy.

Source is not saying that good and evil are both expressions of love, or that they are the same. Even though we're not judging hatred or evil, we're not saying that they're the same as love. They are not. We're saying that love allows all expressions. Source's original intention is only love, which is a dynamic and creative force. It is non-judgment, unlimited potentiality, freedom of expression, welcoming, acceptance, innocence, harmless causation, and unlimited opportunity to realize higher and higher expressions of itself without end. When we behave counter to that, love doesn't judge it, because it allows it all. Imagine for a moment if you were never told that you were bad or wrong. Imagine that there was no incrimination or disapproval, but only acceptance and welcoming. Would you be a different person? Would you look on others differently and behave differently? You would, as you would be transformed by the experience.

Q. WE'RE ALL TOLD THAT AT THE END OF OUR LIVES WE WILL
HAVE A LIFE REVIEW OF OURSELVES. ISN'T THAT BEING JUDGED?

A. No. What happens is that you see a movie of your life and you experience everything—every action and reaction—as the cause and effect of your choices, both high and low. You will experience yourself in a relationship with all life everywhere. Whatever someone else felt by your actions and behaviors will be shown to you as if you were experiencing it yourself. You will see what qualities or lack of quality you have donated to life—all life. You have either contributed to the experiencing and awareness of more love or you have deterred it. It could be a mixture of both. You will realize that you're partaking of everything and you are in relationship with everything. When you realize this, you will see how important and powerful you are.

For example, let's say that a mass murderer crosses over. The same process or review will be as true for him/her as it is for everyone else. Both the acts of love and the acts of harm will all be experienced as if the doer was also the receiver. We will all be shown what effect our beliefs and actions have had on everything, positive as well as negative. We'll be able to see it and experience it all. And that's as true of you as it would be of someone very evil.

There is no one waiting at the gate to send you to heaven or hell. You will experience yourself through your own behaviors, actions, victories and failures.

Q. THEN WE CAN GET AWAY WITH A FEW BAD THINGS?

A. Not really, because you're going to experience what the other person experienced as a result of you—good and not so good. You'll get to know that it's all one relationship with everyone and everything. So, there's no escape or separating yourself from your own cause and effect.

Our perceptions are very interesting because we use our perceptions to separate things and put them in categories. We put others in categories by our perceptions of them. We say that things are separate from us, and we label things. The truth is that there's no separation at all, between anything or anyone.

Here's another way to explain it. Remember when you were little and you'd have a bubble bath? You'd splash the water and make more bubbles. In this Field of all expression we're all making more bubbles. Whether we know it or not, every time a bubble is made, we experience it on some level of our being. It goes into our cells as knowledge or experience. Each "bubble" has a unique wavelength because we created it, which means that everyone will know it on some level, because we're all immersed in the "All That Is." The bubble is in the collective "soup." It's like adding another spice—everybody gets to "taste" what you've added to the All That Is at some level.

Q. YOU MENTIONED THAT THERE'S A CLEANSING GOING ON, AND PEOPLE OF ONE VIBRATION WILL GO TO A REALITY OF LIKE KIND AND OTHERS WILL GO TO REALITIES BASED ON THEIR VIBRATIONS. COULD THIS PROCESS BE CONSIDERED A JUDGMENT PROCESS?

A. Not in the sense of God Source judging us. What is true is that like attracts like, which is the Law of Cause and Effect in operation. Each spirit attracts to itself the place or vibration that matches its consciousness, until it awakens to remember God Source, which could happen at any moment. This is why we can't say that everyone is going to the fourth or fifth dimension, for example.

Q. SURVIVING CONCERNS ME. ARE THOSE WHO ARE MORE OPEN, ACCEPTING AND INTEGRATED MORE LIKELY TO SURVIVE?

A. Perhaps love's response to your fear is to show you that you *do* or will survive. It could be survival on this dimension to allay your fears if that will serve your awakening, or it can be you leave this dimension and see that you still *are*. Remember that we all survive as our spirit selves, whether we stay in a body or not. I know you are concerned with your physical-body survival. I can't say whether those who are more aware of

God Source than others are more likely to survive or not. Everyone has their own personal life plan going on. It all depends on individual soul contracts. Some may be meant to stay here and some may be meant to leave, and that may be determined by their soul contract rather than their frequency.

A Course in Miracles addresses the idea of conflict. It says in order to not experience conflict in our lives we have to forever give up the *idea* of conflict forever. The belief in it has to go. So here we are talking about hatred and evil, and we're being asked to choose only higher and higher standards of love. It isn't that you don't see evil things happen. Obviously, if someone's behaving in evil ways, it can't be denied, and there are those who appear "soul-less." We're not trying to say that unloving behavior is love. It isn't. Instead, when you consciously choose to hold yourself to higher and higher standards of love, you lose interest in judging others. You recognize that beneath the surface, all evil behavior is a call for love. How do you handle it?

If you have someone who's behaving insanely and criminally, you still have to remove them from society. You can't allow them to continue victimizing others, perpetuating the victim-victimizer game. The loving thing to do is to stop them from continuing to harm. I'm not talking about killing anyone. You can remove someone from society while understanding that all unloving acts are degrees of insanity and are calls for love. If you said, "I love you" to a person committing a crime, it may or may not have an effect on them, depending on the degree of their insanity. They may not be vibrating at a level where they can hear or accept that thought. Obviously, someone behaving in unloving and destructive ways has no self-love but within your own being, you can know that they are as unconditionally loved by Source as anyone else, and therefore, at the level of Source, there is no judgment.

There is still the Law of Cause and Effect in place as long as there is time. This is the law where like attracts like. Even so, in your own heart you can know that one brother is all brothers, and we can look on a brother with love and harmless intent no matter what the circumstances. You can do this while you lock the jail door, until the one who is behaving insanely chooses love and lives from love. This happens when the person is ready—it could take one or many lifetimes. Redemption can happen in an instant. It is not our place to magnify a person's guilt with our thoughts—it is our job to forgive and love, while removing a person from society who is harming others. Again, we are not talking about killing anyone—that is not our place.

In light of the extreme example above, we all need to look at our own behavior and thoughts to see how well we are choosing high standards of love, for ourselves as well as others. We may be causing as much damage with our own unloving thoughts or actions each day towards ourselves or others as a criminal would by an outward action.

Many believe that we need the yin and the yang—the good and the bad. However, I keep hearing Source say, "No. No." Those things that would be considered evil are not equal to Source's love. The problem is that we believe both good and evil are *real* and we think both are necessary. Only love is real. Evil is based on false perception. It has no self generative power of its own. Many people believe that in order to know love, you have to experience hate, or, in order to know good, you have to experience evil. Source is not agreeing with that. When you encounter love, it is a full experience in its own right. If you experience evil, you automatically know it is not love—there is nothing about it that feels loving. Neither is a requirement for the other to be known.

Q. THERE ARE UNLOVING EXPRESSIONS —THE HIGHER THE FREQUENCY OF A PERSON, THE MORE LOVE THAT IS EXPRESSED, THE MORE SOMEONE IS AWARE OF IT, THE MORE IT'S PERCEIVED AND FELT, THE MORE IT'S INTEGRATED, *ETC*. WHAT IS THE DIFFERENCE BETWEEN FREQUENCY AND VIBRATION. IS THAT A POLARITY?

A. It's possible to see it that way, although you are talking about forces of Nature that concern the material universe. The Earth is more magnetic, therefore its vibration is heavier. As vibration increases, it becomes denser or heavier—more compact or "physical," not lighter. We're trying to raise our oscillation rate to bring in a higher frequency—or electricals—and have less vibration—or magnetics. We're trying to fill our Earth bodies with more spiritual consciousness, which is light based or more electrical. Magnetics are vibration, but frequency is oscillation. When you increase your vibration, you make yourself heavier. When you increase your frequency, you make yourself lighter.

Our bodies are more carbon-based or magnetic because the Earth is more carbon-based. But as our Earth body incorporates more light, its biology also becomes more light based, as does our body, which means that we become more electrical in nature.

Q. YOU MENTIONED THAT WE ARE MADE FROM LOVE. IF SO, WHY DO WE FEEL SO BEREFT OF LOVE?

A. I just got an image of Santa Claus with a big bag of gifts. Source is saying, "You've forgotten that Santa Claus is real, and there is no coal coming to you—only good." Every time you judge someone, you will feel bereft of love because you can't judge someone and not feel the consequences of it somewhere in yourself. The belief in judgment makes you feel guilty, and when you feel guilty, you believe that you are not loved and are going to be punished. You can't feel or be love if you're doing that, which is why we feel bereft of love—because we're continually in judgment, which automatically creates fear, which blocks out the awareness of love's presence.

If you didn't believe in judgment, and you knew that you can't judge, and you understood that Source loves everyone the same, you would be in a state of harmlessness within yourself and with respect to others. In this state, you would never feel bereft of love. You feel bereft of love because you are in fear of punishment, which comes from judging yourself or another. Love demonstrates its reality when we're ready to welcome it and become it.

Q. WHAT'S THE ROLE OF GRACE IN RELATION TO LOVE?

A. Grace is an action or quality of love—it is the blessing that is love that forgives and returns to the state of innocence. It affirms and confirms that goodness not only exists, but it is also deserved.

When someone's really annoying you, bless them instead of judging them. Intend grace for them, and allow it to express itself however it can be expressed for that person. Grace is the blessing that comes out of love. You won't know how it will manifest in a person's life, and you don't need to know. You're not being specific and saying, "I'm blessing you because I want you to do this, this and this." You're blessing them by acknowledging that they are innocent in God's eyes, just as you are, even if they're not behaving like it, or they don't know it.

Q. SO IF YOU'RE SENDING LOVE TO SOMEBODY'S HEART, IS THAT GRACE THAT YOU'RE SENDING THEM?

A. Your motivation determines that. In other words, if you send love to someone out of a pure intention without any motive of your own, then it is an offer of Grace, which is a pure offering with none of your own agenda. Some people say they're sending love, but they really want to change something in the other person. In these cases, they're really sending judgment.

Q. YOU SPOKE ABOUT LOVING OTHERS BY WAY OF FORGIVENESS AND GRACE, BUT HOW DOES THAT APPLY TO OURSELVES, AND WHY DO WE HAVE SUCH DIFFICULTY LOVING OURSELVES?

A. It does apply to ourselves—self-forgiveness is necessary for each of us. When we don't forgive ourselves or someone else, we stay in guilt together with them. This means you and they are locked together into an event or a perception, and neither can be free. It serves no one to remain in unforgiveness. It does not allow for the experience or the awareness of love, and is not Source's will. Source would prefer that we learn from our mistakes and choose higher-loving expressions in the present and the future rather than to stay bogged down in the past. It desires this for all concerned in a situation or event.

Q. SO WE JUDGE OURSELVES, TOO?

A. You can't love yourself if you're judging anybody, including yourself. It's all one thing. Judgment is judgment, and it has its effect, which is the belief in guilt that demands punishment. If you judge another, then you will bring a perceived deserved punishment upon yourself, because somewhere within yourself you will know that your judgment has no foundation in love's reality. This will manifest as fear of loss, or an actual loss or illness—all determined by you at the subconscious level. Remember also that judgment against others keeps you in karmic bonds with them and prevents love from entering your and their awareness. In these situations, no one is freed.

Q. IS SELF-JUDGMENT LIKE, "I'M TOO FAT, I'M TOO THIN, I'M TOO TALL, MY HAIR'S THE WRONG COLOR, ETC.?"

A. Those are surface examples, but it can be much more tragic than that. We cause our own death, our own illnesses, our own lack and losses.

Think about what's beneath this, really — the belief in judgment that has to go, not just the act of judging or not judging. It's the belief in judgment. Judgment is also the belief in guilt. As long as you believe in guilt, you will project that belief in victimization upon yourself and out into the world. If you believe in victimization, then you can't believe you're loved, that you're made of love, or that you reside in a vast field of love now and always. Further, you won't believe in your own innate goodness, which deserves the best of everything, because that's how God Source made you and everyone and everything. The belief in victimhood and love don't go together.

Surrendering to forgiveness really means that you are willing to give up all those beliefs in judgment, guilt and victimization. Close your eyes and imagine just for a minute that those concepts and words do not exist. Let yourself feel what it feels like. Imagine that no one ever made you wrong or judged you in any way. Imagine that you never judged anyone or yourself. Imagine that you were never guilty. Instead, when mistakes were made, you were met with loving kindness and compassion and were given more love and grace to make a better choice. Imagine that you were always given another opportunity and another and another. Imagine that you did the same for others, which is what love does. It is ever patient and keeps offering opportunities to know and experience greater and greater realizations of love.

The choice to give up the idea and the belief in guilt, conflict and judgment is always available, whenever we are ready. The reason we haven't come to this realization is because we want other people to be guilty so we can feel justified in our grievances. We all do and have done this. There's no way we can know that we're loved or experience what real love is as long as we're doing that. Beneath the surface we'll always have the fear that God's going to punish us, because we know at some level that judging brings its own consequences through the law of attraction, as do all loving actions.

Q. IF WE STOP BELIEVING IN GUILT, IS IT AUTOMATICALLY REPLACED WITH LOVE?

A. Love is what's there and has always been there. You will now be aware of it and feel it more deeply.

Q. SO YOU DON'T HAVE TO WORK AT LOVE?

A. No, love is what's there when you give up the belief in guilt and judgment. This Field of Love has always been there. It has not gone anywhere and isn't going anywhere. You don't need to work at love, you need to work at releasing judgment.

Q. DO YOU HAVE TO WORK AT FORGIVENESS?

A. Only if you're not really willing to surrender your beliefs in guilt. If you had to ask Source for something, say, "Help me surrender these beliefs." What may be "work" is when you begin to notice how many times judgment surfaces in your daily life and how many times you have to remind yourself that guilt and judgment are not real.

Q. SO WE DON'T HAVE TO TRY TO LOVE OURSELVES OR OTHERS?

A. No, not when you truly forgive and bless. When you take away the beliefs mentioned above, suddenly you're in communion with life at a much deeper level. Your awareness and sensitivity to subtler energies increases. When you're in communion, or communication at these deeper levels, you feel love's presence more and more. All you feel is love when you're no longer interested in judgment. You realize and experience everyone and everything as yourself. You realize that you are good and God's will for you and all life is goodness. You determine how able you are to receive that goodness.

Participant: Communion seems to be such an interesting term.

Other participant: "Say it very slowly...Comm-union... Come into union. Come into unity. It means that we belong."

Participant: I feel that guilt and the belief in judgment form a disconnecting or separating energy that makes us feel alone and deprived.

Aingeal: Yes, that's right! Communion is also communication with all. People say, "I feel disconnected. I would like to be more in tune with everything. I would like to be more psychic." Those are things that are naturally there when you give up the beliefs in guilt and judgment. Your ability to give and receive information from this Field of Love is just there.

These little things we use judgment for—somebody's fat or thin, or unkempt or neat, poor or wealthy, etc.—underneath all that is still the belief in guilt and punishment. You may think this or that person should be more perfect in your eyes, more pleasing in God's eyes. They should dress better, they should be neater, smarter, richer or whatever. Even if you say, "I have to perfect myself, or be more perfect," that's a belief in guilt. Beneath all of that we're saying, "I'm better than them because at least I'm becoming a vegetarian. At least I'm doing this and I'm doing that or I'm better than the person who's eating meat," all of which is still a belief in guilt.

Source is basically saying, "Who cares? I allow everything—fat, skinny, neat, dirty, hobo, mansion—I allow it all." Source cares more about the state of your inner world, which is what you will be looking at in your life review.

We are all immaculate conceptions. You see, there's really no way out of love, thank goodness! You will always be given further opportunities to choose and realize love. Love will always be there for you whenever you are ready to accept it.

Q. ARE THERE EXAMPLES OF MOMENTS OF PURE LOVE?

A. There are times when you bless or express love with no agenda, or when you love another, desiring only their joy or happiness. These are moments of pure love. You can also include acts of courage for yourself or others, or acts of service to others done out of pure love without expectation of being paid or getting a return. Love does always return, however, in some way. Giving is receiving.

Q. WHEN I WATCH A BEAUTIFUL SUNSET, IS THAT A MOMENT OF PURE LOVE?

A. Yes, it could be, when you are in communion with the sunset—when you recognize that the sunset is you, and that you are the sunset—otherwise, it's just an experience of beauty. If the feeling of ecstasy you get from watching a beautiful sunset makes you feel loving or makes you feel a magnificence, it would be called an experience of love.

From Source's perspective, an example of the pure love that we're talking about is when you give as a natural extension of love. When you give for the joy of giving, it is an act of sharing or joining. It comes from a natural desire. You extend a hand just from kindness. More than that, it is a way of being where you are love itself—allowing, harmless in thought, word and action, desiring only to extend yourself as love.

Consider these examples of love in action. I was driving to Philadelphia to attend a seminar a few years ago, and I had to cross a bridge. When I got to the other end of the bridge, there was a stoplight, where these young boys wanted to wash my windshield for money. I didn't want them to because I didn't have any extra money to give them. I had five dollars with me for lunch, and that was it. I kept saying "no" to the boys. They ignored me and kept washing my windshield. I was watching how furious I was getting, and I thought, "Now I have to pay them." Or, "Don't pay them, because they didn't listen to me." Suddenly I heard Jesus's voice say to me, "That's your son." I felt Jesus meant it literally that these little boys were my own sons—my own children. I was so overcome by the truth of what I heard that I took out my fiver and I opened up the window to give it to them and right then the light changed, so I never got to give them the money.

But, when I got home that evening, my own three children had been busy making popsicle stick trivets during the day and they ran up to me saying, "Mommy, Mommy! We each sold a trivet today and we made $5.00!" It was so obvious that my willingness to give those boys my last $5.00 benefited my own children, proving that we are all in relationship with each other, a relationship that affects us all in each moment. How we look at, see and treat others affects what happens in our own lives and family. I didn't want to give. I was in full judgment. When I got to the point where I was willing to give up my lunch money because I realized that these boys were also my children, it benefited my own children the very same day for the same amount of money.

Another time I had gotten in an argument with my former husband. I was really angry with him, and I went down to the park. I was calling him every name in the book under my breath. I went and I sat on a swing, fuming. Again, I heard Jesus's voice say to me, "You are making this up."

"What do you mean I'm making this up?" I asked.

"You want him to be guilty, so you made up the whole argument so he'd be guilty. You know, you could choose peace instead of this."

In that moment I realized that I didn't want to choose peace. I had my reasons for being angry, and I was sure that I was right. I also knew that what I was hearing from Jesus was correct. I sat with the whole thing for a long while, and then I said out loud, "OK, I choose peace!" At that moment the entire memory of the argument with my husband got erased from my mind. I literally couldn't remember what he and I had been arguing about. I tried to remember, "What was I mad about?" but I couldn't remember. Choosing peace literally erased the argument from my mind. When I got home, my husband wanted to chat about the argument and I said, "Well, there's nothing to talk about because I can't remember any of it."

I had to have the willingness to see peace instead of guilt. When Jesus presented me with that choice, I got to see how much I didn't want to choose peace—I was choosing anger and the belief in guilt over peace.

Most often we aren't aware of the choices that could be made in any given situation. We certainly aren't aware in angry situations that we are making up the idea of someone opposing us in order to reinforce our belief in guilt. But actually, all situations devoid of peace are really asking for peace, and that is our choice in those moments: Do we choose peace over anger or not? Seeing what we are willing or not willing to do shows us where we really are in our own consciousness.

Q. YOU'VE BEEN SPEAKING ABOUT QUALITIES OF LOVE THAT SEEM TO BE BIG, UNIVERSAL QUALITIES. IS THE PERSONAL SENSE OF LOVE BETWEEN TWO PEOPLE A DEGREE OF UNIVERSAL LOVE?

A. Two people in a relationship have opportunities to share love and become love in the higher sense, but it's not a given that the attraction between two people is love. The relationship is an opportunity to love and to practice love. You could have someone in your life to whom you are attracted, but then, after a time, the relationship may not stay loving, because the attraction lessens. You might still be attracted to the other person, but there may not always be loving behavior between you. Sometimes what is considered personal love turns into an exercise in making the other person feel guilty, which is obviously not an act of love. Nor are relationships based on physical attractions necessarily love, although they could be.

Your own intimate relationships are exceptional opportunities because they're in your reality every day and you can see yourself mirrored in another. You can take what you learn and extend that way of being to those whom you meet. Each relationship is an opportunity to practice and learn about love. You're practicing either love or judgment.

You can do the ascension process with another person if you both truly practice and actualize love. On the other hand, you could choose to be single and do it with the whole world.

You do not have to live with someone with whom you're incompatible, or where there's neglect or abuse going on. Loving another person in higher love does not mean that you accept bad behavior from that person. In a compatible relationship both people are consciously practicing and actualizing love. In relationships where mistreatment, control or abuse is present, real love is not present, so no real relationship is happening. In these cases, the loving thing to do is to realize that both people would be better off letting go of an unloving situation where the willingness to become love is not present.

We said that love upholds the highest standards. It is an act of higher love to make choices that uphold yourself in loving ways—do not accept abuse or mediocrity for you or for those you love. Hold all to the highest victory in your heart and walk away from situations or people that do not reflect that.

Q. WHEN TWO PEOPLE ARE IN A RELATIONSHIP AND PERCEIVE THAT THEY LOVE EACH OTHER, WHY DO BREAKUPS HAPPEN?

A. Breakups happen because one or the other, or both, aren't doing their work or they may be meant to go in different directions for further growth or to fulfill a particular path. It can also be about learning that attractions aren't always love, which I mentioned earlier. When two people say they love one another, they demonstrate it by seeing each other in their innocence.

Q. I'M TRYING TO GET PAST THE CATHOLIC *IDEA* OF "'TIL DEATH DO US PART." IF ONE IS NOT PRACTICING FORGIVENESS AND THE

OTHER IS, CAN IT BE A MORE LOVING THING TO SEPARATE, EVEN IF IT VIOLATES THE LAWS OF RELIGIOUS BELIEF?

A. It can be the more loving thing to separate because you're not in a real relationship at all, if it's based on making the other feel guilty. Ultimately, it doesn't matter if you stay together or break up. There's no judgment around it. The decision has more to do with whether or not you are practicing love together. However, love has the power to transform any negativity where there is a willingness.

Q. SO WE ARE THAT LOVE?

A. That's right. You have a choice to resonate with it and keep merging with it in an ever-greater way or deny it, in which case you will feel separate and alone by your own decisions.

Remember that love is. There is nothing we can do to change what Source created. Love is always there whenever we are ready to live out of that field and that's why whatever you do or don't do doesn't change the fact that love is. The quality of your own experience of love is directly proportional to your willingness to choose It.

Q. IF WE'RE REALLY PART OF THE WHOLE THING, THEN WOULDN'T SOURCE SUPPORT US?

A. Source defines love as allowing. Love's quality is life and expression. Even if you're doing something that attempts to reverse that or doesn't allow that in you, the loving energy of Source will still always be with you. It's within us, and it naturally draws us to want to know more and to come into communion with it, which is why Source's love allows. It knows that the life urge is in you and that at some point you will desire only love. Love's intention is already there for bliss. Even if you're not experiencing bliss, you still have something in you that's going to drive you toward wanting to find it, which is how Source supports you.

You're made of Spirit. You're made of Source, which is love. Once you understand that your body is Spirit—once you get it that it's all the same thing—you start to practice forgiveness, because it's the only sensible thing to do.

Q. WE'RE ALL SO ATTACHED TO OUR LIVES, AND WE DON'T WANT TO GIVE UP OUR BODIES AS IMPERFECT AS WE THINK THEY ARE— OUR PERCEPTUAL IDENTITIES ARE CONNECTED TO THEM. IT WOULD BE WONDERFUL TO BE SO HARMLESS IN MY INTENTIONS THAT MY BODY COULD RADIATE ONLY PURE LOVE AND EXPRESS ONLY LOVE. THEN I WOULD BE FREE. I THINK DYING IS PART OF THE REVERSAL THAT WE ACCEPT AS NATURAL, BUT I DON'T THINK IT IS. I THINK IT'S A CONSEQUENCE OF OUR FEELING GUILTY—I THINK WE KILL OURSELVES.

A. That's really what we're doing. But you see, sickness and death are consequences of judging other people and ourselves, because it's our belief in punishment. The belief in judgment and punishment are the same things.

Sondra Ray of Rebirthing used to say, "All death is suicide." That's a whole other topic, but in principle it's true. It's because we feel guilt that we kill ourselves.

Examples of this are: "I'll make myself sick before God does. I'll put myself through cancer, through all this horrible suffering. I'll self-debase, I'll make my life miserable in order to atone before God sees me. And then maybe it won't be so bad."

It isn't something you do consciously. The belief in guilt is in the subconscious, which is the cause and effect process produced by associations. The subconscious association with guilt is that it demands punishment. When you judge, you suppress your own God urge as well as your own immune system.

The body is a miraculous invention. Even if you argue that it is predominately used as a vehicle of separation, it has a safeguard within it called the kundalini. The kundalini is literally the God-force energy within our bodies that rises and purifies all that is less than love when it is awakened. It can merge us with Source and turn our bodies into light, and it can overcome death, for it is the fire of love. If we understood this, our emphasis on external youth and beauty would give way to the inner ascension chamber within our bodies. Then we would begin to truly know ourselves.

Q. HOW DO WE GO ABOUT DOING THAT?

A. There are many practices that focus on raising the kundalini. There is Kundalini Yoga and Tom Kenyon's CD called "The Magdalene Meditations" to name two. There are various other yogic techniques that focus on this as well. Still, it can be done by our own consciousness by taking on the process of purifying our lower nature, or ego self. This purification is the practice of becoming diligently aware of our motives and thought processes. It asks us to choose higher virtues when we are presented with things that tempt us towards judgment or unkindness. This process purifies our lower nature and in so doing, our kundalini rises through the chakras and integrates our higher nature within us.

Q. I ALWAYS WANTED TO LIVE IN MY IMAGINATION. WHY MUST I CONTINUE TO LIVE IN THIS LIFE? I WOULD RATHER BE IN THAT OTHER PLACE. I OFTEN WORRY ABOUT TRYING TO LIVE IN FAIRYLAND.

A. What it's really about is bringing more Heaven (electricals) into the Earth's (magnetics) sphere, but you can't do it so long as you judge, which is why it's a discipline — simple in concept, but not necessarily easy to do. Stepping away from judging is a wonderful opportunity to break the chains of too much magnetic energy, which allows the physical body to change and carry more of God's love. We are all here to actualize love in this dimension. It is needed on this density level.

Q. WILL WE RECOGNIZE THIS CHANGE?

A. You will feel it. People are already feeling it, actually. I get calls from people saying they know that they are changing; and it's happening in varying degrees with people from all walks of life. They are becoming more aware of love, telepathy and past-life memories. They are desiring different foods and are seeing and feeling more unity.

Q. HOW CAN I DETERMINE WHETHER MY SELF-LOVE IS SELFISH?

A. Being loving to others and most definitely to yourself is a natural result of finding out that we are all innocent and composed of love. When you truly understand that you're not guilty, it's easy to be loving. There's nothing wrong with self-love; in fact, it is one of the most important things that is required. If you don't love yourself enough to be good to yourself, you will not be able to be good to others. We must choose higher standards for ourselves so as to bring more love into this reality. Remember, it's about the quality of our choices — the higher the quality, the more refined the love.

Let's talk about the judgment that people place on the path of service vs. the path of self-love. The path of love is really only one, all-inclusive path. You can't truly give to others if you don't love yourself — you will see it as sacrifice. How will you know that everyone deserves the highest degree of love if you can't allow yourself to have it? You're forcing it at that point. We're talking about giving up the belief in guilt for all time for everybody, regardless of who they are and what they've done, and that includes ourselves. When we can truly do that, loving our self will be easy and sensible. If there's a decision that you need to make that is self-nurturing, you'll know to make it, which may mean saying "no" to certain people, circumstances or ways of life. On the other hand, if there's someone that to whom you need to give, you'll know that too, and you'll just naturally respond to them.

Making the choice for yourself to no longer accept certain things or people who make you feel worse about yourself is a victory for everyone.

We all receive love when you choose to love yourself more fully or to say "no" to unhealthy or unloving ways or treatment. If you think you're guilty, you have to think the world is guilty too, so choose to believe that we are all good and deserve only good. It's all or nothing.

Q. WILL I EVER FIND TRUE LOVE? OR IS IT MY FEELING OF GUILT THAT'S BRINGING ALL THIS UNHAPPINESS UPON ME?

A. Check to see if you have released your judgment of others and yourself in order to find and remember true love. If you were truly to do that, who knows how that would play out in your everyday life? You could suddenly find love in places you didn't before. Others around you may suddenly seem different. Or, your whole relationship could blow up and fall apart, leaving an opening for someone more loving to come in. You could move to Spain by yourself and be blissfully happy. You really don't know the form that it will take, but the reason that you can't experience it yet could be because you still may not believe you can have it. That's when you ask for help. Ask a higher part of yourself to help you say, "I'm willing to see things differently."

Participant: I have been doing that, and things have changed around in the last few days. I'm more peaceful now.

Aingeal: That will keep increasing. The more you can do that, the more you're going to be able to apply it across the board to everybody and everything. Like attracts like.

Q. MY MAIN PROBLEM WITH CHRISTIANITY HAS TO DO WITH LOVE. IN ISLAM IT'S MERCY — ALLAH IS MERCIFUL. WE END UP WITH TWO DIFFERENT CULTURES WITH AN EMPHASIS ON EITHER LOVE OR MERCY. THEY BOTH SEEM TO BE CONCERNED WITH FORGIVENESS. IS MERCY SOMETHING DIFFERENT THAN LOVE?

A. Christians may say they're about love, but both of these religions still project judgment onto each other. Both still believe in guilt. It doesn't matter if you're Muslim or Christian. Islam's version of mercy wouldn't necessarily be that everybody's guiltless. It may be that people are guilty, and now they're going to receive mercy. Christianity believes in sin, and then you're forgiven of sin. Both religions are judgment based. They're not that different, actually. There's usually a judgment first and then there's forgiveness. If it's Christian, its forgiveness; if it's Islam, it's mercy. If these religions were truly based in love, they wouldn't be seeing each other as enemies or as separate. That wouldn't be happening. "My God's right. Your God's wrong." That nonsense wouldn't be happening if each religion were really based in the love we're talking about today. We still assassinate people who try to bring peace. We kill them or threaten their families.

Choosing only love is a decision—a choice—all or nothing. You're either choosing to see and be only love or you're not. So, if somebody is saying, "I'm going to be merciful, you thief! I'm going to only cut off your right ear instead of both ears," there's still a judgment first. You can't say that being kind and only half-killing the criminal is merciful or loving. Merciful to most people is, "I could punish you severely, but I'm not going to. I'll overlook it. I'll forgive it. I'll only punish you a little." It's still the judgment game. It's still making somebody guilty first.

That form of forgiveness can actually be dangerous when you make somebody guilty first and then say you're going to forgive them. You're just reinforcing the belief in guilt. The greatest gift that we could give anyone is to know that they're innocent. We give up our belief in judgment, even if the other person doesn't. They may still think they're guilty or horrible; they may still think they've made too many mistakes and that they're worthless. You can't change that for them, because that's their decision, but, you can see them as innocent and by doing so you're donating grace to them. That grace may be what tips the scales for them some day.

My dad in the last few years of his life started being verbally abusive to my mother. He always had a bit of a temper at times, but this was worse. He had a cold that didn't go away for a few months. I thought this was unusual for him. A year later, he came down with throat cancer, and he asked my sister, "Do you think this is God punishing me for what I said to your mother?" My sister told him "yes" because she was mad at my father, which of course reinforced his guilt. But the truth is that the answer is "no." It's not God punishing him—it was my father punishing himself.

We are not saying that people don't do things that are unloving or criminal; we are saying that the repair is to affirm that they deserve love, no matter what. Then you can put a criminal in jail and lock them in so they don't project their own guilt on another person through violent actions. You can walk away from an abusive person and still know that they deserve to realize love.

Your walking away is you loving yourself and in so doing, you affirm love. You make that affirmation not only for yourself, but also for anyone who may need the strength to make the same choice. We either bring the actuality of love's presence into realization, or we keep it hidden through our belief in guilt. Whatever we choose, love still allows and is still present beneath everything.

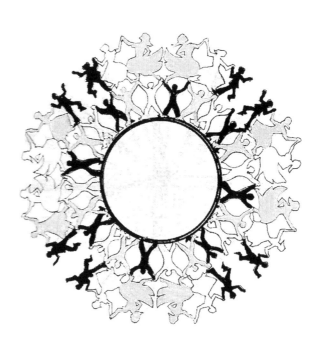

Chapter 6

Miracles

As I say the opening prayer, the room fills with red light—the same light that appeared during the group sessions on Trees and the Art of Prosperity.

Q. WHAT IS A *MIRACLE*, AND UNDER WHAT LAWS DOES IT OPERATE?

A. A miracle alters the laws and elements in any given dimension. It intersects a particular paradigm vertically, allowing for a dimensional shift in the moment from one form or experience of reality into another. It replaces fear with love. It corrects at the cellular level, but it also corrects the mind. It replaces dis-order with divine order. It comes from the Law of One, which recognizes God as One, love as law and love as order. Miracles correct perception as well as matter through the opening created by re-establishing love. Miracles occur instantaneously, because they do not follow, nor are they limited by, the perceptions of time and space.

Q. WHAT IS THIS RED LIGHT ABOUT AND WHAT DOES IT HAVE TO DO WITH MIRACLES, PROSPERITY AND TREES?

A. The red light is really from the violet-light spectrum. The violet-light spectrum is inherent in all life everywhere in this dimension we call Earth, even though it operates in a higher-frequency range. It is the color of transmutation and forgiveness, which go hand in hand. Miracles come under the heading of transmutation of matter or conditions. Prosperity works this way as well, as it is about turning poverty consciousness into prosperity consciousness or turning base thoughts into higher thoughts.

Red light has a lower frequency than violet light and is necessary to ground a "miracle" or a transmutation into this physical plane, thus creating a different "appearance." Using the principle of "as above, so below," we see violet being above, and red being below.

Q. HOW CAN YOU SAY TO THE MOUNTAIN, "MOVE," AND IT WOULD MOVE?

A. It is possible because matter only appears solid. Everything is consciousness, and density is only an agreement made by minds who are experimenting with the idea of separation. Remove the perception and belief in solidity, and anything can move.

Q. IS THERE SUCH A THING AS A BAD MIRACLE, OR A MIRACLE IN REVERSE? IN OTHER WORDS, IF SOMEBODY CREATES A BAD EFFECT SOMEHOW, IS THAT ALSO A MIRACLE?

A. The "miracle" I am seeing is a change for the better, or a higher change based in love. It is moving something from an unhealthy state to a healthy state, or from a lower frequency to a higher frequency. More than that, it is reestablishing Source's original intention for life in a situation or condition that has forgotten it. This can occur on any level—spiritual, emotional, mental or physical. So, there are no "bad" miracles.

Q. WHEN SOMEBODY USES THE FORCES OF CREATION TO MANIFEST SOMETHING NEGATIVE, IS THAT A MIRACLE?

A. Miracles are from the order of love. Our ability to manifest desires in our lives using thought, intention and desire is indeed a miraculous process, and it implies that we are all "geniuses." We consciously use the Law of Cause and Effect when we do this. Our very ability to manifest comes from Source's underlying intention. It's in the nature of the life principle. However, we understand that a "miracle" is a phenomenon that instantly changes a physiology, a state of consciousness, or an event without requiring the conscious intention of the receiver of the miracle. This makes it something of a different order that operates under different laws—specifically the laws of love, which automatically "forgive" all that love is not. It follows that any state of consciousness that is not love is unnatural, and that is where all pain, illness and suffering exists.

Q. IS THE PROCESS OF "MIRACLES" EQUIVALENT TO THE QUANTUM FIELD OF SUBATOMIC PARTICLES WHERE YOU HOLD THE IMAGE OF WHAT IT IS THAT YOU DESIRE TO MANIFEST, AND THE IMAGE ARRANGES THE SUBATOMIC PARTICLES INTO YOUR IMAGE?

A. Miracles occur under the laws of love, which would be the laws of communion and sharing. In your example, the Law of Cause and Effect is still in use, and very often it only involves the separatist desires of the thinker. On the level of mind, imagination and intention, it works that way. Your intentions work quickly because your belief actually alters the quantum field. Being a fluid field, it responds to your will and desire. A miracle, however, can occur without your conscious will and intention.

Q. WHAT HAPPENS TO THE BODY WHEN IT "RECEIVES" A MIRACLE?

A. There is an immediate "whitening" or purifying effect in the body. You could also say that all misperception is corrected. "Time" is suspended or interrupted in the moment, and an alteration of the person's reality takes place, which allows for a literal dimensional shift to occur within the individual, altering the individual's bodily programming, thus making the body "new."

Q. MY UNDERSTANDING OF A MIRACLE IS WHEN JESUS RAISED SOMEBODY FROM THE DEAD OR CURED AN ILLNESS. THE PERSON PERFORMING THE MIRACLE MAY HAVE BELIEF, BUT THE RECIPIENT MAY NOT BELIEVE ANYTHING AT ALL, AND YET, THE MIRACLE APPEARS TO HAPPEN. HOW DOES THAT WORK?

A. Jesus didn't provide miracles for everyone. The miracle has to be in alignment with the individual's soul purpose.

Q. WE GET THE IMPRESSION THAT JESUS COULD GO AROUND PERFORMING MIRACLES ANY TIME HE CHOSE, BUT YOU'RE SAYING THAT HE WOULD HAVE BEEN VERY SELECTIVE?

A. Yes, because it's not appropriate to offer a miracle to everyone. It has a lot to do with where people are in their own soul development. It may not be appropriate for their soul growth to receive a miracle in certain instances.

Q. CAN WE SAY THAT EVEN THE CREATION OF THE HUMAN BODY IS A MIRACLE? BUT WHOSE INTENTION WAS IT?

A. The "miracle" about the body is the fact that the process of creation itself is divine—there's a divine blueprint for life that other beings may learn about and modify in different ways to create assorted life forms, like the cloning we're doing now. It doesn't mean, however, that those who created various life forms or are doing cloning are highly spiritual or evolved beings, because they're not really causing miracles. They're taking information from an existing design as a template and using existing materials to create new life forms. The miracle in these cases is life itself—the fact that life *is*, that life exists at all.

Q. IS THERE A LINK BETWEEN A MIRACLE AND INTUITION?

A. No, there is no link in the context in which we are speaking. Intuition belongs to your innate instinctual nature, while a miracle is a spontaneous intervention in our paradigm from a different order of reality.

Knowing that something is going to happen before it happens is not a miracle. Intuition is something you were born with. It's part of the divine imprint that you have. So, Source wouldn't call intuition a miracle—It would say it's part of our inherent make-up, similar to how animals have instinct, plants know to face the sun and close up at night, etc. You would say that these examples are evidence of the intelligence of life built into every living thing. Humans have their instinctual self as well, which we call our intuition, which allows us to receive higher impulses (illuminations) from Source that go beyond survival. We have the ability to discern many different frequency bands of information. The center of our intuition comes from our solar-plexus area, which is why people say, "I have a gut feeling..."

However, there's a higher knowing that involves our whole system—where every cell knows at the same moment. To use it we just need to evolve to that level of knowing and awareness. This inner knowing is not called a miracle. A miracle causes an instantaneous change—a vertical intersection in this reality—and doesn't require intuition. It alters the physical laws, because it comes from a Field of Love that supersedes this reality and has no polarity or duality.

Q. SO, ARE WE ALSO LOOKING AT PERSONAL POWER? IN OTHER WORDS, IF PEOPLE WERE REALLY IN THEIR KNOWING, IN THEIR UNDERSTANDING, IN THEIR TRUE SPIRITUAL CONNECTION TO SOURCE, COULD THEY PERFORM MIRACLES?

A. If they were in that degree of knowing, yes. However, they may not choose to specifically cause a miracle because with that degree of knowing, they would understand whether or not a miracle would be appropriate in a given situation. A person who has achieved this level will naturally radiate a vibration of love that naturally allows miracles to occur. We read about masters who can cause miracles, and you can do the same when you know your true spiritual connection to Source.

A. BECAUSE OF THE GROWTH OF AWARENESS NOW, SHOULD WE EXPECT MORE MIRACLES AS PEOPLE COME INTO THEIR POWER?

A. It depends on how each person wakes up. In other words, waking up for one person might be that they suddenly find out that chakras exist. For another, it may mean they realize who they are in Source and move into mastery. As people become aware of more things, there's the potential for them to wake up and realize the God power within themselves that has always been there. Ultimately, it is the recognition that they are, have always been, and will always be, love. These words sound nice, but the realization and actualization of being love is usually a process of unfolding. It involves deep love of self and the behavior that naturally accompanies that, and from that comes the natural desire to extend the same love to all life everywhere.

Q. I STILL HEAR QUITE A DISTINCTION BETWEEN MANIFESTING A DESIRE AND CREATING A MIRACLE. AS OUR INTENTIONS BECOME PURER, WILL WE BE BETTER ABLE TO PERFORM MIRACLES AND TO MANIFEST OUR DESIRES MORE EASILY?

A. Here's the distinction: The truth is that you could have a black magician sitting here right now who knows that something will materialize because he's intending it to. That's just a fact. He could cause an instantaneous change, but that change wouldn't be a miracle. A miracle has love and purity attached to it. A miracle is an instantaneous expression of love, or an instantaneous change, in a loving way. The manifesting process—if it's devoid of love—is not considered a miracle. When someone intends something dark, or negative, their resulting manifestation will eventually compact in on itself. When something compacts, ultimately, it's going to turn in on itself and be destroyed. When this happens, it goes under the heading of death, or molecular compaction. A miracle, on the other hand, promotes more life. It causes life expansion or "correction," rather than contraction, or error.

If someone has a desire to manifest something in their lives, and the desire is not ill-intended, they may do so, knowing that the power of thought and desire are the key components of manifesting. This is fine to do, but it would still not be considered a miracle—it would be considered manifesting. A miracle is love in action, devoid of the necessity for anyone to think about it or desire it. It comes from the field of love, which is not affected by anything here. It corrects.

Q. IF EVERYTHING IS PERCEPTION, WHERE DO MIRACLES FIT IN?

A. True communication with Source and with All That Is automatically causes miracles. We are talking about a consequence of real love, which is communion and acceptance with all life. Communion dissolves perception, which is an aspect of the belief in separateness. The miracle comes from Source or love, which is beyond perception. Love is a reality in which there is no duality. Love can intersect this or any other dimension at any point in time and alter its physics because it comes from a "place" where only love, or unity resides, which is also divine order. There is neither perceived separation nor any division. Nor is there guilt or judgment.

Q. ARE MIRACLES HAPPENING NOW? IS IT LIKE 100 A DAY...?

A. Oh, much more than that! More than thousands are happening all the time. We just don't hear about them. *(Suddenly the room is full of orbs!)*

Q. CAN THE ORBS THAT YOU SAID WERE HERE IN THE ROOM FACILITATE A MIRACLE IN SOME WAY? ARE THEY CONNECTED WITH MIRACLES?

A. My feeling about the orbs in this room is that they came in to listen. They're very interested in what goes on in certain places. Source wouldn't say, "Go to the orbs for a miracle." Source would say, "For a miracle, go to love, which is in the realm of Source." Can orbs perform miracles? No. Orbs are manifestations of thought. They come from the billions of thought forms that humanity thinks or imagines daily. Many orbs have become actual "beings," others have coalesced into colors or geometric patterns. For this reason, orbs can be perceived as "visitors" in that they are thought forms that have become conscious, or "alive."

When orbs appear in a room, they oftentimes are parts of consciousness traveling and stopping in to listen. Once an orb has become conscious, it can now learn and evolve in that consciousness.

Q. I REALLY FEEL THAT THERE ARE MIRACLES HAPPENING EVERY MOMENT OF EVERY DAY, AND EVEN HERE IN THIS ROOM. YOU CAN SAY IT'S A MIRACLE THAT I GOT HERE, THAT WE DROVE ALONG IN THE CAR, AND THAT WE SURVIVED DRIVING THROUGH TRAFFIC. AREN'T THESE ALL MIRACLES? WHAT ONE PERSON SEES AS A HUGE MIRACLE, SOMEBODY ELSE MIGHT SEE AS A SMALL MIRACLE.

A. In those examples, yes, life is a miracle—the fact that life is here and it all works, is definitely a miracle. The miracle that is life is one level of miracle. The other is when our physical Laws are reversed—such as an interruption in the Law of Cause and Effect where the outcome of a situation is altered and love enters in. In those cases, we are talking of a higher order or a higher law that comes into effect where something intersects our linear reality and causes either a reversal or a complete change in a condition, state of mind, event or situation instantaneously.

Q. YOU SAID THAT ALL MIRACLES HAVE LOVE ATTACHED TO THEM. THAT'S A BEAUTIFUL CONCEPT. BUT ARE THERE ALSO DEGREES OF LOVE? LET'S SAY THAT A GIRL IS ILL, AND HER MOTHER UNCONDITIONALLY LOVES HER AND DESIRES THAT SHE BE WELL. IF SHE DIES, IS IT BECAUSE HER MOTHER DIDN'T LOVE HER ENOUGH?

A. No. This child, depending on her own soul journey, is either going to take the mothers love and heal or, if the child has a soul contract according to which she's leaving soon, she will die. You must always consider what's going on with a person on a soul level, which is why miracles do not happen for everyone.

If someone wants to develop a particular quality or virtue before they leave this world, a miracle may actually interfere with that purpose. We are all here doing many things, and each one of us has had a hand in orchestrating our soul contracts before we entered this world. Miracles and love do allow our contracts to be suspended or altered for higher purposes, but such changes would be made by either the individuals or their higher selves. The question would have to be examined: Would the experiencing of a miracle promote the soul growth required for the individual, or not?

Q. MY HUSBAND AND I WENT TO LOURDES 7 TIMES FOR OUR THREE SONS. WE DEEPLY BELIEVED AND PRAYED THAT OUR CHILDREN WOULD BE CURED. COULD OUR CHILDREN'S ILLNESSES BE PART OF THEIR SOUL JOURNEYS, WHICH IS WHY THEY WEREN'T CURED? WE BELIEVED A MIRACLE WOULD OCCUR, BECAUSE IT HAD SUPPOSEDLY HAPPENED FOR OTHER PEOPLE THERE.

A. Remember in another group session we asked about your deceased sons, and talked to them? We saw that it was in their soul contracts to leave when they did and also, that they had wanted to stay together. I know it's hard to accept that when they're your children, but it had a lot to do with the two of them being together, and not being apart.

Q. MY OTHER SON IS ILL, AND I KNOW HE DOESN'T WANT TO LIVE. HE WANTS TO BE WITH MY OTHER SONS WHO HAVE CROSSED.

A. The difference here is that there's a part of your son now that doesn't want to take the responsibility for living, which is why he is being asked if he wants to live. I wouldn't assume that his soul contract is the same as your other children. Your remaining son has had other lives in which he's given up on living, where he hasn't really pushed hard enough. He's a soul that's being tested with challenges in order for him to push through and succeed this time. I don't see that his soul contract is to die young. He's causing that to happen. He can get well if he makes the decision to do so, and maybe you could facilitate that by talking to him.

It is his liver that is sick, and the word "live" is in the word "liver." The liver filters the blood, and the blood is the life-force energy, so if he's losing life-force energy, it suggests that he doesn't want to live. He will heal when he decides that he does want to live. He can turn this around for himself.

You can intend or ask for a miracle for anything or anyone you desire, and it will be held within their auric field—it will be available. What the person does with it is between themselves and their soul.

Q. IS THERE ANY DIFFERENCE BETWEEN A BODY RECEIVING A MIRACLE AND *ALCHEMY*, WHERE SOMEONE TURNS A SUBSTANCE FROM ONE THING INTO ANOTHER, OR THE PERFORMANCE OF *MAGIC* ON SOME LEVEL?

A. You're talking about two different things. Magic is different from alchemy. When a base metal is turned into gold, it is working within the physical laws of Nature. You could say, in a way, that miracles are alchemy insofar as they transmute something from one form to another, but a miracle is not coming *from* the physical laws of Nature—it is *altering* the physical laws in an instant. It is rearranging elements and forming them into something new. Turning base metals into gold is a long, lengthy process taking years, but it can be done.

Magic is different, because it is the calling in of various forces, substances and spirits to effect a change, and it doesn't necessarily use love as an abiding principle. It incorporates rituals and other talismans to cause a desired effect or outcome. It would still come under the Law of Cause and Effect. Magic is very different than the miracles we've been talking about, where it's an action or intention based on love and knowing. Magic is very different.

Q. DOES THIS ASCENSION CYCLE THAT WE'RE IN BRING POTENTIAL TO US TO PERFORM MIRACLES?

A. It brings a potential for more awareness of truth. We've always had the ability to facilitate miracles.

Q. HOW CAN WE FACILITATE MIRACLES?

A. We need to address this question on a few levels. To facilitate a miracle, you have the power of the Emerald Green Ray in your hands. When you offer this to someone, you are facilitating in them an opening for peace and love to enter, which allows a miracle to be received by the person you are helping. The rest is between the person and Source.

In the bigger picture, everything that comes from pure love is a miracle. This is an all-encompassing statement.

Scientifically, star energy also facilitates (not causes) miracles. You have a core connection to star energy at a point at the tip of your sternum, or breastbone. Star energy raises your body's frequency into a temporary "ascended state," allowing the body to correct. For yourself personally, meditating on this point can create an opening for healing on many levels. Star energy is also called the "blue-white fire core."

Q. WHAT IS STAR ENERGY? AND WHAT DOES IF HAVE TO DO WITH MIRACLES?

A. Nuclear fusion. Star energy can drastically change the form of something from one state to another. Its blue-white fire core is literally inherent within everyone. However, it is not activated in most of us. If it were activated, healing or "miracles" would be occurring naturally. Scientifically and physically, we are formed from star energy or star elements.

You can be helped in realizing your true connection or communion with Source, or "All That Is," through meditating on your "star seed" at the point at the tip of your breastbone just below your breasts at your sternum. It is a "gateway" to the remembrance of your origin and your connection and interrelationship with all life, which is love. To connect with this part of you, just sit or lay quietly and focus your attention inward at the point at the tip of your sternum. Keep focusing there and intend to connect with your own star essence within. You may feel an opening there, or heat. You can ask this star point to heal your body of any infliction. Allow this energy to go to where you need it. Come out of the meditation when you feel ready. You can repeat this meditation whenever you like.

Chapter 7

Time & Dimensions

As I'm saying the opening prayer, there are many spheres at the ceiling level. These are not orbs, but moist and liquid *spheres*. Some look like they're shimmering with silver, some with gold and some with white. They feel aware, and I feel a consciousness with them, but I wouldn't say they are full beings. They don't belong to our dimension.

Q. WHAT IS *TIME*?

A. Time is being shown to me as an actual living web of light particles and sound tones that is a consciousness field.

   I can see beyond it, and it becomes dark beyond or outside of it. Time *curves*. It's round, and it arcs. It does belong to a certain dimensional space in that it has boundaries, which is what differentiates it from the darkness that I see beyond it. It exists within a given dimensional space, and it is made up of a living web of consciousness and energy; all of our thoughts and desires are there. It has its own particular quality. You do go beyond it into what you might consider a void or hyperspace, but hyperspace doesn't have anything to do with the time matrix that I'm looking at.

Q. IS THERE A SPECIFIC NUMBER OF THEM?

A. Yes. There are only five or six. They look like a Christmas ball with an elliptical shape in the middle. They're telling me, "You're getting it now." They're being really clear about their shape, but yet they feel moist. They are from a different dimensional space, not familiar to me. I've not encountered them before. They pop in and out of our dimensional space.

Q. HOW MANY OTHER DIMENSIONS ARE THERE INSIDE AND OUT OF PLANET EARTH AT THE PRESENT TIME?

A. There's an unlimited number of other dimensions intersecting our reality. We really don't have any concept of how many dimensions there are in, around and through us.

These dimensions intersect our third-dimensional reality, appearing as vertical and diagonal lines that intersect our dimension at different angles. Some of them go right through our dimension, crossing over it or just passing through it. They don't affect our dimension, and we don't notice them, because their frequency and angular rotation is very different from ours. Some of those dimensional spaces don't originate in our time field. We could be aware of them or fall into them, however, at the point where they intersect our time web.

There are stories of people who have visited places where some past historical event occurred, and they reported seeing a scene from that event playing itself out in living color, as if it were just happening. The scene would appear with the same figures from the past, dressed in their period clothing and re-enacting the same event as if it were still alive and locked into a time warp. Those visiting the place felt as if they were in a strange portal watching an alternate reality take place. Some people experienced it as being out of their bodies, when they really just popped into and back from a different dimensional space. The only way you can experience another dimension in your 3-D waking state is if you're at that point of intersection where our 3-D and the other dimension meet. If you weren't at the point of intersection between dimensions, you wouldn't be aware of anything unusual.

Q. COULD SUCH A DIMENSION BE DESCRIBED AS AN ALTERED STATE OF CONSCIOUSNESS?

A. The effect of being in a portal could produce an altered state of consciousness, but the altered state wouldn't produce the portal. You can also experience your alternate selves in other dimensions. You could come upon an intersection point where another you is in another dimension, and you could experience that as a living-now timeline.

Q. ARE TONIGHT'S SPHERES OTHER ASPECTS OF OURSELVES?

A. No, they are not other aspects of you.

Even though I'm feeling them there, they're not coming down into our dimensional field. They're outside of it, even though I'm aware of them. They do not want to come into our time net for some reason. They're hovering right at the edge.

Q. COULD THEY GET TRAPPED HERE?

A. Yes, and they don't want to. They have a particular moisture that makes me feel that they are not compatible with our environment.

Q. CAN WE GET OUT OF TIME?

A. Yes, time is definitely something you can get in and out of. It actually has an edge or an arc to it.

Q. DOES TIME STOP?

A. Time is a living consciousness made up of our consciousness. It's not going to stop until we stop—until we ascend out of our perceptions of this physical reality. We may see it change in its properties as mass consciousness changes, however. It also has parameters.

Q. DOES THE BOUNDARY OF TIME EXPAND, CONTRACT, OR STAY CONSTANT?

A. It seems to stay within fixed dimensional limits or within certain parameters. I don't feel that it extends. It has a certain frequency range, or belt. It is round, it has an arc shape to it, like a disc. It feels held in place by other forces in the cosmos. It feels elliptical in its motion.

If you look at the Earth spinning on its orbit, around the center is this big, elliptical energy field. If you were to tip the Earth the other way, you might get another elliptical the other way. Time feels like that.

Q. Does time have a heartbeat?

A. It is more of a breathing rhythm as opposed to a heartbeat, similar to an in-and-out breath.

Q. Can time speed up or slow down?

A. I'm getting a *no*. It's not going anywhere, but stays within its boundaries. What people perceive as a speed-up or a slowdown is really just a *ripple* in time. Think of it as a big energy blanket with a woven pattern of light that can ripple and vibrate at different rates. It's a fluctuating field. When you encounter a ripple, it can make you feel as if things are speeding up or slowing down. You could experience time as speeding up today, but tomorrow you might think that it has slowed down again. It's not a stable field in this sense, but it is stable within its parameters.

Q. Are we multi-dimensional? Could our mental body be in one dimensional space or angle, while our emotional body is in another?

A. I have to be very careful here with words. I can't say that it's that separated. Source doesn't want us to think of ourselves in that way. What I'm seeing instead is a pillar. I'm looking at little cells in the pillar—the different aspects of us are different cells in the pillar. The pillar is complete and whole, and it's contained—all is contained within it. Source doesn't want us perceiving that parts of ourselves are separate realities, because they aren't. It would be easy to think that way, because different parts of us may function at different rates of vibration, but all our bodies are contained within us. It's not the same as having an experience of an alternate self in a different reality. Your emotional and mental bodies are contained within your own pillar of light.

There are a wide variety of experiences in the time field, and what we perceive dictates what we see. We may want to call them realities, but Source wants us to call them experiences. There are not different realities in the time field, but there are definitely a lot of different perceptions and experiences there, and many other sets of realities beyond the time field. How you think and perceive determines what you tap into.

We don't see beyond the time field because we are locked into our beliefs and perceptions of time. Our frame of reference for reality has limitations at this point. It's only when people release their attachment to the idea that the time field is real that they actually start to have an experience of what it's like outside of it. The time field is what holds your body together. Beyond it, you wouldn't have a body at all.

Q. ARE TIME AND MATTER SYNONYMOUS?

A. Matter comes together because of the time field, which holds matter together. This is exciting because when people ask, "How do you dissolve your body into light?" or "How do you walk through a wall?" You do that by dissolving the time field within your consciousness, and it won't happen unless you understand that. Most of us are locked into a frame of reference or reality about time, which is why we can't seem to shift matter. The stories you may have heard of beings materializing or de-materializing are factual, because they have freed themselves from the time field. They can reassemble their material form by coming back into the time field. They can get in and out of time.

Q. IS AN "*ALIEN ABDUCTION*" ACTUALLY A DIMENSIONAL SHIFT OR AN ALTERED STATE OF MIND, OR ARE THEY ALL THE SAME?

A. Good question! An "alien abduction" is an experience in another dimensional space out of our time field. It is not being made up in a person's mind.

Q. IS IT THE SAME AS AN ALTERED STATE OF CONSCIOUSNESS?

A. No, it is an actual experience. The "alien-abduction" experience is occurring in a dimensional space that intersects our time-space but is not *in* our time space. The "abductors" can manipulate the properties of our time-space in order to get in and out of it. In an "alien-abduction experience," the person is taken temporarily into another dimension and then returned. The person is having an experience in the "alien's" reality and then brought back into this one.

Some "abductees" have experienced seeing a blue light. When the "door" opens, that blue light shines into our reality, and people experience it wherever they are in this reality. Not every experience of blue light relates to "alien abductions," however, because the properties of blue light are also involved with the art of teleportation.

Q. IN OTHER WORDS, THE PERSON EXPERIENCING WHAT THEY TERM "AN ALIEN ABDUCTION" HAS SIMPLY SHIFTED INTO A DIMENSIONAL SHIFT IN THEIR OWN CONSCIOUSNESS?

A. No, they're *actually being taken* into another reality. It's not just something that's happening in their minds. It's an actual event. Those "beings" know how to manipulate our time field, but we don't yet know how to do so ourselves. They come here and take us into their reality.

Q. SO THEY'RE ACTUALLY OPENING UP A PORTAL?

A. Yes, a dimensional portal, and we slip through that interface. They actually take us through that interface.

Q. WAS 2012 ONE OF THOSE INTERFACES, OR AN EXIT POINT TO ANOTHER DIMENSION?

A. No, 2012 was not an "exit" point, and did not push us out of time since then. It was more like taking the blanket of time and shaking it, giving all of those little filaments that are woven in the web a chance to rearrange themselves. And because they rearrange themselves, things can look, feel and function very differently.

Time as we know it will start to have more of these shifts. Since we're in the blanket of time, we're going to ripple with it and experience reality in a different way.

What we see will be different, because the old pattern is going to be shaken up. It has actually been shaking for some time and will continue to shake until 2017 at least. Individuals will have different experiences, depending on their own state of consciousness. We're still not out of the time field, but the carpet of time to which we cling is being shaken.

Q. CAN WE GET "OUT OF TIME" DURING THIS PROCESS?

A. As I consider being "out of time," I feel like I'm in hyperspace. Being beyond time is so big that you can't even imagine it. You may experience a very expanded state of awareness, but you're really not out of time until you can dissolve your body, materialize, de-materialize, and teleport yourself. Our consciousness can catch a glimpse, but we won't actually experience being out of time as long as we believe we are locked in our bodies. We can only experience a limited perception of it.

Q. HOW DO WE ENTER HYPERSPACE?

A. Transcend your body beliefs and perceptions as explained above. Time looks like a big dimensional wheel. When you start to get into hyperspace—and I'm getting very hot—you become one with All That Is. Your perception of yourself as a being with a particular identity disappears. In fact, perception itself disappears, and only pure consciousness remains. When you're into hyperspace, you're in a field of All That Is, and you *are* all of it. So, when you ask how to get out of time, the answer is that you have to get off the wheel of time, which is all about the perception of identity, which creates karma. It's all about perceiving yourself as something different, separate and distinct from something or someone else. In perception, you are in relationship with something or someone, as opposed to *being* All That Is.

I have to be clear—it isn't that you dissolve into the oneness and have no awareness. You literally are everything. You no longer can define yourself as any one thing, because you're all of everything.

Q. IS THAT *ZERO-POINT*?

A. No, zero-point is an actual location.

Q. IS ZERO-POINT BEYOND THE TIME FIELD?

A. Yes. When you say "zero point," I have an experience of traveling really fast in hyperspace, heading toward a center, which feels out beyond this time field. I'm having the sensation of going into a funnel; I'm going in and in and in, and I'm not coming to the end yet. I'm going inward, and I'm going to be arriving at a point. I'm heading in toward something that is either a starburst or a sunburst. It's a point of interchange or interface. Zero-point would be that concentrated point of energy—if you can call it energy—or a point of intensity that is an interface to an entire other reality field or world.

Q. IS THIS WHAT IS CALLED A BLACK HOLE?

A. No, I'm not in a black hole. The point that I'm heading in towards is not black at all—it's bright!

Q. IS IT *HOME*?

A. Going Home is going into the field of All That Is, and would not be going to zero-point; it would be *becoming* All That Is. That's Home.

Q. IS THAT WHERE ZERO-POINT ENDS?

A. No, because there are many zero-points in the Universe. In terms of the one that belongs to us, I'm heading towards this bright point, and then I'm at this burst, which opens up into an entire other field of life that we don't really know about, because it isn't in our time frame. It's not in our experience of time. So, as much as that would have an intersecting point, there might be another zero-point somewhere else where the same process happens. Zero-point is being explained as a concentration of energy that's an interface point. The universe is so huge that even in our broadest perceptions, we can't imagine.

Q. IS *TÍR NA NÓG* REAL? (IRISH MYTHOLOGY: THE LAND OF ETERNAL YOUTH, OR THE OTHERWORLD)

A. What I see with Tír na nÓg is very different from moving through hyperspace and experiencing All That Is. It is a level of space, but there's something very static about it. I'm seeing it as being in a different layer, or overtone, above our own. It's not here in the same space, but it is in another spherical layer above this one. It also is an elliptical shape — the same shape as the time field — and it rotates the same way, but it's at a different resonance, which is why things there stay in suspension.

You can go there, but I honestly don't think that you'd want to stay there forever—I don't see that it's a desirable place to stay. It feels like a place where you could get caught indefinitely. If you were there — you'd want to change and continue to grow and expand. Someone could desire to go there and could create that for themselves, but once they got there, they wouldn't like the unchanging nature of the field. They'd be cycling around in it eternally

Q. WHAT HAPPENS IN *DÉJÀ VU?*

A. When we sleep there is a part of our consciousness that disengages from our body, but is still connected to it by a myriad of threads. Our consciousness floats off and has experiences in those other states. *Déjà vu* is when the physical you here in the third dimension catches up to the experiences your consciousness had while you were out of your body.

Q. WHEN WE HAVE A *DÉJÀ VU* EXPERIENCE, ARE WE JUST GLIMPSING IT, OR ARE WE REALLY IN THE EXPERIENCE?

A. You are in the experience when you glimpse it or remember it. When you remember where you've gone, you are having the experience in 3-D. You don't experience the déjà vu until the body catches up to where the consciousness went. The catching up *is* experiencing the event in 3-D.

Q. CAN WE EXPERIENCE OTHER DIMENSIONAL SPACES?

A. Yes, you can experience other dimensional spaces by making the intention while in a meditative state. The focus to experience other dimensional spaces actually sets the grids in place that allow you to get there. Make the intention "Where do I want to go? What do I want to experience?" There are some dimensions and many random holes in the dimensional field that you definitely would not want to experience, so, be careful what you're asking for. Another option could be to ask for a dream to show you a dimension that would expand your experience of Source. Quantum Jumping is another great way to experience other dimensions and your other selves in them.[1]

Q. ARE THERE DIMENSIONS FROM WHICH YOU MIGHT NEVER COME BACK?

A. It could happen. If you found yourself in a not-so-nice dimension, the experience could be so traumatic that you may not realize that you're the one who put yourself there and that you can also choose to get out of it. You may get caught in the fear of being in it. When you're traveling in other dimensions, you need to have your wits about you concerning coming back. You need to be able to declare, "I'm going back now." You could easily lose control of that faculty if you suddenly found yourself immersed in a hellish place.

---

1. Burt Goldman's Quantum Jumping: www.quantumjumping.com

Let's talk about fears for a moment. I knew someone who made the intention to experience a specific aspect of himself in another dimension. His intention was positive. However, when he opened the door to the other dimension, he was met by a negative spirit. He closed the door and assumed his travels to the other dimension weren't working. Nonetheless, he tried again and was again met with a negative scenario. I talked to him about any fears he might have had about going to another dimension. Sure enough, he had various fears about it. Once these were dealt with and cleared, he was able to successfully meet other aspects of himself in other dimensions.

Q. SO IF I WERE TO END UP IN ONE OF THOSE HELLISH DIMENSIONS, WOULD THAT CORRESPOND WITH SOME ASPECT OF MY CONSCIOUSNESS OR MY OWN PATTERNS?

A. Yes, as in the example above. It is important to have your intention be clear and to be sure that you are not being wishy-washy or fearful. Otherwise, it would be better to wait until you may be more ready.

Q. WHEN WE TALK ABOUT PEOPLE WHO HAVE A LOT OF WISDOM OR SPIRITUAL KNOWLEDGE, DOES THAT EQUATE TO DIFFERENT LEVELS OR DIMENSIONS?

A. It equates to achieving a higher frequency level. You could have a person with much wisdom and spiritual knowledge, and they could still be living here in our 3rd dimension. Integration of knowledge and experiences occurs within you, which is similar to something being woven. The degree of integration one acquires brings you to a place of balance and understanding within yourself which is called wisdom. You now have knowledge, which is what wisdom is based on. This is not book knowledge, but knowledge that comes from integrating experiences. A person who is wise has integrated that knowledge within him/herself.

There would be beings in other dimensions who could have experienced or learned more and integrated more. Integration of knowledge catapults you to another level of *awareness*, thus changing your frequency level. Integration of experiences is a prerequisite to achieving higher levels of awareness.

Q. CURRENT PHYSICS IS CONCERNED ABOUT THE AMOUNT OF DARK ENERGY AND DARK MATTER—WHAT ARE THEY? SCIENCE POSTULATES THAT 96% OF THE UNIVERSE IS MISSING. COULD OTHER DIMENSIONS EXPLAIN DARK ENERGY AND DARK MATTER?

A. Dark energy and dark matter are two different things. Dark energy appears like tubes or cylinders of other dimensions or realities. They look hollow and are vertical. They co-exist in our time web and are interwoven into it. They're part of our time web, but because they're cylindrical or tube-like, they're not accessible in the same way that an intersecting or angular dimension would be. Other dimensions and realities intersect at angles, and you could most likely find the angles and the exact points of intersection. Dark energy, however, looks like cylindrical, vertical tubes that intersect our time field and then go through it. Because it's cylindrical, there's no intersection *point*. It's difficult, but it looks like it's a type of alternate reality that has a completely different shape that isn't based on angles. It's based on a cylinder or a tube.

Dark energy hasn't been defined, because it really doesn't fit into the web of time neatly in terms of degrees and angles. It doesn't have the same dynamics or shape that we're used to. It is a cylinder or tube without any door that you can get in. It might spin around inside itself and it might move, but you can't access it.

Dark matter has to do with a vacuum. Dark matter are particles that are vibrating at a heavier rate than light would be. Light particles sparkle and dance. Dark matter feels heavier and has a magnetic quality to it. I get a sensation of being pulled into a vacuum by it. It's a different type of particle. It's still part of what makes up everything, but it has different properties and wavelengths, even though it is still part of the stuff of creation. Everything's different in it—the spin rate, the electricity, the magnetics are all different in it.

I feel it in the bottom of my feet—it's a buzzing feeling. What's its function? The qualities of it are responsible for making vortices. In other words, the spin rate of dark matter makes vortices. It can coalesce things into form. It has a motion to it. Gravity would be connected to dark matter because it has a force in it that can pull things into form. I keep seeing vortices with a vacuum-like effect.

Scientists know more about dark matter than they're telling us. They're already using it. It's actually connected to gravity and anti-gravity. Tesla most likely had a lot of information about it.

Q. IS OUR TECHNOLOGY JUST ANOTHER DIMENSION IN WHICH WE COULD GET STUCK?

A. It depends on how it's being used. Technology is learning about different properties and how to use them. In other words, whether technology advances in a certain way depends on how scientists put together the properties that have been discovered. It could either be something that traps people or something that allows them access to other dimensions. Technology itself is not another dimension, but it can be a tool to access other dimensions.

Q. COULD WE GET STUCK IN IT?

A. Only to a point, because the universe only allows things to coalesce in a certain way before it ping pongs back the other way. Nothing is ever really stuck forever.

Q. SO WE CAN JUST ENJOY THE LIFE THAT WE'RE HAVING?

A. You can. Negatively, technology can be used to create a more confined field for us, and take more and more of the life-force energy out of things. But there's a safeguard in the universe where Source basically says, "That's it. No more." Technology can also be used to advance our knowledge and understand more of the life force energy in the universe.

Q. SO WE'RE NOT AT RISK OF GETTING CAUGHT UP TOO MUCH IN COMPUTERS AND MOBILE PHONES?

A. It depends on what we're using them for and also what kind of frequencies they emit. All low frequencies weaken your immune system. The dependence upon too many artificial things also dulls your own innate communication system with your higher abilities and aspects.

Q. IS THERE MORE INFORMATION FROM THE MOIST SPHERES?

A. You know, they've actually turned a creamy-white color, and they're shimmering.

Q. WHAT ARE THEIR NAMES?

A. They're places, not names. They're other reality fields. They have a consciousness, but they wouldn't want us to identify them as persons or beings. They can hover above our heads and not be caught in our time field. They can give us an experience of another realm of consciousness. They're alternate realities from higher, expanded states.

We can try an experiment. If you like, put your hands above your heads. Ask them to come over your head and see if you can feel them. They actually feel like they have skin, and they're watery—like a water balloon. They're saying that they're an *opportunity*, because they come from a reality that is not affected by our time matrix. Because they're not affected by it, you'll be able to access healing waters; you'll be able to access keys, which are in the form of little sound shapes that come directly in and give you the experience you are asking for. So if you're asking for knowledge, or a healing, or clarity, they can download that to you. *To be clear, they themselves are not coming into you.* They're really clear that there's nothing about them that's going to come into you because they're outside of our time matrix. It is an opportunity for us to experience a different type of information and access an experience that you wouldn't be able to access in our reality field.

Q. CAN I ASK ON BEHALF OF ALL OF US? DOES EVERYONE WANT TO ACCEPT THIS OPPORTUNITY?

A. We can let each person decide for themselves if they want this experience or not. I already accept. I can feel it, so I know it's positive, so if you want to, you can accept it. It's not like anything I've ever seen or experienced. The shape feels cool in temperature. They're watery, but this water's different—clean and regenerative, like an elixir.

Q. CAN WE ACCESS IT NOW?

A. It's above your head now. The more you use it, the more results you'll have, because they are conscious, aware and alive. It's a collective, so it wouldn't want to be called one thing. I don't feel that they come to everybody, and their appearance is not a common thing. I'm hot from that! Very hot and yet they don't feel hot. I feel a skin, like a bag, but somehow it's making me very warm.

Q. CAN WE GIVE THIS GIFT TO OTHERS?

A. They're telling me, "No, it's for you." However, by being in communication with them, you can make intentions for others.

Q. WE HAVE BEEN GIVEN THIS OPPORTUNITY BECAUSE WE CHOSE TO COME HERE WITH AN OPEN MIND AND ASK THESE QUESTIONS?

A. No, it's because of the topic of Time and Dimensions. If we weren't having this topic, they wouldn't have come in. You could say they are another type of consciousness, but they're not locked into our time field, which is why they can intersect it and cause different things here without becoming involved in it. I think there's great learning from them as well. All you have to do is focus your intention, and you could have a question-and-answer session with them. You each can have your own personal relationship with them tonight.

Q. SO, THE MORE WE KEEP ASKING THESE KINDS OF QUESTIONS, THE MORE WE OPEN UP TO KNOWLEDGE?

A. Yes, questions promote the knowledge. If you don't ask the questions, how would you know? It's the topic. They came because we're discussing Time and Dimensions.

Q. IS THERE ANYTHING THEY WANT TO TELL US THAT WE HAVEN'T ASKED?

A. Each one of us has to focus in to get our own answers. We'll do it right now. Ask the question: "Is there anything they want to say to you or to the group?" Let's all focus on that.

Time is taken for participants to have their own experience...

Aingeal: They're readjusting everything in my body. Quite interesting. They're saying it's like having your higher brain. I could feel the water in my body adjusting; my heartbeat was being regulated. I'm totally peaceful and relaxed now. They showed me places in my body where I have held trauma, and they were fixing it. They kept saying, "Higher brain. Higher brain." I feel as if it were a higher brain that we all used to have. The higher brain looks like it is filled with pulsing light—glowing and beautiful yellow light— and it is much bigger than the brains we have now.

Participants: "A song just stuck in my head, 'Burning down the house.' It burned down all of my assumptions, expectations, and perceptions. I am all of that: I am time, and I am non-time, I am zero-point, I am beyond the dimensions, the whole lot. Anything I want to think of, anywhere I want to put my consciousness or focus or intent. But I won't burn down the house!"

"Restraining your imagination is like applying a vice onto your life. That's the first thing I got. The next thing was: 'You bought in. Now buy out.'"

"You accepted an extraordinary thing tonight. Now continue to accept extraordinary things."

"Recognition is gratitude. Gratitude is recognition for this consciousness. I got a final piece of advice that said: 'Meditate more.'"

"It was like looking down at all this."

"I feel that the whole experience of time is a collection of people's ideas and beliefs and an experience of watching yourself create. Watching yourself have experiences is what it feels like to me."

"I feel like creation goes on forever. It is so big that we just can't fathom it. Even when you get out of this particular time field, this is only one little time field. You're never going to be tired. You'll love being part of everything. It's just so, so amazing. What's the point of it? I feel joy and fun."

Q. WHAT IS THE POINT?

A. From Source's point of view, creation is fun. The fact that creation *is*, is joy. It goes on and on: Isn't it wonderful, isn't it awesome?

We have no idea, because we've made ourselves so limited in our perceptions in this time field that we're focused in. If our perceptions were freed, we'd see everything as joyful and magnificent. Even within our own field of time there's so much to see. However, compared to what I'm seeing, our time field is a very sticky field. We have a lot yet to know.

Chapter 8

Dreams

With our questions about dreams, we found that there are many levels to dreams, and many dimensions intersecting other dimensions in the dream state. Therefore, some of the questions have multi-levels to the answer.

Q. WHAT ARE *DREAMS*, AND WHAT IS THEIR PURPOSE?

A. Dreams are composed of ribbons of colors or color bands. They are part of a wave movement that is happening around and through us continually. They flow and congeal into various shapes, and then they move on. They appear very transient, yet they are very alive and dynamic.

The purpose of dreams is multifaceted—they bring in more light (color-nourishment) to us to rejuvenate us; they bring understanding and enlightenment to us; they are a medium for our creative minds to manifest and express our desires and see our fears; and they can be the bridge between worlds and dimensions. Dream frequencies interact with our brain waves while we're sleeping. If we were aware of these living color frequencies during the day, we would be able to receive them and be nourished by them all day, without thought interference. In other words, we wouldn't have such a great need to sleep, because we would be revitalized constantly. Because we are using our brain frequencies during the day to think, decide, observe and receive data, we are not conscious of dream frequencies. Sleeping is a time when these color frequencies can come in freely and communicate through and to us in myriads of expressions.

This level of dream energy is designed to bring more light into our bodies to replenish and nourish us. This revitalization process could take the form of a dream in which you are dreaming of events that occurred during the day or some other situation in your life. These alive and conscious color bands come in and help you process events in your life so as to bring you back into balance. If you didn't have an issue or event that needed to be processed or balanced, these color bands would still be in your sleep process, bringing more light and color into your consciousness and your body. Often dreams are about organization and putting something in your life back into order.

Q. IS THERE A PARTICULAR PLACE IN OUR PHYSIOLOGY OR OUR BRAINS FROM WHICH DREAMS ORIGINATE?

A. There doesn't seem to be a particular location in our physiology or our brain, but dreams do have to do with the way our brain fires or is firing when we sleep.

Q. DO OUR BRAINS AND THE NERVE NETWORK IN OUR SOLAR PLEXUS CONNECT TO OUR DREAMS?

A. The nerve network in the solar plexus connects to the mass consciousness. It has a horizontal movement to it, and connects to things linear. Brain chemistry, in contrast, is nonlocal, and its firings go off sporadically in many different directions. It's interrelating with the field on various electrical levels, which is why the brain is the relay station between many different dimensional levels.

Q. WITHIN OUR TIME REALITY, HOW LONG DOES A DREAM LAST?

A. The average dream is 30 seconds to a minute, but some can last up to five minutes. Most don't last longer than that. You're in a "no-time" place when you dream — time collapses in the dream state.

Q. DO WE CONTINUALLY GET DEPLETED OF COLORS AND LIGHT?

A. Yes, we are made of color, light and sound. We do get depleted of these elements in our daily lives. Colors have a very strong connection to the minerals in our bodies. During times of stress, we become depleted in various colors, sounds, and minerals. Minerals are very important to us, because it is through them that we can absorb color and sound frequencies into our bodies. Therefore, if your body is deficient in minerals, you will not be able to absorb the amount of color frequencies that you need to keep yourself enlivened and in balance, even if you were out in the sunlight all day. Dreaming rebalances and re-nourishes us.

Q. WHAT DOES IT MEAN IF YOU DREAM IN BLACK AND WHITE?

A. When this happens, you have ventured into an alternate reality—what we might call a hibernation zone, realities that are not necessarily positive. This is actually how you can tell that you may be in a negative place. There are alternate dimensions that are devoid of certain qualities of light and color, and finding yourself in one while you're sleeping can help you understand how to deal with negativity. This can be a signal that you may be deficient in certain vitamins and minerals, or that you may be becoming ill and need to check in on yourself. Dreaming in color tells you that you are within a normal dream state.

Q. WHY IS EVERYTHING POSSIBLE IN DREAMS?

A. Dream states are not subject to the same laws of gravity that are present in our conscious awake state. These color frequency bands are free flowing, and they do not have the density to them that we have while we are in our bodies. The truth is that thought is continually creative, but it may take longer for our thoughts to manifest in our physical reality than in a dream, precisely because our reality is denser and the color frequencies or elements needed to easily manifest may not be present. In the dream state we do not have this densification or color deficiency that we experience in our physical reality. Therefore, our thoughts can manifest instantaneously in the dream state. Different dimensional levels have different laws of physics, and many other dimensional levels do not have the same type of gravity that we have here on Earth.

Q. When did dreaming become necessary?

A. We have had the ability to dream since we have been in dense physical bodies and began to lose our memory of who we are. We have dreamed since we lost the ability to communicate with all life everywhere. Dreaming isn't only a human quality — animals also dream. The ability to dream is within any species that has a brain and requires the ability to communicate or interrelate with different aspects of reality, while in a body. It is how species get nourished.

Q. Is there any way we can be more active or conscious in the dream state and use our dreams more productively?

A. That is a great question, because our spirits would love us to be more consciously aware while in the dream state. It is easy to do by putting our attention on the subject, much as you do in meditation or any other type of practice. There are many books out today on lucid dreaming, where you can begin to be "awake" while in the dream state so that you can influence the progression and outcome of dreams.If you were to put more attention on this and make it an actual discipline, it would be a way for you to see our physical reality much differently and help you manifest your desires. You would also be able to cause your dream state and your conscious waking state to become one continuous flow.

We currently go to sleep and go into a dream state, which feels like an entirely different reality from our waking state. As conscious dreamers, we can meet our guides consciously while in the dream state, control the outcomes of dreams by making choices, and manifest our desires deliberately while in the dream state, which would help us immensely in our physical waking lives with direction, abilities, and clarity of purpose. In other words, our lives could become more deliberate and more focused, with much greater meaning and purpose. We could wake up remembering the discussion we had with our guides. There would be no more separation between waking and sleeping. A bit of a discipline is required, however, and it does require practice.

Q. WHERE IS THE PLACE WE GO TO WHEN WE DREAM, COMPARED TO WHERE WE ARE IN OUR PHYSICAL REALITY?

A. I'm being shown a large circular sphere of energy. Actually, we really don't go anywhere—it is rather that we interact with levels that are already around us. We actually interact with this sphere constantly, not only when we sleep, but also when we're awake. We just aren't conscious that we are doing so.

Q. SINCE DREAMING IS AN INTERACTION WITH THE SURROUNDING DIMENSIONAL LEVELS, ARE WE ACCESSING SOMETHING NEW, OR DO DREAMS FORM FROM WHAT OCCURS IN OUR AWAKE STATE?

A. Both. However, dreaming wouldn't be necessary if we were in a more conscious alignment with this field around us that is interacting with us all the time. Dreaming occurs because we are not consciously aware. Think of it like frequencies accessible on a radio station. If we were more conscious of this field around us and of the living colors that interact with us, their integration into our lives would occur throughout the day rather than just while we sleep. Dreaming occurs because we become depleted and need to be revitalized by these color rays. Since our consciousness is only focused in a linear fashion, we are not aware of the communication that goes on between the many different levels surrounding us. Therefore, we inadvertently block the integration or flow of various nourishing life-force energies.

Can you imagine what a greater effect these color waves could have on us if we each were in a conscious co-creative relationship with them throughout the day? When we direct our attention to so many other things that really have little importance, we actually block our own awareness of these other levels of reality. Therefore, we are not aware of the communication that we have with all life, and because we are not aware of this communication, our ability to consciously interact with it is diminished.

Think of your consciousness as nerves or wires that need to be kept free-flowing in order to have a give-and-take type of reception. When we use our thoughts to focus on things that actually cause static in this communication system, we can't receive the messages from the relationships that are going on between us, others and the universe. Because of these disruptions, sleep is necessary to temporarily close off our conscious mind so that we can be replenished without interference.

Dreaming happens as a consequence of our linear focus of attention. Nourishing energy, our spirit guides and other levels of our subconscious all need to have a way to get through to us, because our minds are never quiet throughout the day. Jiddu Krisnamurti once said that if we were consciously awake, we would have no need to dream, which is why we are being encouraged to begin a conscious relationship first with our dream state and then with our complete reality.

Q. DOES IT FOLLOW THEN THAT THOSE WHO DON'T DREAM OR REMEMBER THEIR DREAMS ARE HEALTHIER THAN THOSE WHO DO?

A. No, we can't deduce that. People still dream, even if they don't remember their dreams. When someone has reached the state where they no longer need to dream, they will be fully conscious and will know they are. Most people are unconscious and still dream because they need to be replenished or re-nourished. Some people are awake at these levels and don't need to dream, but they are exceptions rather than the rule.

Q. WHO ARE THE PEOPLE IN OUR DREAMS?

A. They can be symbolic representations of aspects of yourself taking on particular forms to get a message across to you or they can be a visit from someone in another plane of existence. Many of the actors you see in dreams are created by aspects of your own self, so that you become aware of these aspects. They appear in certain ways, doing certain things, because of the associations that we make in our minds about our world and our lives. At other times, these "actors" can be fragments of your own consciousness that come from your own thoughts, beliefs and desires. If you are not consciously aware of the symbolism in your life, things will be arranged for you in the dream state to help you become aware of certain things. Many things happen in the dream state: guidance is received; your color frequencies are adjusted for nourishment purposes; you process out events of your everyday life; and you may be actively traveling to other dimensions or carrying out a mission.

Those who show up in your dream, portraying themselves in certain roles and sequences, have everything to do with whatever you may need to see or have affirmed. Perhaps you are being warned of something that could show up in your everyday reality — something that you need to look at or change. You'll be aware because of the emotional impact the dream leaves on you when you awaken.

> I have had dreams that affected me emotionally that I thought meant a certain thing, but when I sat down to write about what the dream meant to me, its message was entirely different than what I had originally thought.

Something that can feel ominous in a dream can actually be a very high message about transformation in your life. It's a good idea to look at dreams as symbolic dramas that show you something about yourself and what you're doing or not doing in your life. Do this by asking yourself what the scenes and sequences mean to you, because everything in our consciousness is associative or has a symbolic meaning to us on a subconscious level and it is all very personal to each one of us.

You may meet alternate selves in the dream state. These would be other versions of you living in different dimensional spaces having their own lives. It doesn't really matter whether these alternate selves are fragments of your thoughts and desires playing themselves out or actual aspects of your soul. What matters is if they show up in your dream, look into what they mean to you, just as you would any other image showing up, and you will still make tremendous progress in understanding the workings of your own being, whether on the 3-D or multidimensional levels. Remember, we are in relationship with our other selves even if we are not consciously aware of them, and what they do in their dimensions affects us here and vice-versa.

There is an active relationship going on continually between what happens with our thoughts and our brain chemistry and how that gets translated to the different dimensional levels around us. A co–creative process is happening between our own thoughts, feelings, and beliefs, and the forms, colors, and shapes they become in this reality and other realities. The dream state doesn't act upon you; rather it is responding to your quality and what your consciousness is emitting—*i.e.,* everything about you is creative and has an expression in other dimensions.

Which alternate dimension you experience when you sleep may be guided or directed by a higher aspect of you, depending upon what message you may need to decipher from the formations that your own consciousness is displaying. This is the opportunity that our own internal guidance uses to give us a message or direction when we wouldn't be aware of it in our normal waking consciousness.

Not all dreams are important messages—some may just be the healing or the de-stressing of events that have occurred through the day. However, it is important to look at what aspects of your daily life are appearing in your dream state, because there could be some important information there for you to examine.

If we were more conscious in our everyday life of the different dimensional levels around us, we would be co-creating much more often with much greater clarity and deliberate focus. If we were more conscious, we wouldn't need to receive guidance in our dream state. Instead, we would be consciously and consistently interacting with our own guidance throughout the day. We would also be fed all day long by color and light, because we wouldn't be using our brain power for decisions or actions that deplete our energy. Instead, we would be in the flow of life, which would be one continuous action without the need to sleep and dream to replenish ourselves. We would be more in the moment.

Dreams in which you dream about certain people can be a message or warning for a particular person, or they can represent some aspect of them, you, or both that needs attention or has a message. The fact that they are showing up in your dream means that you can offer them healing energy or a blessing, which may make a difference in some aspect of their lives and yours. Do not assume that dreaming about death or illness concerning someone you know means that such a condition is coming to that person. Sometimes it is that a person's spirit self is asking you to convey to that person a message about something he/she may need to take care of. Always offer a blessing or healing energy in those cases.

Q. DO THE THOUGHT FORMS OR BEINGS THAT APPEAR IN DREAMS COME DOWN INTO THIS PHYSICAL REALITY?

A. Particular beings or events can materialize into this physical reality from the dream state, because you are co-creating with yourself through the process of dreaming, whether you are consciously aware of it or not. This is also why it is a good idea to become a conscious dreamer, so that you are deliberately choosing what you would like to bring back from alternate dimensions to enhance your present physical reality. Usually actors or events in a dream do not materialize for any lasting period of time, because the dreamer does not focus on them long enough for them to become solidified or lasting in this dimension. That would be the case in normal dreams or unconscious dreams where we are not deliberately and consciously creating the scenario. We need to know, though, that any thought form we create can attach itself to other people with similar energy and become something more, even if we ourselves are not energizing it; this is true, whether we are waking or dreaming.

> Here is a story in which my dream state and my everyday reality merged. I was asleep and dreaming that I was walking through a forest. I was aware of a dark cloud above the tree line that was following me throughout the dream. It felt very evil and ominous. I was trying to get away from it and trying to

find my way out of the forest. I could see a clearing and a light at the edge of the forest, but every time I took a step in that direction the dark cloud would advance upon me. It seemed that there was no way out of this. Just at that moment, my dog in my everyday life began to bark, waking me up from the dream. My husband got up to check the house to see if there was someone in the house. When he went to turn on the lights, he found that the power was out. This was very strange, as there were no storms or anything to cause such a power outage. While my husband was checking the house, I lay in my bed thinking that I couldn't leave the dream that way. I had to go back into the dream and try to overcome the evil presence. My husband came back and said there was nothing strange going on in the house, and we all went back to sleep. I immediately fell back into the dream, and it continued exactly where it had left off before I awoke. I was still fearful of not being able to find a way out of the forest, and in my mind I called the police. The police arrived immediately and looked up at the dark cloud looming above us and told me that this was out of their league. They said they couldn't help me.

Suddenly a voice said, "There is only one God." As soon as I heard this, the dark cloud disappeared, and I was at the edge of the forest and out in the sunshine. At that same moment, the power came back on in the house, the alarm clock went off, and all the lights came on. What had happened? I feel there really had been an evil energy present in my physical reality during the night. The dream was relating that fact and showing me a dream to let me know what was going on. How it ended up had a lot to do with the voice that came in to remind me that there was only one God—in essence one true reality — in which evil does not exist. As soon as that reality intersected the reality of the negative forces, the negative forces disappeared.

To clarify, we are making the point that evil is based on false perceptions of reality and therefore is not a living presence in and of itself.

This is a case where higher guidance was at work teaching me a very valuable lesson about what happens with our consciousness, and what we believe a reality is like. In other words, in the dream I was in a reality where I was being threatened by dark forces, and I was in extreme fear. However, another part of me intersected a different reality where only Truth exists. When this happened, I was now in a completely different reality that was based in safety, love and support, which evidenced itself in my physical waking reality at the same moment by the power going back on. In hindsight, the dark cloud could have been a malevolent ET abduction attempt which my higher guides thwarted, by first waking me up with my dog barking and second, by getting a truth message through to me when I went back into the dream the second time. Since ET ships often affect the power in the areas they appear, it would make sense that the power would go off and then back on again when the "dark cloud" left. Perhaps the dark cloud was really a cloaked ship.

Q. DO OUR DREAMS FORM OUT OF OUR OWN EXPERIENCES, OR DO WE ACTIVELY CREATE THE DREAM SCENARIO AS WE GO ALONG?

A. There are many levels of dreams. There can be times during the night when you are processing your waking 3-D life and another part of the night where your guides are downloading scenes or information to help you. While you're sleeping, you can sometimes float off into an entirely different dimension where you've never been before. It may be positive or not. Sometimes dreams are your subconscious giving you a measure of your progress in your life or as a soul. For example, it may show you what your attitude is, or it may play out a scenario to let you know what you've been doing with yourself—what your thoughts have been manifesting. That's why it's important to look at all dreams as symbolic dramas giving you a message about yourself on various levels.

If you get proficient at paying attention to your dreams, you will notice that each dream carries a particular energy or feeling with it that will help you determine what type of dream it is. A given dream might help with your everyday experiences, like rejuvenating yourself or relieving stress; or it might be a message from your higher guidance. Possibly, a frightful dream may be evidence that you wandered into a dimension that isn't necessarily so positive, while a happy dream may suggest that you have visited somewhere that is very euphoric.

> In my story mentioned above, the dream had many layers. It was an actual event that was happening on a dream level, but it was also happening in my everyday life, as it had turned the power off in my house. I was under some type of threat, and my higher guidance came into the dream to help me—most likely because I was asking for help (calling the police in my dream). I was also learning a lesson about the truth of only one God, and how no other realities different from this are real. It was also a test of my courage, by me going back into the dream to overcome the fear and the evil presence. Once the evil presence left, the power came back on in my house, showing that the dream and my everyday reality were coinciding.

Some types of dreams can be prophetic—as in doomsday scenarios or some other type of disaster. In these cases, the dream can be implanted by negative beings. What I mean by this is that sometimes negative entities use a person's dream state to create images of doomsday scenarios as a way of using the dreamer's mind and emotional body to encourage disastrous effects in the 3-D world. Many people who experience prophetic dreams and then see that they have manifested in 3-D think this is proof that they are tuned in to the future or are highly intuitive. However, what can really be going on is that they are being used by dark forces to create catastrophic scenarios on Earth. Anyone having a doomsday dream should quickly reverse the scenario with their mind by asserting that all is well and no disaster will occur. In this way, they contribute to a positive future instead of energizing a doomsday future. Dark forces know the power of imagery and how our emotional bodies can create futures based on pictures and feelings, which is why they use us to create doomsday events in our world, since they do not have enough power of their own to affect our physical level of reality.

> One recurring dream I have exemplifies higher guidance. I dream that I am about to board a huge white jumbo jet. I need to get to the gate on time, and I find interferences or obstacles in my way. Sometimes I get on board just in time by some fluke, while at other times I don't make the flight. Sometimes the jet is already in flight, and I am on my way to somewhere very beautiful, loving and bright. Usually I know the people aboard the jet are soul friends whom I've known for many years, and my husband is always traveling with me. Other times, I will be getting off the jumbo jet at some new place, and find that there are ETs in this new place, all of whom I know. The symbolism of the white jumbo jet always lets me know that this is an important dream—a measure of my progress or lack of progress, depending on how it turns out.

If we were conscious dreamers, we would make choices in our dreams so they would turn out great, which would affect our everyday lives by putting us on tracks that support our highest growth and progress. By becoming conscious dreamers, we will gain greater degrees of control over the outcomes of our dreams, and we will be able to interact with their various levels consciously. As conscious dreamers, we change the scenarios of many aspects of our dreams in varying dimensions by consciously choosing our outcomes, so we no longer have to feel that we are a victims of forces outside ourselves in our dreams. This practice will also help us merge different levels of reality into our 3-D waking life so that they serve our highest desires, rather than thwart us in our progress.

Q. SO IN ESSENCE, THE MORE CONSCIOUS WE BECOME IN OUR
DREAMS, THE STRONGER OUR CONSCIOUSNESS WILL BECOME IN
OUR WAKING LIFE. IS THAT RIGHT?

A. Yes, that's right. The stronger you are in your own consciousness, the less you can be affected by negative forces. You begin to see that there is no separation between your subconscious and your conscious mind—nothing need be unconscious to you any longer. The greater your degree of conscious awareness, the more deeply you will know yourself. You will also begin to see the symbolism and connections in your 3-D waking life in the events and situations in which you find yourself. You will understand the thoughts and beliefs beneath any experience or situation. You will also understand what is being reflected back to you. You will be able to consciously make decisions in your 3-D life much more easily, because you will have clarity on what the choices are and what they mean.

Becoming more conscious and disciplining yourself to become a conscious dreamer will cause you to be more awake in all levels of your life. The advantage to sleeping is that the part of us that is subconscious can display itself as dramas, symbols, other people, scenarios, *etc.*, which only needs to happen because we are unconscious of what is going on beneath the surface of ourselves. The more conscious you become, the less you will need to sleep. You will in essence, become a conscious creator in every dimension of your life. The idea that there is a barrier between your conscious mind and your subconscious mind is really an error. It is only because we do not understand the language of symbolism and reflection in our lives that it appears that we are unaware of things that are going on beneath the surface of our conscious mind. The fun part of becoming a conscious dreamer is when you see the intentions you have manifested in your dream state begin to appear in your 3-D reality.

When people die or have a near-death experience (NDE), they usually find themselves in a place of knowledge and understanding. Suddenly they see how everything is related and how everything makes sense. All the pieces fit into place. Things of which they were unaware in their 3-D lives suddenly all flow together and they get to see that life is a single movement of consciousness. It isn't necessary to die or to have an NDE for this awareness to come to you. It can be done by becoming a conscious dreamer or by learning to see the symbolism in your everyday life. In a way, your 3-D life is also a dreamscape—a drama, or a collection of thoughts and beliefs being acted out through your relationships, situations, and experiences and your reactions to them.

Q. Can a conscious dreamer heal another person from the dream state?

A. Yes, with their permission. It can be more powerful to consciously manifest from the dream state.

Q. If you do something like that without permission, would you invite the same kind of intrusion upon yourself?

A. You could, and you would also be creating karmic chords with the person you're trying to heal, which means that you have taken on some of their karmic burden by becoming involved in their energy without their permission. You create psychic chords between yourself and them. It's actually a loving thing to *not* interfere in another person's situation unless you are asked. Some situations people are in are because they are being challenged to become more self-masterful in some way.

Q. Can anybody or anything monitor our dreams?

A. Other aspects of yourself can watch your dreams. You interact with higher parts of yourself all day long, and especially in your dream state, because the barriers of 3-D waking consciousness are not there. If you're having something play out in a dream that is the result of your own thought processes, I don't see the other aspects of yourself interfering with the process, but they may watch it unfold, looking for a message to send to you that might help you in your 3-D life. If you allow them to inspire you, they will send a particular frequency to you when they find an opening.

Let's say a higher part of myself was trying to interact with the 3-D me throughout the day. It could be more difficult for it to get through to the 3-D part of me because I am busy and my mind is filled with other thoughts of what I have to do during the day. This 3-D part of me may block communication. In this case, the higher parts of me would probably go off and continue doing their own thing on their own levels until I am sleeping, when I may be more available for them to communicate.

Q. LET'S SAY WE WANT TO SEE SOMETHING MORE CLEARLY, COULD WE ASK FOR A DREAM THAT WOULD SHOW US THE ANSWER TO A SITUATION OR GIVE US CLARITY ABOUT SOMETHING IN OUR LIVES?

A. Yes, of course. In fact, it's a very good idea to practice doing that, so you establish more of a conscious rapport between your conscious self and your dream-state self. You've probably heard that it's good to record your intentions in a notebook before you go to sleep, and when you wake up, no matter what time it is, immediately write down your dream in your notebook before you forget it.

Q. WHEN SOMEONE WISHES YOU "SWEET DREAMS" BEFORE YOU GO TO BED AT NIGHT, WHAT KIND OF EFFECT DOES IT HAVE ON YOUR DREAMS?

A. It's a nice sentiment to offer someone when they go to sleep at night, but the truth is that a person's own consciousness follows its own journey when it is sleeping. What the sentiment will do is offer someone a greater degree of protection in a dream. Ultimately, it is the person's own consciousness, and what's going on with them, that determines the quality of their dream state.

Q. WHAT IS GOOD TO SAY TO CHILDREN BEFORE THEY SLEEP?

A. Don't forget that children as well as adults are still under the protection of their holy guardian angel, and it might be a good idea to call on that presence to be active with them throughout their sleeping/dream state. When you consciously solicit the protection of your holy guardian angel and that of the child, they will be more active and better able to do more for you. It assures that they won't be off playing.

We need to remember that angels are evolving too. They may not always be available or on duty to serve you. The same is true of your holy guardian angel. Your holy guardian angel would most likely be aware if you were in significant danger, but it may not always be interacting in every aspect of your life. It may be off on another project or doing something in another dimension, for example. If you deliberately call on your holy guardian angel before going to sleep at night and ask it to provide a particular service, it will guarantee that they will be there.

Q. CAN ONE'S DREAMS BE INFILTRATED BY NEGATIVE FORCES?

A. If there happens to be a negative energy in the vicinity of your consciousness while you're dreaming, and you are in a vulnerable place, it's possible that negative energy could interfere with your thought processes while you sleep. Keep in mind, however, that there always has to be some resonance between the negative energies' frequency and your own on some level. We have to remember that like still attracts like on all levels. The planet is always turning, and at times parts of it align with certain grid patterns, and at other times it aligns with other grid patterns. It's the same for us when we sleep. The particular time when you go out of your body to sleep determines what grid patterns are in place. Another example is the exact time you were born, which determines your astrological configuration depending on where the planets were at the time of your birth.

The configurations of the grids of the planets determine the kind of energy or place you initially slip into. If you happen to be feeling vulnerable or upset when you go to sleep, and there was a likeness in the ethers at that particular moment, you could easily slip into a different dimensional space that vibrates at a lower frequency and you may find yourself amongst other beings that are also vibrating at a low frequency, which is why the practice of lucid dreaming, or waking yourself up while in a dream, is very useful. You will realize that you are dreaming and be able to choose yourself out of a particular dream or space that you find unpleasant.

The more consciousness you hold, the more control you have over where you end up in your dream state and in your waking life. The only way you are acted upon in any given situation is when you're not in conscious choice. The more you upgrade the quality of yourself or your own frequency, the greater protection you have from low-vibrational energies. When you are consciously watchful of patterns unfolding and scenarios manifesting, you can choose a different outcome in the moment. In contrast, if you are unaware of them, then you will be driven by those situations rather than driving them as a conscious chooser. Understand the power of consciousness itself is unlimited and very great, and the more aware and conscious you become, the more power you have. The more power of consciousness you have, the faster your choices and decisions become manifest. Remember also that the quality and power of your own consciousness contributes to the quality of the whole.

Q. ARE WE MORE POWERFUL IN THE DREAM STATE THAN WHEN WE'RE AWAKE?

A. Not necessarily. It isn't that the dream state is more powerful than the waking state. You are always powerful. It's just that your logical mind isn't interrupting you in the dream state with useless thoughts and perceptions.

Q. ARE DREAMS MORE REAL THAN 3-D REALITY?

A. No. This idea comes from the thought that there is some sort of division or separation between worlds in which one world may seem more real than another. Shamans called the subconscious world the dreamtime, implying that it was a place of archetypal images that was somehow more real than our waking world. The truth is that it only appears to be separate, because we have not yet developed our consciousness to the point where we can be awake to the various levels of our own being or to the collective unconscious.

Q. IS OUR 3-D LEVEL OF REALITY ALSO A DREAM?

A. On a certain level, it's all a dreamscape. You could say that creation and all image-making is a dreamscape in the sense that we are imagining it all or coming to conclusions about reality, and then seeing it manifest before our eyes. We're actually making it all up as we go along, but there is a core truth in creation—and that is the love that is behind all powers of manifestation. It is obvious that we don't always create loving manifestations; however, the principle that allows image-making to congeal into a manifestation is still the life principle behind the scenes. In this way you can see that you either make your own heaven or your own hell; you feel as limited or unlimited as you believe. When you know this, the possibilities are endless as to what you can experience according to your beliefs. Ultimately, though, if you play with manifestation, you will eventually want to experience only pure love. You will recognize that all these other scenarios are just ideas of consciousness playing themselves out according to our desires. When we get to the place where we desire to be only love, our creations will be entirely different.

Q. DOES EVERYONE DREAM THE SAME WAY?

A. Everyone has the same potential in their dreaming states, but not everyone has the same language in their dreams. Since the language of dreams is symbolic, it is personal to the dreamer. The way a dream is organized or comes together is also personal to each person, and each person has a personal associative meaning to each symbol in their dream and in their waking life too. This is why it's beneficial to ask yourself about your dreams in terms of what the sequence of events in a dream mean to you personally. Until you become adept at being a conscious dreamer, this is how you can discern your own messages from your own unique symbolism.

Q. WHY CAN'T I DREAM IN RUSSIAN OR JAPANESE, IF I SPEAK ONLY ENGLISH?

A. You don't dream in a foreign language because you have created a symbolic association with your dominant language, which is the language that your subconscious uses to convey messages to you. This is not to say that you couldn't have a dream where you are speaking a different language—in these cases, the message coming across would be very interesting, and most likely you would have lived a life where you knew that language in order to discern the message. Chinese or Russians dream in their own languages because that is the language they have used to associate the events in their lives. If you really want to dream in Swahili, go ahead and ask to dream in Swahili.

Q. PEOPLE WHO BELIEVE IN JESUS WILL DREAM OF THE IMAGE OF JESUS THAT WAS PORTRAYED TO THEM WHILE GROWING UP. WHEREAS SOMEONE FROM ANOTHER COUNTRY WILL HAVE GROWN UP WITH ANOTHER IMAGE. SINCE NO ONE CAN REALLY PROVE WHAT JESUS ACTUALLY LOOKED LIKE. ARE YOU SAYING THAT WE ALL MAKE UP OUR OWN ASSOCIATIONS, AND THAT IS WHAT APPEARS TO US?

A. Yes, this is true, but remember the purpose of dreams oftentimes is to get a message across, which is why dream language is so personal to each person. It's all about association.

I had a friend once who was not very spiritual. His dad had passed away, and I happened to meet with him at a shop that I owned. He told me that he had a very strange dream about his dad where his dad appeared to him in the dream and said to him, "I am perceived only by you." He was a bit confused about what that actually meant, but it makes the point that much of our imagery of people, places, and things is relative only to us in our own minds. Another example is when you tune into someone who has died. They will appear very much as they did in their Earth life, perhaps younger at times or more radiant, but still with the same basic face or body appearance as when they were alive. Do they really look like that once they're in spirit? It's possible, but they may also appear a certain way in order to get a message across to family and friends still here.

Q. CAN YOU ASK ANY QUESTION, OR CAN YOU ASK FOR A VISION OF SOME SORT IN A DREAM?

A. Yes, of course. You can ask for insight, clarity, inspiration, anything.

Q. WHAT CAN I DO TO HELP MY PATIENTS WHO SHARE THEIR DREAMS WITH ME?

A. You can encourage them to be conscious dreamers, because it is really important for people to establish their own language for their own dreams. This will empower them on a personal level to be able to decipher what their own dreams are telling them. It is also important for us not to interpret others' dreams, but rather to encourage them to describe what their own dreams mean to them. Remember that everybody has an associative mind, and we each know what things mean to us personally. It's just a matter of inquiry, and taking the time to sit and feel what the scenario in a dream might feel like, or what it may mean to you symbolically. The reason it's so important to encourage more conscious dreaming or even to encourage someone to examine the meaning of their own dreams is so they can monitor their own personal progress in their lives and get very clear on what their choices are.

If you were to encourage your patients to do this and keep a notebook, they can then bring you the results of their own interpretations, and in so doing you would be better able to know how to help them, and it would be a co-creative interaction between your patient and yourself. You would also be able to offer your own insights. At that stage you would be having a lively discussion about what feels right, or what other options are. In this way, both of you would be coming from a place of strength where neither one has authority over the other. Rather, you would be helping to co-create the highest possible outcome for both your patient and yourself. It is important that we be careful not to put our own language into another person's dreams, but rather help them discover their own language through their own inquiry. You can then repeat back to them what they are sharing with you about their own interpretations so they can hear it and decide if it feels right or accurate to them, which will allow them to strengthen their own communication language with themselves.

Q. DOES A SEPARATE CONSCIOUSNESS DO ALL OF THE CREATING, OR DOES CONSCIOUSNESS INTERRELATE WITH OTHER DIMENSIONAL LEVELS TO CAUSE A CO-CREATIVE EXPERIENCE?

A. It is more that we are relating with the field of All That Is, which is interacting with us and manifesting our thoughts and reflecting them back to us. In other words, conscious creation is a co-creative endeavor because everything is alive as consciousness, so therefore everything is always inter-relating with everything else. The thing about becoming a conscious creator is that you consciously interact with the field of All That Is, which can cause a very different type of co-creative relationship with the intelligence of all life. The only reason that things seem to be going on without our conscious awareness is simply because we are not directing our attention to this relationship that we have with all life everywhere.

Q. THERE ARE MANY DIFFERENT BOOKS AND IDEAS REGARDING DREAMS, LIKE JUNGIAN, FREUDIAN AND METAPHYSICAL, NOT TO MENTION THE NUMEROUS BOOKS OUT THERE ON WHAT OUR DREAMS MEAN. ARE YOU SAYING THAT NONE OF THEM ARE BENEFICIAL? IS ANY ONE BETTER THAN THE OTHERS?

A. It isn't that one is better than the other, or that there are some that are more accurate than others. There may be some interpretations of dreams that resonate with a person when they are trying to find their associations within their own dreams.

For example, I have gone through periods in my life when I was attracted to certain books or other people's opinions about dreams that would resonate with me at the time. Later, as I grew and evolved, those same books stopped resonating with me. Eventually, I realized that I was my own best interpreter of my own dreams. Whatever people need at their own level of consciousness to help them decipher their own language would be best for them at the time, for as long as it serves them. Some people may be attracted to the Jungian interpretations of archetypes and the collective unconscious, while others may be attracted to the Freudian sexuality symbolism. Another person may go into the shamanism version of the dreamtime. Perhaps none of those apply, which is why ultimately your own symbolic language is best.

Q. YOU'RE TALKING TODAY ABOUT THE BENEFITS OF DREAMS, AND YET MANY OF US WAKE UP, AND THE DREAM DISAPPEARS, AND WE

HAVE NO RECOLLECTION OF IT. DOES THE DREAM SPHERE DISAPPEAR AS WELL WHEN WE WAKE UP?

A. Every thought form has existence on some level. Whether it dissipates or is attracted to a thought form stronger than itself depends upon how much it is energized or what is in close proximity to it. These factors determine whether the thought form becomes a thing in and of itself or dissolves into nothing.

Much of the reason people don't remember their dreams is because as they wake up, a different part of their brain switches on as they once again become part of their 3-D waking world. As one awakens, an entirely different hormonal process begins to occur before a person has fully awakened. Therefore, the brain has already begun to switch modes, and the events of the night have been put into the background. It isn't always important to remember your dreams. As mentioned earlier, some dreams are designed to process events of the day and others are for replenishing the colors in our light bodies and physical systems. When you have a message dream, it will most likely gnaw at you throughout the day, or you will remember it soon after you wake up, which is why it is good to have a notebook and pen nearby so you can write down your dream before you get too involved in your 3-D activities.

Q. DO PEOPLE WHO HAVE CROSSED OVER DREAM?

A. They have no need to dream, because they are already in the spirit world.

Q. CAN DREAMS FORETELL THE FUTURE? WHERE DO PROPHETIC DREAMS COME FROM?

A. Prophetic dreams are probable realities that are floating around in the mass consciousness. They will always have a resonance with the person who is doing the dreaming. In other words, there is something about the person that resonates with the prophecy on some level. We can actually help a negative prophecy dream manifest by becoming emotionally involved in its scenario. By doing this, we actually give it energy, even though we don't realize it.

I had a dream a couple of months ago that the financial system had collapsed, everyone was scattered, and there was chaos everywhere. In the dream we were living in a very tall, white, high-rise. When we heard the news we went downstairs, and everything was covered with a gray ash, almost like a nuclear winter. Two store owners gave AHONU and me packages of food that had to be mixed with water. They gave them to us for free, because there was no water to be found anywhere. Of course I woke up from this dream horrified, because it felt like something that was going to be happening soon, or in the near future. I was definitely feeling the emotion of this possible scenario. But then I had to get a hold of myself and remind myself that I was looking at a possible future, and not necessarily an absolute future. Once I realized this in my mind, I said "no" to the scenario and chose to see peace instead. Immediately, I regained feelings of peace and safety. In this way, I didn't give any more energy to the negative potential future.

Sometimes people do dream of scenarios that are occurring now. This happened to me once when I was dreaming about a plane crash near a small island, and I was watching the small plane fall down into the water. There were other people around on the island who seem to be involved somehow in this crash. The next day the news covered the plane crash of John Kennedy, Jr. off the coast of Martha's Vineyard. In that case, I was dreaming about something that was occurring at the moment I was dreaming it. This was a case where I intercepted the same timeline as John Jr.'s timeline and was an observer in the situation.

People who dream of disasters seem to like it when their dreams come true, which they view as proof that they are psychic, or that they can somehow predict events through their dreams. They don't realize that they may be helping to manifest those scenarios by giving them validity and energy. If you talk to people who continually dream of things that come true, you will find that most often they are dreaming of someone dying, or some disaster. These people may think that they are really psychic and able to tune into the future, but what is most likely really happening is that they are being used by dark forces to help manifest those probabilities. We need to remember how powerful our minds are. If we remember that every thought takes form on some level, we will be more conscious of what kinds of thoughts and visuals we are giving our energy and emotion to.

When you dream, you can tune into many possible futures time-lines. No one is more psychic than anyone else in this process. We all travel to different probabilities when we dream. It is valuable for us to become conscious creators in the dream state so that we can defer nega-tive-dream probabilities and replace them with better outcomes. In other words, be a creator of miraculous futures instead of catastrophes. The frequencies that we broadcast across the nerve network in our solar plexus determine what we help manifest in our world. We are all affected by what we collectively contribute energetically. We are all con-nected to each other through the nerve network in our solar plexus, which connects to the grids around the Earth. Walk away from fear, and choose to broadcast miracle scenarios across the Earth's electro-magnetic grid.

Q. DO DREAM CATCHERS REALLY KEEP NEGATIVE SPIRITS OUT?

A. Dream catchers are talismans. Talismans are objects that are made or used in rituals that are imbued with particular meanings, geometries or intentions for a desired outcome. A talisman can be very powerful depending upon the intention that's put into it and the ancient history that it holds. Dream catchers can help keep negative spirits out because they have an ancient ancestry connected to them as symbols of power and protection. Dream catchers carry a particular vibrational frequency that does offer an energy of protection, based on its original intention. Many rituals use talismans that are very old.

Q. ARE OUR DREAMS BEING INFLUENCED BY THE CURRENT TIME CYCLE THAT WE'RE IN?

A. What I'm hearing is that the gap or barrier between the spirit world and our 3-D world is thinning. Because of this, we have access to many other dimensions in our dream state that would have been difficult to reach previously. The consequences are that you can manifest faster, which applies to positive as well as negative. Another reason to be miracle-minded!

Q. IS IT POSSIBLE TO COLLABORATE WITH OTHER PEOPLE IN OUR DREAMS? IN OTHER WORDS, COULD YOU DECIDE TO GET TOGETHER WITH SOMEBODY BEFORE YOU EACH GO TO SLEEP AND DECIDE TO MEET EACH OTHER IN A DREAM FOR A SPECIFIC PURPOSE OR TO DO SOME MANIFESTING?

A. You could definitely do that! It would be a great experiment. You could even make an agreement to arrange to meet certain geniuses who have passed on to obtain knowledge about a particular subject if they are willing! You can also make arrangements to meet people who can give you information about healing the Earth or breaking through perceived barriers or limitations. These are just a few suggestions. You can start your own dream group!

Q. DO WE NEED THE CONSCIOUS AGREEMENT OF THE OTHER PERSON TO MEET THEM IN A DREAM?

A. Yes, you do, if you are talking about doing an experiment with a friend who is in 3-D with you. You can't go collaborate with others without their knowledge. How would it be a team experiment if you didn't agree to meet the other person first?

If you are trying to meet with someone who has already crossed over, if they show up in your dream it would be obvious they are agreeing to meet you- if they don't show up, they obviously don't want to meet you!

Q. CAN WE USE DREAMS TO MEET RELATIVES WHO HAVE CROSSED OVER?

A. Yes, but first ask if they are available to meet with you, and then make sure you have a good reason for calling them in. This is really a good procedure with whomever you may decide to communicate with.

> One night many years ago, I went out of my body, but not in the dream state. I decided to go see what this guy was doing that I was interested in. It was about 3 a.m. I immediately went to where he was—at a friend's house with a group of other people. I could see through the walls of the house, and I could see him walking back and forth from his van to the house, possibly smoking pot. I was only watching this for a moment when I was put back into my body by my guides who gave me a very strong message that spying on someone else when I was out of my body was a no-no. So, you get the point.

Participant: I knew a homeopath who had conversations with Samuel Hahnemann, the founder of Homeopathy, in her dreams,. She did this by taking remedies that allowed her to have conversations with people who had passed on. There were things on which she disagreed with him, and she told him so!

Q. WHEN A PERSON HAS A SEXUAL DREAM WITH ANOTHER PERSON, IS THAT COLLABORATION? IF NOT, WHAT IS GOING ON THERE?

A. Obviously, if you're having a sexual dream involving another person, it's likely that there is an agreement on some level between the people involved. There's no judgment in it, but you could ask when you awaken what its meaning or purpose was for you. You might be attracting an entity or being to you that is not in your best interest, or the dream may just reflect a fantasy of yours, or some unfulfilled part of you. Most sexual experiences on the astral levels reflect unfulfilled desires, although some are unions with other energies, depending on what they symbolize. Bringing this back full circle to the realization that everybody in a dream is an aspect of yourself suggests that you could learn much by knowing yourself more deeply.

Q. ARE SLEEP DREAMS THE SAME AS DAYDREAMS?

A. No, daydreams are either fantasies or imagination, which are not the same as the process of sleep dreaming, because your consciousness isn't actually going to different frequency bands or dimensions when you daydream. People who daydream are taking their focus away from their current physical reality and going into their imagination. A daydream can also be an inspired creation being received from higher guidance. You're not in the dream state when this is happening in your waking life. If we were more conscious, we'd receive more genius inspiration more frequently.

Q. WHAT IS *REMOTE VIEWING*?

A. Remote viewing is becoming aware of the intersecting points of current events or probable realities and reporting on "the scene." It is also a form of spying by going to particular coordinate points and looking into what's going on there. The other thing we need to be aware of is that whenever we view or observe probable futures, there is a tendency for us to make that reality more likely, simply because we've energized it by observing it.

Q. COULD WE DO THAT IN A POSITIVE WAY TO ENHANCE POSITIVE OUTCOMES?

A. Instead of that, just imagine a world in which everybody is in the flow of their true creative powers, which would be more appropriate, because someone in the flow of their own creative powers would naturally be creating positive futures and outcomes moment to moment. If people were in the flow of their own genius, they would naturally be creating paradises, which is what freedom and love really are. As we become more in the flow of love's natural creative presence, beautiful futures naturally follow. Being more in love's flow also reinforces everyone's divine genius and allows them their own creative expressions.

Q. DOES REINFORCING YOUR OWN DIVINE GENIUS REINFORCE IT FOR EVERYBODY?

A. On a collective level, everything you do affects the whole. If you reinforce your own genius, it is an accomplishment that makes it vibrationally possible for each person to do the same in their own lives. You can't do it *for* another person, but what you are doing is strengthening that potential timeline in the collective field. In other words, you're contributing to the pool in which divine genius is manifesting on Earth. The real reason that people want to project a positive future is because on some level they are fearful of the future. This is very different than allowing higher genius or higher love to come through in the moment for people where positive futures automatically manifest.

Q. WHAT ARE THE EFFECTS OF SOMEONE OR SOMETHING WAKING YOU UP WHILE YOU'RE IN THE MIDDLE OF A DREAM?

A. It may cause a cascade of hormones in the shock of waking from one reality into another. The body will put things back in rhythm before too long. However, there are times when you're not fully back in your body, and you may feel off for a time before you come fully back in.

Q. FLYING DREAMS, BEING-CHASED DREAMS, DREAMS OF
FALLING—WHAT ARE THEY ALL ABOUT?

A. Flying is the natural state you are in when you are dreaming. It is
what happens when you're temporarily free of your body.

Dreams in which you are being chased usually have something
to do with subconscious fears that you haven't cleared yet.
These dreams are trying to show you what the fear is, especially
if they're recurring. They could also be about a demon or some
other entity attachment. They can also represent your trying to
run away from something in your everyday life or from
something much deeper.

Dreams of falling are dreams in which you feel out of
control in some aspect of your life. They may also represent
issues of safety, security and trust. Oftentimes in these types of
dreams, someone will either wake up before they actually fall
or land, or they will land, but land softly, showing that the
danger they perceived was not as bad or real as they thought it
was. If you were to wake up in this type of dream before you
actually land, it might show you that you're not ready to face
whatever the perceived danger or threat is. Conversely, if you
do land in the dream and find that the landing is soft and
without danger, it can show you that you have overcome some
type of fear within yourself.

Q. DO YOU HAVE TO BE COMFORTABLE IN YOUR BED, OR SITTING
UP IN A CHAIR FOR EXAMPLE, TO HAVE LUCID DREAMS?

A. It has more to do with where the brain is at the time, and what types
of frequencies are running through it. In other words, the brain-wave
activity of your brain determines what types of dreams are unfolding in
your consciousness. I'm also being told that hormone levels determine
what types of openings the brain can access during sleep. In other words,
are you in a light sleep or deep level of sleep? Hormones and the chemi-

cals they produce have a lot to do with our state of enlightenment. Grid conditions also play into it, as mentioned above.

If you deliberately make a practice of lucid dreaming the chemicals and hormones that you produce while sleeping will begin to change. Remember also that each hormone and the chemicals in them contain colors. Hormones are like keys that unlock doorways that create openings in the brain. Whatever you focus on determines what types of chemicals and hormones you produce. Your thoughts create hormones of certain quality and color, which is why when people say they wish they were more psychic, they're not, because they're not producing the right chemicals and hormones to open up that particular part of themselves. However, if you make it a deliberate practice to establish communication with different parts of yourself or your higher parts, your consciousness will listen to you and begin to produce the types of hormones and chemicals you need to accomplish your desire.

It is always preferable that your state of consciousness be formed by your own conscious will and intention, rather than by drugs that artificially induce or produce certain chemicals in the brain. Drugs can produce certain chemicals and hormones in the brain, thereby temporarily opening up certain parts of the brain, but remember that you are allowing an outside stimulus to do what should be done by your own will and learning. Also, the centers of the brain that drugs open can be damaged through this practice. In the book, *Change Your Brain, Change Your Life*[1] by Dr. Daniel G. Amen there are many photographs of what the brain looks like after it has been subjected to the abuse of drugs, alcohol, caffeine or pot. What you see are huge areas of the brain with dark holes in it. It's quite shocking to see these pictures, but it underscores what we're saying. If you have a vision, for example, under the

---

1. Amen, Dr. Daniel G. *Change Your Brain, Change Your Life*. Random House, 2008.

influence of LSD, you won't be able to actually *be* that vision. You will have a temporary artificially induced state of consciousness which is different from when your state of consciousness becomes an actuality inside of you.

When we're talking about drugs, we are including prescription drugs and also foods that are heavily laden with processed chemicals. People who consume a more organic, raw food diet sometimes report that their consciousness is able to expand in a much bigger way, which is because they are taking in more sunlight and color through those foods without the interfering chemicals. All of these factors influence the quality of the chemicals and hormones that create our bodies. The quality of our thoughts is one of the biggest factors that influence the chemicals and hormone production inside us.

Q. WHAT ARE *NIGHTMARES*?

A. Nightmares are an interface between a fear and a dimensional reality that matches it. They can also be produced when one's hormones are out of balance, but most often, nightmares can be traced back to the quality of the person's thoughts, or to their diet.

Q. HOW CAN WE PROTECT OUR DREAM STATE?

A. Bring your guardian angel into your dream state with you or your own I AM Presence. Do this by consciously inviting them into your sleep state before you go to bed. We need to remember that our own guardian angel is a powerful presence that gets appointed to each one of us individually to help us complete our soul contract. It has tremendous power to help us, protect us, and intercede for us to help us fulfill this purpose. Establishing a more conscious relationship with our own guardian angel can propel us forward in many ways. In the end, it's all about your own self-mastery.

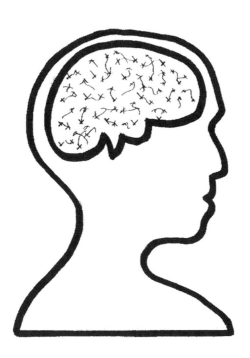

Chapter 9

The Brain

As I say the opening prayer, the room filled with the familiar red light that oftentimes accompanies topics that have to do with the physical world.

Q. WHY DOES THE *BRAIN* HAVE TWO SEPARATE HEMISPHERES?

A. The answer that I'm hearing is that the brain actually doesn't have two separate hemispheres. The two lobes of the brain send signals back and forth to each other, but they don't perceive themselves as separate hemispheres. They don't want us to perceive them that way either. I see them functioning together. There are myriads of electronic signals passing back and forth between them constantly. They each may take on a different *job*, but they don't want to be thought of as *separate*. They work in harmony with one another, and they complement each other even to the point of restoring a deficiency in one part. We can't make a general statement that one hemisphere does only one thing and the other does another. For example, if you remove one hemisphere or part of one hemisphere, the other hemisphere will naturally take on the function of what is missing.

The brain is telling me that it wants to be called a *being,* because it is the connector between your individuated spirit, the Mind field and the body. The brain is a receiving and transmitting station that seems to have a consciousness of its own. It wants to be called a being because it is vibrantly aware. The brain is where the individuated spirit and the Mind field interface with the body. When I look at the brain, I do not see it as solid, but rather as a hollow sphere of *light*. I am looking *through* it. I do not get a sense of denseness about it. It appears *translucent,* with electrical firings going on back and forth. The brain relays the beliefs and thoughts of the individuated spirit and the Mind field to the body.

Even though we think that the brain is the main intelligence, the brain wouldn't necessarily agree with that. It is the receiving station or hub for the Spirit–Mind field–Body complex and relays its information to the body and its organs, like the switchboard operators who used to connect our telephone calls by plugging wires into various openings. You'd look at their switchboards and you'd see various wires criss-crossing each other, which is similar to how these brain firings look. The brain would be the main operator responsible for relaying signals and connections back and forth for a myriad of functions. You can also say that it is a huge mass of highways that send and receive thought impulses or messages. The brain is also non-local, which means that it can transmit and receive signals from and through the universe, as well as to and from any stationary body.

Q. WHY DOES THE BRAIN LOOK LIKE IT HAS SEPARATE LOBES?

A. It appears this way because different parts of it perform certain functions in the *overall process*. Functions dictate shape and size. One part would still cover for another, however, if a part gets damaged.

We had intended to go through all the different lobes of the brain, but the brain has its own agenda tonight!

I'm being shown that all the lobes of the brain work together. If you try to isolate parts of the brain—let's say you try to put cells of the limbic system under a microscope, you wouldn't find any emotions in those cells. In other words, you can't take parts of the brain apart and find the particular function that you think a part does. You won't find it physically or chemically, because it changes all the time. The brain stores certain chemicals in parts of it, however, but even those chemicals are influenced by the spirit and the mind of the individual consciousness. So we can assume that these chemicals are in a constant state of flux. Even when these chemicals cascade through a physical body, or *unit* as they are calling it, the whole field can still change in an instant, depending on what's coming across. *The brain is a limitless relay station.* Anything can be produced in it, anything is possible in it, and it can transfer changes across the fields of the body. It affects all the cells and organs instantaneously. The brain is controlled by the Spirit–Mind field complex of the individual. The *quality* of that interaction has to do with the individual spirit and the Mind field and how they are relating.

Q. WHAT HAPPENS WHEN SOMEONE BECOMES PERMANENTLY BRAIN DAMAGED?

A. There is actually a disconnect happening with the individuated spirit in that it is withdrawing a huge portion of itself and becoming an observer rather than a participator in the Earth experience. The reasons are wide and varied for the individuated spirit having this experience.

Let's talk about the distinction between the individuated spirit and the Mind field. The individuated spirit is the actual *identity* of the person, or the actual being. The Mind field is the *substance or field* that turns the beliefs and conclusions of the individuated spirit into concepts. The individuated spirit needs the Mind field to transfer its beliefs about reality into words, concepts or ideas. The Mind field is the substance that down-steps associations and turns them into concepts or ideas. The brain takes those concepts and turns them into electrical impulses, chemicals and hormones that are then relayed to the body of the individuated spirit.

We always thought that spirit is perfect, but I'm hearing that *individuated* spirits are all at different levels of evolvement, different levels of awareness, different levels of maturity, different levels of benevolence, *etc.* Each individuated spirit is on its own journey of Self-realization. Spirits grow and evolve. They can also digress. As long as the universe keeps expanding, so will the potential for individuated spirits to grow and expand into more Godness.

The Mind field is what allows individuated spirits to have experiences in dimensions of varying types. The substance of the Mind field feels very sticky to me. It takes the observations, associations, belief systems and conclusions of the individuated spirit and forms them into ideas and concepts, which then get sent through the brain into the body. This then makes the *conditions* of the individuated body. The body is fashioned after the quality of these chemicals, hormones and signals. This entire process happens quite quickly—much more quickly than the time it's taking me to explain it.

The brain is explaining to me that it is an interface system—a relay or transmitting station. It of itself does not cause thoughts.

The purpose of having a body is so the individuated spirit can move around and have experiences in this dimension. Earth is a particular level of densification; therefore we need a vehicle in which we can stay long enough to do the things we set out to do. If you were to go into other dimensions or planes of existence that are not as dense, the type of body you would create would be very different. In some less-dense dimensions you do not need a body at all, whereas in other denser ones, you may need an even denser body to survive. The same is true with respect to other planets and their life forms.

The density of our bodies also explains why disembodied spirits hang around us when they don't go into the light. They know that as a spirit they cannot affect our dimension in any significant way. They may be able to knock things over or cause other poltergeist-like effects, but they themselves cannot maneuver themselves powerfully enough to still live in this dimension, which is why they often try to attach themselves to someone who is still alive here.

Q. I'M SURPRISED TO FIND OUT THAT INDIVIDUATED SPIRITS ARE NOT PERFECT. COULD YOU GO INTO THIS A LITTLE MORE?

A. A good example is to think of stars. You can look up into the sky and see stars of all kinds of varying shapes and sizes. Some are huge, while others are medium-sized or very small. Each star has its own momentum of power or influence, depending upon its size. Individuated spirits are much like this in that they are not all created the same size or shape. Some have more mass and influence, while others have much less. Smaller, or less mature, spirits go through a process of evolution in which they may be pulled toward other spirits that are grander than themselves, until they learn or evolve to the extent that they themselves become magnificent. You can see that spirits have great potential to continue to grow and expand or burn out and die, much as stars do.

The *perfection* in all this is that each spirit is made from the same life-force energy as every other spirit. Therefore, it is unlimited in its capabilities for evolvement throughout the universe. The spirit will down-step itself into various forms on various planets and dimensions to have experiences and grow, once it gains the ability to do so.

Q. SO COULD AN INDIVIDUATED SPIRIT THAT TAKES ON A BODY IN THIS DIMENSION DECIDE THAT IT DOES NOT WANT TO ASCEND, BUT WOULD RATHER CONTINUE TO STAY FOR MANY LIFETIMES?

A. Yes, that's possible. It's why many people do not achieve ascension away from Earth. When the individuated spirit gets to the point where it is self-realized enough in its consciousness, it will be done with the physical-body experience and will want to move on, which is when it will go through a resurrection and ascension process *at the physical level.*

Q. SO ASCENSION, THEN, HAS NOTHING TO DO WITH THE MIND, BRAIN OR BODY?

A. That's right. Ascension is the condition of the individuated spirit and its consciousness that has to do with the ascension process. The consciousness affects all the levels below it. We are only talking here about resurrection and ascension in relation to the physical body in this physical dimension. The problem we have with this dimension is that once a portion of our spirit is incarnate into a body, we tend to forget that we are a spirit who is here for specific experiences. However, you eventually do come to a place where you remember what you're doing here, and your consciousness expands. Once you realize that you are not just a body, you will turn your attention once again to your inner-spirit self. When this happens, your consciousness begins to change and grow and expand, until eventually it recognizes itself as one with all. You will also realize that it is *your* spirit who is doing the observing, deciding and thinking.

Q. DO WE RE-ENACT OUR PERCEIVED SEPARATION FROM SOURCE EACH TIME WE INCARNATE? DO WE PERCEIVE OURSELVES AS SEPARATE FROM OUR INDIVIDUATED SPIRITS BECAUSE WE HAVE A BODY THAT SEEMS TO THINK WITH OUR BRAIN AND DECIDE WITH OUR MINDS? HAVE WE RECREATED THE FALL HERE BY TAKING ON A SPIRIT–MIND–BRAIN–BODY SYSTEM?

A. I'm not quite seeing it like that. Whether we have re-enacted the belief in separation or not, we can still return to the remembrance of our spirit selves while in a physical body. I am saying this to avoid our falling into judgment and guilt about being physical. A part of our spirit is within us—it gnaws at us to grow and realize ourselves, which accounts for the restlessness and desire that we feel when it is time to grow further in our self-realization process.

Q. SO IT IS OUR SPIRIT THAT IS REALLY THE THINKER, OBSERVER, DECIDER, *ETC.*, BUT DO WE EVER GET TO A PLACE WHERE WE REALIZE THAT EVEN OUR INDIVIDUATED SPIRITS ARE NOT THE BE-ALL AND END-ALL? DO WE EVER REALIZE THAT IT IS OUR RELATIONSHIP WITH SOURCE THAT IS THE KEY?

A. The individuated spirit that I am seeing, which is us, did not deliberately separate from Source. Spirits are born at different rates of vibration and states of awareness. I don't see us making any big decision to deliberately cut ourselves off from Source. Some of us are like pebbles on the beach, and some of us are huge boulders. What you are and what frequency you vibrate at determine your journey, or evolution, through the universe. The bigger your momentum, the more power you exert through this journey. When your self-awareness increases, you become a more conscious being until you become more and more God realized.

Keep in mind that we are talking about a journey that could extend billions of years. You could be a very small spark of the creator and build your own momentum until you become a force in and of yourself to be reckoned with. Or, you could have been created as a huge spark, in which case you would have had more individual momentum and force from the beginning. Regardless of which it is, everything in creation will eventually become God-realized through the various journeys that it takes, the awareness that it attains, the decisions that it makes once it becomes self-aware, and so on.

An example is when people go to a psychic reader who tells them that they are a young soul or an old soul—implying that you may be a young or immature spirit or a mature or older spirit. If you look out into the world and see the diversity of people and all the different beliefs and thoughts and perceptions of those people, it is easy to see that there is a wide range from the lowest to the highest, from the most enslaved to the most free. It is evident that everyone is at a different place of self-awareness. Some people never gain much self-awareness or evolvement of consciousness in a particular life, or even after many lives, which is when they repeatedly return into the environment where they left off to give themselves the opportunity to choose to grow once again. Eventually those with very limited perceptions and dogmatic beliefs begin to question their beliefs, and when this starts to happen, they are on their way to higher evolution of consciousness.

Eventually you will come to the place where you will be aware enough and will have grown enough to say that you are done with experiencing the physical universe and its physical bodies, or that you're done with whatever planet you may have been experiencing. You will become so much like the Creator that you will want to merge with It. Once that happens, you will be on an entirely new journey.

It is our spirits that are learning, our spirits that are becoming greater and more self-aware and conscious. It is our spirits that are on the journey of self-realization until they become pure spirits. You could say that our individuated spirits eventually become *parent spirits,* implying that they have such a powerful creative life force of their own that they create more and more life.

Q. A SPIRIT THAT WOULD WANT TO CREATE A MIND–BRAIN–BODY SYSTEM WOULD HAVE TO BE IN ERROR, WOULDN'T IT?

A. No, it is more about the level at which you were created. If you're a baby spirit, you have to go through your stages of development to reach maturity. Not all spirits are created equal. This is just the way it is — the way things come off of Source—an infinite supply of sparks of God, each at a different frequency and vibration

> One evening many years ago, I was in a three-hour meditation in which I was shown all the sparks of light coming off the Creator. Some were big, some were small, some were medium, *etc.* The larger ones carried more attractive energy than the others. The smaller or more medium-sized ones were being pulled in toward the larger ones, becoming part of them.

This power of attraction seems to go on throughout the universe. Every single spark at some point will grow to become a parent sun. If you were a small spark with no larger bodies near you when you came off of Source, you would continue on your evolutionary journey throughout the universe. Some sparks can pull things to them, while others repel things, depending upon their make-up. The goal was for all sparks to become parent suns—in other words—*givers of life* unto themselves. Even if a spark takes on a reverse journey and ends up compacting in upon itself, it will still return to a universal element and begin again. It may go through various cycles in which it has no self-will, until it becomes free. It really doesn't matter however, how long it takes for an individuated spark to become a parent sun/son. All will eventually achieve self-consciousness and God realization.

Q. WHAT PART OF THE BRAIN WORKS TO CONTROL PAIN?

A. Give me a moment as I'm seeing the brain light up. It is showing me that it all functions together, not separately. Pain is the reaction of a person's consciousness to an event or experience. There is an association made between the person's consciousness and what is happening to them that actually causes a pain reaction, which is why no one experiences pain the same way. Two people could have the same experience, and each would come away with a personal association and conclusion about the experience. One person may find a situation painful while another person may not. It has a lot to do with how the individual consciousness processes the experience.

The body reacts to the pain stimulus from the consciousness of the individual. The pain comes from the way in which the individual consciousness is processing a situation, experience or event. Therefore, it can be understood that it is not the body that says it's in pain, but rather the consciousness inhabiting the body that *feels* the pain. When the body receives the pain signal, it immediately begins restoring balance as much as possible, *i.e.,* it *responds* to a message that is being sent to it via the individuated consciousness. The individuated spirit projects its pain onto the body—the body itself is neutral.

Q. CAN WE CONTROL PAIN WITHOUT DRUGS?

A. Yes, pain can be controlled without drugs. The body itself reacts to pain signals immediately. I don't see that the body causes pain, but rather that it reacts to pain, going to work to counterbalance the problem. The body immediately sends chemicals and hormones to the painful area to alleviate it or to bring balance to it. It may not always work, depending upon the condition of the person's body and consciousness. For example, the production of hormones and chemicals do not work the same in all bodies, depending upon their condition.

Q. DOES ALL PAIN HAVE THE SAME PURPOSE?

A. Pain on any level — physical, mental, emotional or spiritual — notifies the individual that something is happening to them or their world with which they are not in agreement or which they don't like. The feeler of the pain has an emotional reaction to something going on in their environment, which is actually where pain comes from. What's going on and how the person is *receiving* and *interpreting* it determines the level of pain.

Pain is common here in this dimension because so much happens here that registers as not okay with us. Pain is a signal in our consciousness that what is happening is not what we want to be happening. Now that you know this, it is possible to help others look at what may be going on in their lives that is not sitting right with them. You would do this process individually, like homeopathy, where each person is treated as an individual with a personal set of symptoms.

Pain can be a useful signal to help rebalance a person, but there is no general remedy for pain, because each individual has a personal associative function. When someone tells you they are in pain, you can't really experience what they're feeling, because you, as another individuated consciousness, experience reality in your own unique way.

At another level, someone can be experiencing pain while they are going through a process of change or a shift from the old to the new. Someone can feel pain from an inner resistance to the flow of change. If you feel pain, it would be good practice to do some self-inquiry to see if your pain derives from associations or victim responses, or if it comes from moving to a different level of consciousness. In other words, are you stuck in the old, while things are changing in your life? The change could be physical, emotional, mental or spiritual. Self-inquiry into the pain will determine which it is. Pain can let you know that you need to make a change, or that you are in a process of change.

Conversely, when someone is at peace with their world, they do not experience pain. The events in their world do not affect them the same way.

Q. HOW DO COLORS AFFECT THE BRAIN?

A. Colors break down into chemicals and hormones in the brain as sunlight comes in through the brain. Those chemicals and hormones each have their own properties depending upon which color it is.

Q. ARE CHAKRAS COLORS?

A. Chakras are vortices, not colors. They embody colors, however.

Q. HOW DO COLORS AFFECT THE BODY?

A. They get broken down into chemicals and hormones that affect organs and tissues, depending upon their chemical compositions. Each color has a different chemical composition. This process is not solely dependent upon the brain, however. You could shine colors directly onto your body, which would break them down and produce chemicals from them.

Q. SO YOUR BODY CAN USE COLOR WITHOUT IT FIRST BEING PROCESSED THROUGH THE BRAIN?

A. Yes.

Q. WHAT COLORS RELATE TO THE HORMONE TESTOSTERONE?

A. I'm seeing blue and purple in it. It looks like a beautiful, rosy, plum purple, with a little reddish hue and a bit of orange.

Q. SO THERE ISN'T ONE PARTICULAR COLOR RELATED TO EACH PARTICULAR HORMONE?

A. It looks like they are a colorful combination of colors and elements.

Q. WHAT COLORS RELATE TO THE HORMONES OF THE THYROID?

A. I see gold, white and clear light, with the texture of a light syrup. People often assign blue to the thyroid, but that's not what I'm seeing.

Q. HOW ABOUT PITUITARY HORMONES?

A. I see a reddish-brown color with small amounts of different colors, and I feel a pulsing as I tune into it. The red-brown color seems to be a result of a mixture of other colors. It has small amounts of green, orange, yellow and some violet. It actually may have all the rainbow colors mixed in small amounts.

Each hormone takes on a particular pattern as well as the colors. The pituitary, for example, appears as little rectangles and triangles, and I am aware of a specifically organized geometric pattern. The thyroid appears as a chain, all linked together. Testosterone appears as a DNA chain, which leads me to believe that it may influence the DNA's structure or operation.

Q. WHAT COLORS RELATE TO ESTROGEN?

A. I see pink, white, gold, and a little bit of blue. Chemically, it feels very soft, loving, and nurturing. It has a spherical shape.

Q. WHAT COLORS RELATE TO THE PINEAL GLAND?

A. I am seeing white and gold only. The gland feels rough to the touch. If I were to touch it on the outside, it would feel rough, not smooth, like a nut.

Q. HOW ABOUT SEROTONIN?

A. I am seeing yellow—almost golden, but not quite. Around the outside of the chemical I see a small line of bluish purple that flows through the body, acting as a protector, like a guardian chemical. Imagine serotonin as a security guard checking everything to make sure everything is on or off as it should be. It goes through the body and makes sure everything is connected properly and functioning correctly. It switches things on and off as needed. It makes me feel positive and happy when I tune into it. It also feels like a lubricant as it goes through the body.

Q. MELATONIN?

A. It has a rosy color—like a red-violet with some white. Melatonin seems to have a lot to do with cellular structure. I see a picture of little white cells. Melatonin seems to affect the quality of those cells—how awake they are, how well they can function. Even though melatonin has been known to be the chemical to help people sleep, I'm seeing that its function in the cells is actually to keep them awake and functioning properly.

Q. HOW DOES THE EGO RELATE TO PERCEPTION?

A. Remember that our individuated spirit is really the thinker having an experience with a particular level of awareness and dimension. We mistakenly think that we are a body with a brain that is doing the thinking. We think we are a *person* walking around in a physical body, which is a misperception because our spirits are really doing it all. We have defined who we think we are because we do not remember our spirit self. This self-defined image is our *alter ego* — a false sense of identity. It is a self that is vulnerable to how it is seen and perceived. It makes itself up as it goes along. Sometimes it is grand, other times impoverished. Its sense of self changes depending on how it sees itself at any given moment, or on how others see it. It measures its success or failure on external happenings. None of this is the spirit that is trying to learn in this dimension. If you focus only at the body level, you will perceive God and spirit as *up* and distant, while the truth is that a portion of your individuated spirit has come *down* into this level. The alter ego self that is here thinking it is the thinker is in error.

Once you're down here and functioning only at the horizontal or linear level—you walk horizontally, you perceive horizontally—that makes you think that you are a linear identity, what we call the alter-ego identity. The alter ego isn't wrong, it's just incomplete, so it doesn't recognize itself as an individuated spirit learning to become self-realized. The alter-ego self is vulnerable to being torn down or built up, influenced by others, and subjected to attack from the outside. It is also subject to disease and death *because* of how it sees itself.

In truth, spirit is spherical. Being in the *now* is a spherical action. It is moment to moment, with each moment being complete in and of itself. It's not thinking about the past, present or future, which are all linear perspectives. Our particular orientation determines whether we are in our alter-ego identification or our spirit identification. *Waking up* is when you begin to realize the difference.

Q. WHAT DOES SOURCE HAVE TO SAY ABOUT MEMORY?

A. I am seeing violet-purple. Memory is nonlocal—it is everywhere and in every cell—not restricted to the brain. However, there is a *function* of the brain that can *locate* memories. The brain has the ability to call a memory forth and translate it to you visually, mentally or emotionally. It is an incredible mediator with an unlimited capability to receive, transmit and send signals and ideas. It can also locate a point in outer space if you tell it to. It could find it and transmit that information to you. The brain in and of itself does not hold on to anything.

Q. HOW DOES SOMETHING BECOME A *MEMORY*?

A. Memory is the *incorporation of an experience* into the consciousness of the individuated spirit, which itself is holding the memory.

Q. WHAT IS *LOGICAL THINKING*?

A. All thinking comes from your individuated spirit. So when you say "logical," it all depends upon what spirit is thinking at any given point or what it wants. In other words, if I want to *reason,* I will activate my ability to reason. My spirit sends that message to the Mind field and it says, "Okay, yes, I'll organize that for you." The brain then goes ahead and produces the chemicals to allow that message to translate into a function. It would be the same if your spirit wanted to be creative rather than logical—it would go through the same process. It comes from the individuated spirit through the downstepping process.

When people say the mind is all-powerful, they stop there and don't go any further. They don't realize that it isn't the mind, it is the individuated *spirit* that is thinking, observing and deciding. What is incredible about the Mind field is that it can take any thought, conclusion or association and turn it into a concept, thought, form or idea. It can take anything and turn it into something else. The spirit's request does not always have to do with the body. It may desire to manifest a new house, for example. The Mind field will take that desire and turn it into an organized pattern so it has the potential to manifest in 3-D.

Q. HOW DOES THE PROCESS OF MANIFESTING A DESIRE WORK?

A. This is so interesting—this process actually does involve the brain. The condition of the individuated spirit dictates what can manifest, because spirits are at all different levels of awareness. If the individuated spirit is trying to manifest a desire but is limited in its ideas or associations about reality at the subconscious level, it won't materialize certain things, because *the chemicals won't be produced to bring that desire into materialization.* In other words, the *magnetic field* that is needed to materialize a desire won't be produced, which implies that the *quality* of our thoughts and beliefs determines what chemicals and hormones are created. These in turn generate an appropriate magnetic field. If the generated magnetic field isn't powerful enough, it won't manifest your desire, which is why you must determine what condition your spirit is in and what it has decided or assumed to be true.

The condition of your individuated spirit determines what you can actualize in this dimension, which explains why some people's ability to manifest their desires seems limited or even thwarted. It also explains why some people end up with certain conditions or illnesses. Healing has to occur at the level of the individuated spirit, because that is where ideas, conclusions, associations and programs originate.

Once you start to examine the condition of your own spirit, you can then make different choices. Now that we know that our individuated spirit has limitations, we can also go to our I AM Presence for correction. (I'm experiencing great heat as I'm talking about this) The individuated spirit itself needs a different message for correction from higher up. The change for any healing has to occur at the level *above* the individuated spirit first, so it can filter down to the other levels. This is to allow for more pure thought and perception to be received by the individuated spirit, which then gets conceptualized in the Mind field, received by the brain, and turned into chemicals and hormones for the body system, generating a new magnetic field. In effect, a whole new channel is opening. It can't work from the body up, because it will not be a permanent correction. You can see that modalities that work to make changes below the level of spirit will only produce a temporary correction, until the spirit itself gets healed.

The individuated spirit can and does still have its own capacities for creative imagination, but if there is trauma or damage at the level of the individuated spirit, its capacity to imagine and be creative will be thwarted. Once it realizes that it's being confronted with its own limitations, it can then *ask* for help from a higher source. The ability to arrive at an awareness of one's own limitations is a spiritual evolution. The very fact that we have come to this awareness shows us that something is working within us to take us to a higher level of evolution.

Q. WHAT IS *PERCEPTION*?

A. When the individuated spirit sends its thoughts down to the Mind field, the mind-field makes a perception or concept, which is a way to orient yourself as you move about your world.

Q. SO IS PERCEPTION A WAY TO COMMUNICATE?

A. Perception is an *effect* of the Mind field turning thoughts and ideas into a concept. The individuated spirit uses perception to get concepts and thoughts across to others in a particular reality system. We could say that perception only has the meaning that you give it. In other words, your perceptions could be very different than another person's perceptions, depending upon the conclusions your individuated spirit has come to and how it sees and uses this reality. You can use your body to communicate verbally; you can communicate telepathically amongst yourselves; and you can communicate spirit to spirit without using the body at all.

Q. DO WE NEED TO BE CONSCIOUSLY AWARE OF COMMUNICATING AT OR WITH THESE DIFFERENT LEVELS?

A. No. You are actually communicating with all of life everywhere all the time whether you're consciously aware of it or not. All thoughts go into the Mind Field and get formed at varying levels. Being aware consciously only matters when you are communicating with something or someone deliberately.

All thoughts float around in the Mind field continually, including higher thoughts from higher beings as well as low thoughts from lower beings. However, the ability to *receive* these thoughts depends entirely upon the individuals' orientation and perception of their reality and the condition of their own brain. There are many people today who still can't understand mental telepathy or psychic awareness. They don't believe in it, they say, which puts a huge block to their ability to receive thoughts from the Mind field.

Q. HOW DO YOU RECEIVE THE INFORMATION YOU GET FROM
SOURCE?

A. I receive it through and by love, which is a Presence that I am receiving and am in. I am feeling and receiving it in every part of me. I am in
it, and so it is.

Q. AS A HOMEOPATH, PART OF WHAT I ENCOUNTER IS THE
DEGREE TO WHICH I CAN ACCESS THE PATIENT'S INDIVIDUATED
SPIRIT SELF TO SEE WHAT CONDITION IT'S IN AND WHAT CAN BE
BROUGHT INTO THEIR FIELD OF AWARENESS. WOULD THE
PERSON'S SPIRIT SELF BE READY TO BE HEALED, IF IT IS THAT SPIRIT
SELF THAT HAS COME TO SO MANY CONCLUSIONS ABOUT ITSELF?
SHOULD I INQUIRE AT THE LEVEL OF THE PERSON'S SPIRIT SELF?

A. Yes, that's correct. A healer who could check a person's spirit self
would also be able to see the higher spirit come in when the healer is
asking for the solution. It is the higher being that brings forth a solution
and knows exactly what the individuated spirit can accept and integrate.
I'm getting the feeling that the higher being that comes forward is either
a higher aspect of the individuated spirit itself, a guide, an aspect of
Source Itself, or the person's own I AM Presence. It would be a higher
source connected to the individuated spirit and not some alien or being
who has no connection or relationship to the spirit. As a healer, your
part is easy. You act as the mediator between the individuated spirit of
your patient and the higher spirit who will come in to help theclient.

Individuated spirits are at various level of awareness and evolution,
and because the spirit is both the thinker and decider, it needs to actively
participate in its own healing process. For example, it needs to be willing
to have you check on the condition of itself first. Once you receive the
information about their spirit, you can see what their choices are for
healing, and you can present these choices to them. If they decide they
desire the healing, you then call on their I AM Self to remove the damage or limitation in the individuated spirit. Your client should be able to

feel the effects of this right away on some level. The effects may also continue to be active for weeks or months. These changes can be reinforced through your homeopathic remedies, if need be.

Q. DO I NEED TO GET PERMISSION FROM A CLIENT WHO DOESN'T SEEM TO BE PROGRESSING TO ASK THEIR INDIVIDUATED SPIRIT FOR MORE INFORMATION?

A. Yes, you do. This would actually be a great help to your patient, because until you can get answers from this level, you won't really know what is involved with the individual and what is really needed.

Technique for Healing: Once you have permission, close your eyes and focus on the person's spirit self by making the request to view it. Just take a look at it and observe it at first. See what condition it's in or what it may choose to impart to you. It may communicate with you through a picture of itself, it may say something verbally, or it may impart a feeling or some other sensation. Once you feel you have a good assessment of its condition, you then call forth the higher being in charge of the person and ask it to heal this spirit's condition. It will begin to do this immediately. You will be acting as the observer as this happens. You will also see when the healing is finished and how your client reacts to this process.

Another way to do this is through dowsing, if you're qualified at this method of communication.

This method of healing bypasses all other methods where tedious attempts at trying to resolve problems do not yield a complete healing. Unless you involve the patient's spiritual condition, trying to heal things from the level of the alter ego or the mind level is never-ending. Remember that the alter ego is a false sense of identity that is predominantly linear in its approach to its life. The alter ego is also below the Mind level that conceptualizes everything. The alter ego is a false identity that is wedded to the perception that we are just a body. It takes thoughts from the Mind Field and decides what parts it likes and makes a self that is fashioned after those ideas — it makes up a story about itself. It focuses horizontally and linearly, which is why it feels disconnected and separate, because it is. It hasn't the awareness of the spirit self. The alter ego, being a false sense of identity, actually blocks out spirit's impulses. In contrast, the communication with spirit and its higher aspects is a spherical process that occurs moment to moment.

Q. IS THE ALTER EGO THE SELF THAT IS IN TIME?

A. Yes and no. It is in time in the sense that it is a self that was made while in a body, and which perceives itself to be in time. Indeed, the construct of time is invented by us and our perceptions.

Q. WHAT TYPES OF THINGS INHIBIT THE BRAIN'S ABILITY TO RECEIVE?

A. Thoughts, perceptions, beliefs, personal traumas, the brain's physical condition, pollution of any kind, food quality, grid conditions where you live — all have a lot to do with the functions of the human brain. Chemicals and toxins that you consume through food and breathing affect the brain's functioning. I see a picture of wires being frayed or nerve endings becoming dehydrated, brittle and dry. For the brain to receive and deliver messages, it needs its electrical and nervous system to be in tip-top shape. The condition of the nasal passages also affects the brain — many toxins and poisons come in through the nose and are held in the sinus cavity. This effect is secondary to what we've discussed earlier about the beliefs and programs of the individuated spirit that also limit what the brain can receive and send across to the body.

To help combat these environmental effects, we need to be aware that the body needs an ample supply of good fats for its nervous system and brain to function. We recommend using organic coconut oil as food or in capsule form. We do ourselves a disservice by consuming low-fat foods, which actually cause memory loss and malfunctions in the brain. We also need adequate supplies of minerals and amino acids.

Q. WHAT CAN YOU ADVISE FOR PATIENTS WITH ALZHEIMER'S?

A. I see a picture of heavy-metal toxicity in the brain. There are also dehydration factors involved. So we are looking for a good detoxification process for heavy metals, and we recommend frequent detoxification in general. The person's fat intake needs to be increased, and we mentioned pure organic coconut oil as being a good source of fat. The person's diet needs to change to incorporate more raw and pure foods and more healthy fats. With Alzheimer's sometimes the soul wants time to go back and forth between spirit life and earth life before it makes its transition. This is part of the progression you see with Alzheimer's patients where they progressively are "gone" from this reality for longer periods of time and present for shorter periods.

The image that I'm getting for people with Alzheimer's is that the brain looks like it's suffocating. I'm seeing poor oxygen flow through the brain, therefore signals are not being sent across, and the basic functioning of the brain is deteriorating. The heavy-metal part seems to be quite pronounced in the brain. Years of breathing polluted air, ingesting metals through food, from amalgam fillings, or even food preparation using aluminum pans, can all be contribute to this buildup.

Our Light Bodies

Most of you are aware that we have an aura around our physical bodies that can be photographed and seen as a moving and colorful array of light, which shifts and changes each moment. What may not be as familiar to many people is our *light bodies,* which extend farther than the aura and encompass much more than our physical bodies. Today we explore these light bodies from Source's point of view. As I'm saying the opening prayer, a brilliant emerald-green light is present, as well as a very strange white vortex of light that looks like a very large tunnel leading into infinity.

Q. WHAT IS SOURCE'S DEFINITION OF *LIGHT BODY*?

A. I see beautiful striations of light that appear as woven patterns encompassing us. It's an interesting word, *encompass,* because these patterns of light are not only emanating *from* us, but they are *surrounding* us as well. We are all immersed in this intricate pattern, or network of light, which is everywhere. I also hear the vibrations of this network, which sound like continuous hums or pulses of sound of varying tones. This is an interrelated network of light that connects all things together. We are made up of this network, but we don't *cause* the rest of the network to be what it is.

Light bodies appear as concentrated networks of light in and of themselves. I wish everyone could see this picture! You have these beautiful striations of light that extend throughout all creation, and when you come to a particular life form, it is a concentrated or focused network of light, giving it an appearance of definition and solidity. I see our bodies as beautiful concentrations of light.

Q. WHAT IS THE PURPOSE OF THESE LIGHT BODIES?

A. They are what you are made of. They are points of creation that allow for particular forms of expression. Every life form is made up of light and sound and has its own unique combination of light strands. Each one is having its own unique experience in the creative field. The purpose of light bodies, therefore, is to allow you to experience life in a myriad of ways, to become aware of the Creator and your creative potential and to become a conscious creator yourself.

Your ability to become aware is also in the original design of light and sound. It is easy to see that life forms are at varying degrees of awareness. Some could be considered inert, meaning that their ability to become aware is very limited. Others could be very advanced in awareness. The particular arrangement of light and sound as it coalesces into form determines its potential for awareness. The more potential for awareness a life form has, the more knowledge and understanding it can gain in its experience. Source is saying that the purpose of life is to enjoy life and experience it while becoming aware of the vastness, power, love and infinite potential of creation. We should be looking at creation as a playground designed for our enjoyment. Becoming aware of Source enables us to understand the love that is the basis of reality. Only when we understand love will our creations be harmless and ecstatic. Our light bodies allow us to coalesce into form for this purpose. We can become many forms, not just human. Each form coalesces for a limited time, then unravels and becomes a new form at another time or place.

Q. CAN WE CONTROL HOW LIGHT AND SOUND COALESCE INTO FORM?

A. As you become more and more aware, you begin to understand how to mold light and sound, causing them to come together and coalesce into shapes and forms, which then unravel and become striations of light once again. This is an ongoing process, and we can focus our attention so as to communicate with these strands and intend them to come together in particular forms or experiences. We are in a sea of interwoven sound and light particles. You can call them to you and mold them. So yes, you can play with these striations. They hold the intelligence of Source, and they know how to rearrange themselves according to the focused attention of consciousness.

It would be good to begin exploring this process through your own body by focusing on yourself and looking at your own particular light and sound arrangement that you call your body. If there are things you'd like to change about it, you could begin to communicate with your light body and give it a new image to form. Everything about you—your organs, glands, bones, blood and skin—is made of light and sound. All of it can be altered and rearranged, once you know you have the power to work with yourself in this way. You can become your own scientist.

Regarding *control* over light and sound, Source would rather that we use the word *play,* as it more accurately describes the joy of the creative process. Obviously, your level of awareness and the quality of your consciousness has much to do with your ability to mold light and sound to affect your own body.

Q. HOW DO WE EXPAND OUR AWARENESS OF OUR LIGHT BODIES?

A. This conversation is already expanding your awareness of them. You can sit down, close your eyes and focus inward. Put your attention and intention on your light body, and see if you can see it. It should appear as a myriad of glowing and sparkling light strands. You should be able to see the intricate patterns that are woven to make up your body. There will be points of light that are distinct from the woven patterns as they crisscross and intersect one another. Realize that you can communicate with your light body and ask it to show you areas that may need reinforcement or repair, or it can simply show you its condition via a feeling or by drawing your attention to a particular area of your body. As you scan yourself thoroughly with your attention and you look at all parts of your body and its systems, you can begin to mold or alter specific areas that may need attention or that you would like to change.

You can change the patterns that you see to *mean* something new and different. Consider that the particular patterns in your body have come together by more than a few causes. One cause is the genetic pattern you inherited from your parents; another is the past-life imprints that you bring forward into this life; and another is your collection of beliefs and feelings about yourself, your life, this reality, *etc.* To play with and change your patterns, you may first need to become aware of what those patterns are. While you scan your own body and see the patterns that make up your particular identity, see if you can also get a *feeling* of what those patterns are composed of. Do you like them? Are they patterns that you'd like to keep, or do they feel heavy and inhibiting to you? Once you make an assessment of yourself, you can then go in with your consciousness and give those patterns a different direction. It is as simple as telling your light and sound patterns how you would like them to rearrange themselves in your *body and life*. Make this a weekly practice and record your findings and any results you notice in a notebook. If you are doing this diligently, you will begin to see the expanse of yourself and your connection to the universe of light and sound. This will greatly contribute to your self-awareness, and it will reveal your relationship to all of life. Your perceptions of yourself and the world around you will change greatly as you begin to realize what unlimited potential you have.

Source is telling us that this discipline is not to be used to manipulate any other person into doing your bidding.

There is really nothing solid about us. In fact, the entire universe is simply an array of light and sound that arranges itself in a wide variety of appearances. This network is pliable, and it responds to our conscious intentions. We are continually forming our quality without using our consciousness. Now that we are becoming conscious of our ability to change our own structure, we are moving into another level of self-mastery.

Q. IS OUR SOUND BODY DIFFERENT FROM OUR LIGHT BODY?

A. When you mention sound, I see this brilliantly vibrating blue light. It has a bit of aqua-green color to it, but it is predominantly blue, and I can feel its vibration. We do have a part of us that is a sound body, and it is music. The sound body is made up of musical tones and vibrations. Sound and light interrelate to create form. Both bodies seem to have been created simultaneously. I do not see either sound or light coming first and causing the other; rather they seem to have come from the same original idea of creation at the same time. You can't have one without the other—each is part of the other. Sound in particular is how a shape or geometry comes into being, because there's a series of harmonics that go into the manifestation of forms. Sound *is* something that has coalesced, and it has coalesced because of a particular pattern of light. As a pattern of light starts to define itself, it begins to vibrate, which creates sound-tone frequencies.

What I find interesting with what is being presented is that the human shape coalesces into a musical *orchestra*. If we could see and hear our own light patterns, we could hear our own songs, which we each have depending upon the makeup of our particular light and sound bodies. I find this incredibly fascinating, because if we were to begin disciplining ourselves and go within, we could hear the sounds of our organs, bones, blood, *etc*. Every life form has its own song, and sound is a vibratory field that is filled with musical notes, tones, hums and harmonies. Our light body and sound body are interrelated.

The closest I've come to this is when my spiritual activations allow me to hear my cells hum and feel my whole body vibrate, which I hear and feel from within. Another time when I've heard my own sounds is when I've gone into a flotation tank, which is completely soundproof and lightproof to the outside. You float in a bath of Epsom salts and water in complete darkness. When I was in this, it was so quiet that I began to hear my cells hum. It is a wonderful experience to hear.

Source is saying that the area of sound technology is something we have not yet explored to a wide degree. The ancients had a greater knowledge of sound and its ability to assemble and disassemble matter. The mineral kingdom has many sound tones held within it, which is how large stones could be moved by sound technology. It is also why the use of stone in buildings and structures provides unique healing energies and uplifting feelings.

The reason why it is important to *know thyself* is because we will all be pleasantly surprised to discover the inner workings of our own nature! Not only can we work with our own particular form and shape, but we also can expand it, travel on waves of light with it, and experiment with it.

Q. WERE THE LEMURIANS LIGHT BEINGS?

A. The Lemurians looked like standing columnar waves of light and color. Their bodies were light bodies. The light that you are describing is what they were composed of. The Lemurians were never as densely physical as we are now. They were on this planet at a time when the Earth herself was not this dense.

Q. *A COURSE IN MIRACLES* MENTIONS THE SON OF GOD, AND, TO ME, THE SON OF GOD AND THE SUN SEEM TO BE THE SAME BALL OF WHITE LIGHT. ARE THEY THE SAME?

A. There are many levels to this answer, but it is believed that as we achieve more awareness and God-realization, each of us can become an actual *sun* — not the sun we see in our sky, but each of us can ultimately become a radiating ball of light that becomes another *source* of life. Because we are not yet at this level, we need the external sun to provide a source of light for us while we are in this dimension. We are nourished by it; it causes life to grow here; and many of us need more vitamin D, which comes from the sun. However, as we become masters, we become more radiant from *within* and no longer need an external sun. You can notice this when you are around highly evolved people — you feel good around them; and you feel stronger and more positive, because they have evolved to a place where they hold much light and love. This force can heal you automatically. You can also notice the reverse when you encounter a very dark or negative person, who exudes a power that draws you in or drains your energy because the negative person is *taking* your light, whereas someone who is highly evolved is *giving* you light. Here's a story:

> A few years back a woman came to me for a reading. She was interested in looking into the Akashic Records to see where many famous deceased people had gone. She wanted to know what they were doing in their spirit forms. She asked about 30 famous people, one of whom was Gandhi. In looking at him, I found that he was the only one of the 30 who had become a violet ball of light.

So, the *son* of God is what each of us is, and a *sun*, or ball of light, is the potential that each of us can become.

Q. WHAT FURTHER TECHNIQUES COULD HELP US BEGIN TO SEE OUR LIGHT BODIES?

A. Seeing your light body is like developing your psychic abilities. The light body is here right now. Our psychic sight, as it has been, has not developed to see finer levels of light and sound. We can see the *effects* of light and sound such as when sand is vibrated and begins to take on varying geometrical shapes depending upon the vibration induced, but we do not normally *see* light and sound as they coalesce into form. One of the best ways to develop your psychic ability or inner sight is simply to focus inward daily for at least 10 to 15 minutes as mentioned earlier. It is the practice of giving attention to a specific goal that brings success. This practice is easy. You can focus inward sitting up or lying down, lying on the beach, or relaxing in a tub, or just about anywhere. Close your eyes and just focus within with an intention to see, hear and learn about your light body. If you practice this three or four times a week, you should begin to see not only your own light body, but the light body in all its forms. You will begin to develop your inner sight, which will allow you to see at finer levels. Becoming psychic is like developing a muscle—in this case, your pineal gland. As you practice your inner focus, you exercise this gland, which begins to become activated. The more you use it, the more it develops.

Q. DOES MY LIGHT BODY HAVE THE SAME SHAPE AS MY PHYSICAL BODY OR AURA?

A. I'm not seeing a distinction between your physical form and your light body. Your physical form is *composed* of your light body, and your aura is an *emanation* coming from your body. We have to think differently about how we see ourselves. What we see as our physical body is really our light body that has coalesced into a particular shape and form. Our physical body is the shape of our light body, because it is made of our light body. The only reason our bodies seem to stay a certain way is because our consciousness hasn't changed in its core beliefs about the body, its limits and the reality of 3-D.

The aura is an *emanation* from your body, and it changes in its appearance depending upon the condition of your body and consciousness. I'm not seeing the aura *as* the light body—rather, it is an emanation *from* your light body/physical body.

> When I lived in Chicago, I would often get my auric photo taken, and for many years it showed the same colors—white, violet and blue. It wasn't until I began to change my body and incorporate some new spiritual techniques that my aura also changed color. It began to take on bright yellows, greens and pinks, showing me that I was becoming more vibrant in my physical self, something I greatly needed at the time.

The aura is a *result of* the condition of the physical/light body. Auric photographs of leaves, plants and human body parts also show light emanating from them. The emanation of light from fingers does not *cause* the fingers, but rather it shows the frequency of light coming off that particular form. The aura is the discharge coming from the object, like the rays of light that come off the sun are not the sun itself, but are emanations from it.

Q. DO ALL CREATURES, PLANTS, MINERALS, AND ANIMALS HAVE LIGHT BODIES?

A. Yes. Source is saying that everything is composed of light and sound. Each form has its own unique woven pattern that makes it what it is. Some may think that a rock doesn't have much light in it, seeing as it is so compact. However, it may have more sound in it, because of its density. It is still composed of both light and sound, but its woven pattern would be different than that from another form, like a tree, for example. It's the same principle for all forms that we see, which is one of the wonderful aspects of the diversity of which we are a part: Humans can be consciously aware of their own composition, and they can mold and change their own patterns as well as those of other life forms with their consciousness.

Think of the awakening consciousness in people and all the healing modalities that have come on board in the last few decades. These healing modalities provide a supply of light and sound to us through the practitioner, providing healing on various levels. As advanced as all this is becoming, it is still not the same as going within and learning to change your own biology. The incredible potential of knowing ourselves by going within is enormous. Not only that, but the discoveries we may encounter along the way can be the greatest adventures we've ever had. Throughout this second book in the series, Source has repeatedly encouraged us to go within and not measure ourselves through the outer world. It only takes 30 minutes a day for you to begin to change the entire structure of your world. The possibilities are endless! If you feel you are not ready to do this, however, the use of energy practitioners and healing techniques can still be of great benefit to you and may help activate your higher centers.

Q. Do HEALING DEVICES LIKE LIGHT TABLES OR THE MACHINES THAT SHINE LIGHT ONTO THE BODY THROUGH COLORS AND CRYSTALS REALLY WORK?

A. Yes, they do provide color frequencies, which are very nourishing and regenerative. Colors affect your light/physical body since light is composed of colors as we discussed earlier. Putting more colors into your body will begin to change your light pattern, depending upon the particular colors chosen. What needs to be monitored is whether a person needs certain colors or has too much of a certain color. Colors change hormones and chemicals in the body. If you have a deficiency in a particular color, it will improve your health to add that color. If you have too much of a certain color, adding more may make you ill. Color therapy is a very powerful modality in and of itself, so yes, the devices you mention above can have a positive effect. When you receive a needed color or light, you can repair at every level. Healing energy can help heal physical conditions, but it can also change your emotional state and your perceptions. The key is to hold that new emotion or new perception, so that you don't revert back to a previous pattern. Lasting change comes from allowing the *knowledge* you gain to permanently shift you. Knowing your inner woven pattern of light can produce much faster results then going to external healers, who may not be aware of or be able to see the subtle levels of your light body. However, anything that moves us to greater enlightenment or improved health is beneficial.

Q. ARE WE MOVING TOWARD LIGHT-BODY ASCENSION?

A. Source is saying that we certainly have the *potential* for it. Light-body ascension is when you come into full recognition of yourself as a light body and you master the patterns of your light body and the physical world. Ascension is when you understand that the densification of the body and form are perceptions in our consciousness. When you begin to work with and change the patterns of light and sound, you are no longer bound by the physics of this world — you've gone beyond the beliefs that the physical world is solid and unmovable. You begin to experience yourself as a being of light and demonstrate your ability to alter things in this world. Ascended beings come to know themselves on levels that go way beyond the physical. We can go as far as we can into light-body ascension, but it does require that we become masters of our own makeup and acquire the ability to unravel ourselves and turn our bodies back into only light any time we choose. Light-body ascension is not some magical occurrence that will happen to us on a particular date or through any specific event. What *has* been occurring, however, is an increase of light from the cosmos, which has been activating the light patterns of which we are made, which increases our awareness.

Q. IS DEATH A PART OF ASCENSION?

A. Death is not part of ascension — it is the result of your consciousness. Ascension is the spirit mastering the conscious belief in death and demonstrating this through its ability to move in and out of the physical body at will. An ascended being is not affected by anything it does not want to be affected by. An ascended being takes its body into light and does not go through the death process that we do. The biggest challenge in working with our light bodies, as stated earlier, is undoing many of our false perceptions concerning our physicality and the physical world.

In physical death, your spirit essence leaves your body but is still only at the level of its own consciousness. I'm not talking about the light body right now, which is only a woven pattern of light that forms your physicality. Your spirit is your God essence that is growing and evolving to become God realized, or God Man. When you die, you die at the level of your consciousness or spirit development, which is why spirits go to many different planes of existence after death. What or who a spirit sees when it dies depends upon their beliefs and their consciousness. The saying "In my Father's house are many mansions" indicates the many levels and planes of existence in the spirit world. Therefore, it is not a given that when you die you automatically ascend. Ascension is the mastery of your own spiritual nature and your place in the universe.

Q. Is Earth moving into her light-body ascension?

A. Let's see where she is in her process! What I am hearing from the planet is that she is predominantly still affected by cosmic forces. Planets are all affected by each other and by the cosmic forces that affect them all. What happens on one planet affects all others, *etc.* They are in a vast interrelationship with each other in their particular solar system. The light patterns that we call planets coalesce as a particular solar system. When we speak about different forms being able to cause changes in their own patterns, planets seem to be dependent on one another for their evolution. The Earth is saying that she cannot change herself the way we can change ourselves. She can have her own intention for her evolution, but that evolution is still interconnected to the other planets in this solar system. Our solar system with all its members, including planets and stars, novae and quasars, sun and moon, and cycles, are all interconnected with one another. Since most planets are made of rock and minerals, their ability to consciously change or undo their own patterning is limited. Earth is saying that she cannot be an independent thinker and decider of her own makeup. She is still an interdependent member with the other members of the solar system.

On one level, we could say that the same is true of us, in that we are all connected to one another. However, we can advance in our awareness and consciousness by what we do with our own thoughts and decisions. We can become free of established paradigms by the activation of the God nature within us. We can change our form with our consciousness.

So, when you ask whether the Earth is heading toward her light-body ascension, I hear her saying that she isn't able to yet because of what is happening throughout the solar system. On the other hand, what we do here as humans does collectively affect the entire solar system and its planets. We do have a hand in how other planets evolve. The Earth herself, as powerful as she is with her forces of Nature, is still under the collective evolution of the solar system. Source really wants us to hear this because our consciousness can do so many things. If we decide that we do not want to go within and learn about our true nature or experiment with our light bodies, chakras, or kundalini, we will remain like the Earth—subject to the forces outside of ourselves that act upon us seemingly without our will or consent. We will be affected by all the other consciousness around us and everything that happens as a result. We will be carried along on a particular evolutionary track, completely dependent upon the quality of the masses. Of course, we have a right to stay exactly as we are without ever going within. There is no judgment in Source. What Source is saying however, is that we do have a consciousness that is becoming more aware, and so our possibilities are unlimited. If you take on an inner discipline, you will be someone who can affect the quality of life in this entire solar system in a very positive way. You can do what you want. You can stay in the evolutionary cycle of time and space and cosmic forces, or you can gain your freedom from all perceived limitations. Every person who gains his/her freedom contributes to that potential for everyone. If we stay at the evolutionary cycle and remain predominantly unconscious, we will either eventually evolve and progress further or we will digress into deeper unconsciousness.

Other solar systems have their own sets of patterns with their own planets, and they would be considered dependent upon one another in their system.

Q. DOES WHAT WE EAT, WHERE WE LIVE, OR THE CIRCUMSTANCES WE FIND OURSELVES IN AFFECT OUR LIGHT BODIES?

A. Yes, because the quality of light, sound and color in food either strengthens or weakens your light-body pattern. Let's talk about the difference between *dead* food and *live* food. A piece of white bread, for example, made from genetically modified seeds that have been ground down, with most of their nutrients and fiber stripped away, will not have many nutrients in it. It will be missing enzymes, minerals, amino acids and vitamins. It will have very little light and sound to offer the consumer. If we compare this to eating edible flowers or fresh vegetables and fruits that have been grown organically without genetically modified seeds and not sprayed with pesticides and fungicides, you will have a food that is happy and filled with light and sound particles. This would have much to offer the consumer. Notice, I am using the word *consumer*. We are answering this question from the point of view of someone with normal consciousness who still needs to eat to stay alive in this dimension. Of course, this is 99.9% of the population! We are not talking about someone who has mastered the physical world and no longer needs to consume other life forms to survive.

As for how *places* affect our light bodies, we can use the same analogy as we did with different types of food. Every place carries its own unique vibration and grid pattern. Some places uplift and support your light body and other places weaken it. Remember, there is a bigger picture. The dominant thing that affects you is your state of consciousness. We are talking about different states of awareness when answering this question. All states of awareness from the lowest to the highest are accepted in Source.

To put things in the outer world in perspective, let's consider some yogis who have been known to consume nothing but sugar, tobacco and coffee. There are other stories of yogis who have taken many drugs, none of which affected them in the slightest. These yogis remained healthy and strong and lived to old ages because they found another world within themselves that was not dependent upon externals to be healthy. Some people have also been known to live only on sunlight or the prana in the atmosphere. These examples are extreme, of course, but they show the varying levels of consciousness that can be achieved.

Until we go within and know ourselves and begin to master ourselves as we have been speaking about today, we will be affected by many external things.

Q. DOES THE RADIATION USED IN CANCER TREATMENTS OR FROM NUCLEAR ACCIDENTS AFFECT OUR BODY'S LIGHT STRANDS?

A. We can apply the answer above to this question, but let's see what Source has to say about radiation. Sometimes radiation promotes the growth of new life forms and sometimes it destroys existing ones. It does have the potential to evolve certain species, while in others it creates huge distortions. It can change plant life and animal life, evolving it forward, but, it can also destroy species and mutate them. What effect radiation has on a particular life form has everything to do with how that form's light patterns are configured. You can see that a life form will either be able to use radiation to further itself or it will be destroyed by it. Radiation vibrates at a faster frequency than what we would consider normal in our dimension. If our frequency could handle the frequency of radiation, it would have no harmful effect on us. We have been receiving increased radiation from the sun in recent years, which has awakened many of us, but it has also resulted in sickness and death for others. We are in a great time of change, with incredible potential for both evolution and destruction. Whether a life form evolves or is destroyed depends upon its personal condition, which is why some people get well from having radiation treatments for cancer, and some people die from it.

In concluding this session for today, let us consider getting together in groups to focus inward on our light bodies and become our own scientists. I think it would be a fantastic project!

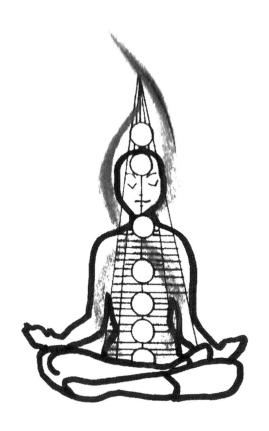

Chapter 11

Kundalini

Today we are asking Source about Kundalini, which many mystical systems describe as the serpent fire located at the base of each person's spine. We will explore this energy from the perspective of Source. As I'm saying the opening prayer, a burst of brilliantly pure white light enters the room. As I was tapering off with the prayer, streaks of yellow and royal blue were penetrating through the white light.

Q. WHAT IS *KUNDALINI*?

A. Source defines Kundalini as *The Path of Courage* — specifically, the courage to become our true self as we were created. The feeling I'm getting is that the journey to our true self is not easily achieved—rather it is something that requires challenges and victories along the way. Conceptually, we have been taught that our true self is something that is already perfect and whole in God, but what I hear Source saying is that to become or *actualize* your true self, as you were created, is a courageous effort and journey. Kundalini is an essential part of this journey.

Kundalini is our ladder of ascension that was put within our bodies and is dormant in its capabilities to the un-awakened. It is the *potential* for God realization that is locked inside our bodies, and certain keys are required to open it. Those keys are related to the journey and therefore related to courage, perseverance, sincerity, honor and all high virtues. The development of virtues is a requirement for God Realization. If you try to activate kundalini without the corresponding virtues on the ladder of ascent, can become ill or cause distortions and imbalances in yourself, because kundalini is a purifying fire. Kundalini *arrives* at radiance — the burst of white light I saw at the beginning of this session. It arrives at this radiance when it is purified and refined. Adepts on the journey *become* this radiance, once they have purified themselves and have become the embodiment of higher virtues. Symbols associated with this accomplishment are the thousand-petal lotus, the sun, the diamond, the swan, the white rose, and the flame, to name a few.

You may have read about adepts in the past who achieved God Realization. They are described as wearing a white raiment, indicating the white light that they have become. They have become the white light themselves and are now *sources* of God radiance. This white light is a powerful force similar to white fire—it's dynamic in its activity and expansiveness. It is not a sweet, gentle ineffective white light, but rather a powerful, purified force of creation, which is also pure love.

Source is saying that there are places or chakras inside the human body that kundalini needs to spiral around and through in order to open up certain keys. There is an order to the spiraling process, and each key along the path within the body has its own corresponding virtues. Kundalini is a raw fire or electrical current that we hold as a regenerative *potential* in our bodies. It is un-purified in its raw state, which is important to know, because the un-purified kundalini can manifest itself in vices. In other words, if that energy or sacred fire is not purified and does not become virtuous, it can remain a force that causes destruction or turns in on itself.

Source is calling kundalini *The Path of Courage* because the bringing forth of the divine presence in kundalini is an honorable and challenging journey of purification that results in the transformation of the lower or animal self within us to the higher God Man. The animal/reptilian nature we spoke of earlier is what requires purification. It is the part of us that is warlike, aggressive, controlling, dominating, greedy, selfish and murderous. It is also judgmental and destructive. We will not get rid of this part of ourselves entirely, because it supports our survival instinct, but this portion of us needs to be lessened by developing our higher nature and higher brain.

Q. DO WE HAVE CONSCIOUS CONTROL OVER THE DEVELOPMENT OF THIS COURAGE?

A. Source is saying yes and no: There are times when the conditions inside a person can cause kundalini to spontaneously arise seemingly out of nowhere. It could be that a person isn't necessarily aware on their path, and suddenly this force arises within them as a predetermined event. In other words, the *soul* would have arranged for that to occur at a specific time, based on its prior experiences and soul contract.

> Here's an example: Let's say that you had things you didn't finish in some past life. It could be that you didn't master some things in physical life. You may have come back in this life to master those things. You could be operating very much in the mundane 3-D world, and suddenly one day you experience kundalini rising. This would be a predetermined event giving you time to master your physical issues in the 3-D world before you take on the continued journey of ascent up the ladder. Kundalini rising changes a person's entire orientation in 3-D.

As for consciously controlling the development of kundalini, you can use certain disciplines to activate the kundalini, but you do need to be ready to take on the challenges and courage needed for the ensuing purification process. As the kundalini rises, it spirals up through your chakras and causes them to move or spin in their rotation. Each chakra has its own unique vice to be purified, so that its higher virtue can be attained, much as a diamond in the rough needs to be refined to bring out its brilliance. So, if you're going to consciously discipline yourself through various techniques to raise your kundalini, you need to be ready for this purification process, so that the kundalini currents can perform in the way they were meant to perform on the path to becoming God Man.

If you've been on the spiritual path and have not been aware of this kundalini process, but you have been clearing your lower self through other means, your kundalini currents may have been slowly rising through this process without your consciously being aware of it. In other words, if you have been achieving virtues by going through various challenges in your life and making higher choices, chances are that your kundalini has been rising slowly as you perfect yourself. It would be doing this very gently and naturally, as opposed to a huge rush that someone who is experiencing spontaneous kundalini rising might experience. If you have been raising your kundalini gently and naturally you will have noticed specific results, such as an increase in psychic ability, heightened senses, deeper communication with all life everywhere, more compassion, harmless intent toward everyone and everything, an increase in sensitivity, a greater ability to be aware of things at subtler levels, increased telepathy and many other higher gifts developing. You will also be having continual experiences of greater and greater all-encompassing love. You may also find that others are naturally awakened or healed in your presence. You may even find yourself taking journeys out of your body, teleporting or bi-locating, meeting other selves in other dimensions, or communicating with spirit beings from other dimensions or the elemental kingdom.

Q. DOES KUNDALINI START FROM THE BASE OF THE SPINE, THE BASE CHAKRA, THE CORE OF THE EARTH, OR SOMEWHERE ELSE?

A. It does *not* come from Earth's core. It is part of our body's spinal-cord system. The spinal column is our ladder of ascent. It has different chakra points on it that are like portals where the kundalini currents can rise and spiral. I feel that I'm in the lower back when I'm looking for kundalini's origin. Source is saying that it originates in the primal self. It's not necessarily calling it the base chakra, but rather it originates in the primal self. In most of us it is dormant, however. We can call it our own potentized life-force energy that allows us to be regenerated when it is activated. It is part of our biology and part of the workings of our central nervous system in the central column of the spine. Another name for this central column is the *pranic tube*.

Q. DOES KUNDALINI CONNECT US TO OTHER PLANETS OR UNIVERSES?

A. Source is saying *no*. The question is a bit of a distraction in that it will take you away from the *journey* of kundalini as a path of courage. When you reach the state of actualizing yourself as white light, you achieve freedom. Once that happens, you are in communication or at one with all life everywhere, and this encompasses other planets and universes.

Q. IS KUNDALINI A NATURAL PART OF ALL OTHER LIFE FORMS?

A. Not in the potential that we are speaking today. Animals, for example, have some of this life-force energy within them, but it remains confined to their instinctual nature. Animals cannot consciously work with this energy as humans can. In other words, animals are not taking on the path of courage, or purification. It is predominantly humans on this planet that can actualize themselves as God Men and become white light beings. Animals do not have the DNA capability to consciously ascend through decision-making and attaining virtues. The same is true when talking about other life forms beneath the animals, like plants or minerals. However, our evolution does affect all life forms on this planet and catalyzes them to a more evolved state.

Q. DO ALIENS EXPERIENCE KUNDALINI?

A. Yes they do, in their own degrees. One of the things Source wants us to know is that there are alien species that are *beneath* humans in their evolutionary process. Therefore, not every alien species has the same potential. Not every alien species has the same kundalini capability that we are speaking of today. Yet, there are some alien species that have gone far beyond Earth humans in potentiality and actuality.

Q. CAN WE STIMULATE KUNDALINI AWAKENING ARTIFICIALLY?

A. *Artificially* is a loaded word. We are assuming that you mean through the use of hallucinogens or various other techniques. The use of these things can stimulate kundalini currents to rise, but Source is saying that if you want to become an actualized God being, you have to do the path of courage to become virtuous. You can artificially stimulate kundalini currents and have visionary experiences through artificial stimulants, which may provide you a glimpse of life at deeper spiritual levels, but the process of actually *becoming* God Man is something that is a complete purification process from the lower nature to the higher nature. If you're going to stimulate kundalini currents in artificial ways, be prepared to do the purification work that will show up as you rise up the ladder of ascent through the chakra system. Only through this process do you actually integrate and become a being of radiant light.

Q. CAN THE RISING OF KUNDALINI CAUSE PHYSICAL, EMOTIONAL AND MENTAL DAMAGE?

A. Yes, it can, if you cannot handle the purification required at the various levels of ascent. Kundalini will not only activate many higher gifts, but it will also drastically alter your perception of reality. Imagine having your orientation of the world being completely turned around, and while that is happening, all of your suppressed emotions and thoughts begin to surface. Everything will change, and clearing and integrating these changes is a huge undertaking. We are talking about uprooting beliefs about the world, yourself and God that you may have brought with you through many lifetimes, as well as clearing any unhealed trauma you may still be carrying from this life or others. If you activate the kundalini at a time when you're not really ready to take on this Path, it can cause damage on many levels.

Kundalini is similar to being struck by lightning. Some people die when struck by lightning, others suffer physical bodily damage, while others have illuminating visionary experiences of God or other worlds. Those who survive such an experience will come back changed, but they may need years of rehabilitation to recover from the physical damage. A kundalini experience greatly affects your nervous system and biology, and its force changes nerve centers as it goes up the spine. It produces an entire new physiology. We need to understand that the nervous system within each person is a delicate and sensitive system, so make sure that you are ready and honoring that sensitivity if you choose to artificially stimulate the rising of your kundalini.

Q. WOULD SOMEONE WHO HAS NEVER HEARD OF KUNDALINI OR NEVER HAD ANY EXPOSURE TO IT IN ANY WAY EXPERIENCE KUNDALINI JUST LIKE A PERSON WHO KNEW ABOUT IT?

A. What I'm hearing from Source is that there would have been some previous buildup or knowledge about kundalini in the person from other lives. Even if a person comes into this life with no recollection of past lives, or never having heard of kundalini in this life, it is most likely that they would have had knowledge or experience of it at some point in some past life. Their soul would know what they had been doing in this area prior to this incarnation. I'm not seeing that someone would have a spontaneous kundalini rising without some prior experience from another time.

Q. IS KUNDALINI A NECESSARY PART OF LIFE OR DEATH? IS ITS RISING SOMETHING WE ARE TRYING TO ACHIEVE DURING THIS LIFETIME? IS KUNDALINI A PREREQUISITE TO A NEW INCARNATION?

A. There are actually many things that stimulate a new incarnation. There is so much to life, people, and their experiences. There are many things people reincarnate for. They come back to resolve issues, to forgive, to play and have fun; some come back for revenge; others come back to continue their path of ascent. Others may come back just to have a family or experience a particular occupation. All of these things are stages or steps along the way to becoming enlightened. Your awakening and that of your kundalini are natural processes. This path of courage does have a sequence to it: If someone has a spontaneous kundalini rising, you can expect there to have been a past history where they would have built up a sequence of events that would arrive at the arising. The rising of kundalini is not an immature event when it occurs naturally. When a person gets ready to become God actualized, it's a deep event inside of them that is a natural result of prior transformative work.

There are those who come into their lives naturally seeking knowledge or exhibiting mature wisdom at very young ages, which indicates prior lives of maturing.

Kundalini is not a prerequisite to a new incarnation—it is the God force that accompanies a new incarnation. It is a necessary part of life because it allows the body functions to occur. At its most primal nature, it is the force for survival and reproduction of the species. At its highest nature, it turns us into light beings. It isn't a factor in the death process.

Q. DOES WHERE YOU LIVE, WHERE YOU'VE BEEN, OR WHAT'S HAPPENING ON THE PLANET, AFFECT THE RISING OF KUNDALINI?

A. What's happening on the planet can affect the rising of kundalini, depending upon the cosmic forces in place. There can be light codes that come from the cosmos that affect the biology of species on the planet. These light codes can stimulate human DNA and cause varying degrees of kundalini awakening. You could say that we all share a collective agreement to be here for kundalini awakening to the degree that we are each ready for it. At some level we all expect to be stimulated by cosmic forces.

There are certain power spots on the planet where the frequency is high enough to stimulate awakenings, but I don't see that these spots will give you a full kundalini rising. However, they wouldn't thwart it either.

Let's look at *places,* not from the standpoint of kundalini rising, but rather from the standpoint of *nourishment.* Different land areas have different qualities and frequencies. Some places work well for certain people, who get nourished and stimulated by the energies there, while other places deplete a person's nourishment. One needs to evaluate such places individually, as one place may help one person but hurt another. *Places* should make you feel good, supported and happy. You should feel healthier and happier when you're in the right place. There is an exception to this, however, in that you can be in a place that feels very nourishing to you and still go through challenges that would be designed to push you further or make you grow beyond your current limits. In these cases, the place would still be considered good for you. There is discernment needed here, because a place that is unhealthy for you would not be giving you challenges that make you stretch your limits but rather would drain your energy and take you down. Those types of challenges are unhealthy. The question becomes "When are challenges good for you and when are they destructive to your growth?" This is how you evaluate whether where you are is the best place for you. So, in answer to your question, where you are does not necessarily determine whether or not your kundalini will rise.

Q. CAN WE FACILITATE KUNDALINI AWAKENING THROUGH DIET OR EXERCISE?

A. Changing your diet and exercising can be part of the purification process by making sure that your cells are in the best condition possible to handle and integrate the higher frequency of kundalini rising. However, these changes alone will not accomplish the virtues necessary to integrate kundalini, because becoming God Man—actualizing that within our biology and consciousness—requires the attainment of virtues.

Cleansing the body and keeping it in a state of vitality can help your nervous system and organs handle the kundalini energy and use it for regeneration. If your body is in a state of ill health because of your diet or lack of fitness, chances are that the kundalini energy will not be able to flow properly through your various channels as easily as it could if you were in a better state of nourishment and vitality. These things are part of the process. There are many breath-work techniques that also help stimulate kundalini energy. Most of these techniques also bring up unhealed issues out of the cells for cleansing, which is another type of purification process. Rebirthing and Transformational Breathing are some examples of techniques that help facilitate this cleansing process.

Q. ONCE I FELL OFF A HORSE AND LANDED ON MY TAILBONE, WHICH SENT A SHOCK UP MY SPINE. CAN INJURIES OF ANY KIND—SPINAL OR OTHERWISE — CAUSE A KUNDALINI RISING OR INTERFERE WITH ONE?

A. Source is saying that injuries can either interfere with kundalini currents or activate them. Traumas can interfere with the flow of those currents if the injuries have affected your spinal cord or nervous system. However, if you are *consciously* taking on the journey of moving the kundalini, there are many things you can do to remove blockages. Even though kundalini is connected naturally to the body, it can also move up the light bodies. You may have heard that we all have what's called a *morphogenetic field,* which is an exact duplicate of our physical organs but is in our energy body and is invisible to us. This field is why people who have lost a physical organ or limb still say they feel as if the organ or limb is still there. You can move kundalini spiritually through the morphogenetic field or through other light-body channels, which could happen as a result of doing clearing work or by consciously moving your kundalini energy. In other words, you can bypass the physical vehicle and still achieve kundalini awakening.

The kundalini does have regenerative abilities as well as destructive abilities, depending upon what it encounters in your biology along the way. Remember that the attainment of virtues contains healing properties, because all virtues are expressions of love. The path of courage is really the path of the mystic, because you become aware of deeper and deeper levels of love and compassion. As you become illuminated in your consciousness, your physical body can become affected in a positive way.

Q. CAN KUNDALINI RISING HAPPEN AT ANY AGE?

A. Source is saying it can, but it's unlikely that it would. Children are being born these days with varying degrees of activation, and some already have a certain degree of kundalini integration put in place within their biology. For normal children, it's unlikely that kundalini would spontaneously arise fully because the biology and consciousness is too unrefined and underdeveloped. However, it has been said that a normal kundalini awakening process occurs at ages 11, 22, 33 and 44. However, it is questionable whether our current DNA strands are working properly for this natural process to occur.

Storms in Nature exhibit incredible power and force, and we can consider that kundalini energy is a force of this magnitude within your own physical body. Its potential is unlimited, which is why kundalini raising should be done with conscious maturity. We are dealing with the literal God force that has been put into our biology as a safeguard not only for our survival, but also for our resurrection and ascension into a God-realized being. If we could truly understand the sacredness of it all, we would treat our physical bodies with more respect. We could say that kundalini is our savior, in that it can get us out of the death cycle we have been in for millennia.

Many people have varying degrees of kundalini awakened, but few understand what it really means to become a blaze of pure-white fire. To actually become the God force — a radiation of the life principle — which is unlimited in its power and potential, is a sacred event. It is an event of pure, dynamic love. This force can transmute your body into light. You can see that this path involves great maturity and responsibility. Many of us have ideas or desires to become Godlike, but few of us understand the responsibility and the purification of the lower self that is necessary to actualize this potential within ourselves, which is why Source is calling it the Path of Ccourage.

Q. IS THE SEX ACT CONNECTED TO THE KUNDALINI ENERGY?

A. The sex act and drive is an *aspect* of kundalini energy, especially when it activated by love. In one way, kundalini is the force that allows reproduction to occur—it is the life-force current that enables us to bring forth a new life form. It ensures the survival of the species. Kundalini rising can be stimulated through sexual exchange and higher love between people, and there are various methods like Tantric sex that focus on raising the kundalini through sexual exchange. This type of kundalini rising can be just as valuable as any other source that stimulates kundalini.

The important thing to remember is that kundalini is an alchemical force that is not meant to stay in the lower chakras but rather is meant to rise up the chakra system into the brain, producing enlightenment and Divine Love at its highest level. The ancient Egyptians also used sexual rituals to cause kundalini to rise, and they deliberately used sexual encounters to promote inner enlightenment. It is not necessary to have sexual encounters or rituals to raise kundalini, however. The sex act is only one way it can happen. Your own inner journey and work also activate the kundalini.

Q. CAN DRUGS LIKE AYAHUASCA OR OTHER HALLUCINOGENS AFFECT KUNDALINI NEGATIVELY?

A. You have to be able to handle the effects of these drug experiences. Some people can have a spiritual vision or an experience of unity where they feel they are becoming one with Mother Earth. The after-effects of any kind of brain opening still requires purification and integration of the lower levels of one's anatomy. The physical body needs to be able to integrate the chemicals that are released during a drug-related experience. If the physical body is unable to handle this shift, these experiences can damage the lower centers, which is why people who have excessive drug experiences become unbalanced in their everyday lives. This is also why Source advises us to work with kundalini in a sacred way, understanding that it is a ladder of ascent up through the chakra system that purifies the alter ego so that the entire body can hold and attain a higher nature. People cannot benefit from experiencing unity or love if they are unable to integrate the experience into their own biology and everyday life. Source looks at kundalini as an incredibly sacred and powerful ladder into God realization, which is why caution is advised if you are going to artificially stimulate kundalini energy through drugs.

Q. CAN YOU DESCRIBE HOW KUNDALINI YOGA HELPS THE BODY AND THE SOUL?

A. Kundalini yoga can be very purifying if it is done consciously and with breathwork, allowing you to be very aware of the energy as it travels up your spine. Because this type of yoga is a conscious process, its practitioner also becomes aware of issues that may arise for purification and thus is better able to deal with them than someone who is less conscious. Kundalini yoga can be very healing and purifying if it is done correctly, and it can both help heal the body and also progress the individuated spirit, which builds the soul energy.

Q. WHAT ARE THE JOLTS, OR *KRIAS*, THAT OCCUR DURING MEDITATION?

A. These jolts are evidence of kundalini becoming active within the body. Other people may call these experiences *activations*, and they can be considered minor kundalini awakenings.

Q. What happens to the kundalini energy when we die?

A. Source is saying that it goes with the person when they die. It moves out of the body at death. It also brings the spirit into the white-light experience after death.

What an incredible fail-safe! We are given a fail-safe, no matter what circumstance or what level of consciousness we find ourselves at. You have the powers of basic reproduction and the ability to expand your consciousness in unlimited ways. You have the ability to overcome death, and if you don't overcome death, your kundalini goes back through the tunnel into the spirit planes. The kundalini also has healing and regenerative powers while in the physical body. It can change your body chemistry and make you an eternal-life being, whether physical or in spirit. Kundalini *is* your God force within, so we can take the phrase *God is within you* quite literally.

When we die, the kundalini acts like an arrow that propels us back into the spirit planes, which is a different process then when someone becomes an actualized God being while in the physical body. The kundalini will take you back no matter what level of consciousness you have achieved in a given lifetime. Once you become a God being, however, you *yourself* will decide whether you turn yourself into spirit or light or stay in a physical body indefinitely. In other words, when you are God-realized, death has no authority over you.

Q. Is kundalini our in-dwelling God spirit?

A. *Yes*! You've got it! Kundalini is your God spirit contained within your body! You can see now how we incarnate, bringing a portion of our spirit with us. It lies dormant at the base of our spine allowing us to live—to be alive in this dimension. It allows us the powers of reproduction, but it also has the ability to turn us into God made flesh once it is awakened. You can now also see how the Path of Courage is a journey we take as spirit beings to the awakening of our own God within-. Kundalini is our spirit in the body. Our spirit grows and develops into maturity and mastery through the purification of the lower, or animal, nature. If we stay asleep in our consciousness, our kundalini will also remain dormant providing our basic survival functions. As our consciousness awakens to the truth of who we are, our kundalini also awakens.Our kundalini *is* our spirit self becoming God realized!

This was a fantastic question, and if it hadn't been asked, we would have missed this realization. Now, when we read over this chapter, we may look at these questions and answers in a very different light.

Q. ONCE, BY ACCIDENT, I HAD A SPONTANEOUS KUNDALINI EXPERIENCE DURING AN ACUPUNCTURE TREATMENT. AFTER THAT, THE ACUPUNCTURIST WOULD NOT USE THOSE SAME POINTS. DID THE PRACTITIONER RESTRAIN MY KUNDALINI'S RISING SINCE THEN, OR DID HE FACILITATE ITS RISING IN SOME WAY?

A. First, there are no accidents. Some part of you would have known that your kundalini was going to be activated by going to this practitioner. So, ask yourself what have been the effects for you of that kundalini experience since that time in your life? What happened after the experience? Did anything change for you in your life, or were you further awakened in some way? As for the practitioner not using the same points again, I would ask myself why a part of me stopped the activation in future treatments. You could also ask the practitioner why he/she stopped using those particular points. We need to remember that we are co-creating experiences with one another. Nothing is done independently of our consciousness. We are all participating in all the experiences of our lives on some level. What the experience has done for you at the very least is help you remember your kundalini and bring you to the choice of what you would like to do next with it.

Q. IS KUNDALINI RISING RELATED IN ANY WAY TO *SPONTANEOUS COMBUSTION*?

A. It's all the same force, you see. It just manifests itself in different ways. So yes, kundalini is related to spontaneous combustion because it does change the chemical composition in the body. Remember that kundalini is a flame of fire within us. Source is saying that even in cases of spontaneous combustion, there is still a soul process going on that is very personal to the person experiencing the combustion. Not every kundalini experience creates spontaneous combustion, of course. Kundalini can totally change your physical body: There are chemical and hormonal processes going on; there are nerve and brain changes happening; and the organs and chakras work differently—it is all quite dynamic on varying levels. Whether kundalini rises slowly or is a spontaneous full-blown experience, it is still a process that can totally change your biology and consciousness.

Q. SPEAKING OF SPONTANEOUS COMBUSTION, WHAT IS IT?

I'm watching a process here so you have to give me a moment. The word I keep hearing is 'implosion.' If I don't say the first word I don't get the rest, and the first word was 'implosion.' I'm hearing that it's a particular chemical reaction that happens inside of a person and it is very rare. I can't explain the chemical reaction but I can tell you it looks like it is a particular thing that happens very oddly, where certain chemicals just happen to collide with each other, or meet each other together. They are odd chemicals like a chemical system that has gone awry. When that happens it causes a spontaneous implosion inside the body. This is what I'm seeing, rare chemicals converging that create new reactions in the moment. It's not like it builds up for days. It is an isolated incident that occurs when chemicals combine and react unusually together.

Q. WHEN A PERSON TURNS THEIR BODY INTO LIGHT, CAN THEY EVER INCARNATE OR TAKE ON A PHYSICAL BODY AGAIN?

A. In the case of people who are conscious beings and are consciously becoming God-actualized beings who can turn themselves into light at will, they can come and go into materialization any time they choose. They would not need to come through the birth cycle to be born into a body. Instead, they can materialize a body of any age or appearance any-time and anywhere. This type of individual can also teleport, bi-locate, or be in multiple dimensions at the same time. They are a fully awak-ened, deliberately decisive being. In other words, they are their own authority in their full God Presence. Keep in mind this is God's inten-tion for all of us.

God Men have achieved their freedom in the true sense, meaning that they are not subject to any laws or physics but are in their unlimited God Presence.

Putting all this in perspective, we have been shown that kundalini is a literal God force within us that is our own spirit energy, which has given us a very big piece of understanding about our innate spirit selves. We see that our spirit selves are not automatically God-realized spirit selves. Each has a journey to go through to refinement, to matu-rity, to become an *adult* in the God sense. It is not unlike our children who contain our DNA — our information — yet are unrealized in their birth state. They grow and develop through different stages physically, mentally, emotionally and spiritually. They make their own choices and have their own results. They can progress or digress as they choose. Our spirit/kundalini self within is much the same. It lies dor-mant in its immature or unrefined state, and must travel a path of courage to become mature. Actualizing our God flame is the ascending path.

Chapter 12

Chakras

Many people have heard of the chakras through various books or other Eastern traditions. Even though there are many writings on this topic, we thought it would be interesting to bring the subject to Source, who always surprises us with Its view of things that we think we know everything about.

While saying the opening prayer, a beautiful sphere of emerald green light with gold around the edges of the sphere appears. Other colors are also emerging—white, red and pink. My initial feeling about these colors is that they relate to the main chakras of this planet, particularly the emerald green and gold. The emerald green has been the main *planetary* and *personal* chakra for this particular time period. Planetarily, and as a species, we move through the various chakra energies through different planetary ages. From the emerald-green chakra of the heart we are now moving into the blue chakra of communication and truth. Our current planetary shift is taking us into the blue chakra of the planet with the *potential* to reach the violet chakra of ascension in this time cycle., which is why there is so much focus on love and moving into our hearts. Emerald green is the color of nurturing, prosperity and love, and if we don't incorporate this color, we won't be moving into the higher-chakra colors. Green is also the color of Nature, indicating that the plant life and their related kingdoms have had much to do with upholding this particular chakra spectrum during this age.

We began this discussion by sharing information on the chakras as they relate to planetary cycles and ages. The evolution of our species into higher realms of consciousness is also related to Earth's planetary evolution through these chakras. The collective mastering of the emerald-green chakra is our current task as a species. We are leaving the solar-plexus chakra of power, which deals with our relationship to our own personal power and the sun, which is why we are seeing so many changes with the sun. We are in the process of moving from our power center to our heart, which is the emerald-green and pink chakra.

Source is putting a very strong emphasis on Nature. If we destroy Nature, we are not going to make it through to the blue-chakra cycle. You can see this process playing out in world affairs: We are in a war between the abuse of power and the correct use of power, which must incorporate the heart to be balanced. This is the task for *all* of us now — not just politics and the governments of the world. It is obvious that the resistance from the power abusers is strong. These factions are doing everything they can to stay in their solar-plexus chakras in a negative way. Their focus is on taking power away from individuals and using domination and control to suppress free will. Our task as individuals is to come into our own true power, which also connects to our inner child through our remembrance of the creative potential and power of our imagination.

Our inner child connects us to Source and to our own personal purpose. Not only do we need to take back our own personal power and lessen our dependency on outer authorities, but we must move from fear into the love of the heart before we can even begin to move into the truth and communication with all life that is implicit in the blue chakra. Anything that enhances the distortion of power must go, which would include all dogmas and agendas designed to suppress truth and the rights of individuals.

We need to progress *internally* up the spiritual ladder and understand *true* authority, which is our relationship to our own *inner* sun. We are moving out of *external* authority and moving into *inner* authority. This is the main purification process we are now in, both as a planet and as individuals. We are reclaiming our own inner sun and our own inner child and releasing our dependence on outer authorities of all kinds.

The inner child is important because it represents the return to the state of harmlessness that can only be found by understanding our own power as creative beings. As long as we believe we are controlled by the outer world, we will not understand ourselves and will not, therefore know our *loving* power. This is why we must return to our inner sun before we can ascend and master the emerald green of the heart. In this purification process there is an emphasis on *forgiveness*—forgiving the past, ourselves, our parents, those who abuse power, and anyone who may have injured our self-esteem. In this way, we begin to reclaim our innate divinity.

Q. WHAT IS A *CHAKRA*?

A. I see strange vortex-type cones that are spinning, and each has a large end that is directed toward our bodies and a smaller end that leads out into various whirlpools, other planes of existence, other dimensions and realities. Each one seems to be a world in and of itself, even though each one is connected to us at various points in our light bodies and anatomy. They form a network of spiraling vortices that enable interdimensional travel. They can take us to other reality fields for different experiences, and when you arrive there, you spend time learning, exploring and having experiences. The chakras enable you to journey to God Man through learning, experience, knowledge and the attainment of higher frequencies and sounds *as they relate to our divinity.*

Every system has its own set of chakras. Our solar system has a certain set of main chakras that lead to different planetary worlds, and supply life-force energy to our bodies. Spirits come into a particular system to learn about the different dimensional realities that are encompassed in that system as part of its journey to self-realization. You do not go to another system until you have explored and mastered all the varying systems that relate to the one you're currently in.

When I look at the journey through these different dimensional vortices, I understand that it could take a person a very long time and many lives to travel through these systems, which may explain one of the reasons that we reincarnate so often. It is not just about the karma we may have created, but it may be more about the mastering of particular chakras and solar systems. Many relationships that people are in focus on mastering particular chakras. They may incarnate together to work jointly on particular chakras. This picture is much bigger than I had thought.

I am not talking about the many small chakras that spiral throughout our anatomy. I am talking about the main chakras that connect us to other realms and also feed our anatomy. You could say that the chakras and the energy that comes through them help create your body.

Q. WHAT ARE THE FUNCTIONS AND PURPOSES OF CHAKRAS?

A. The chakras hold a great ascension potential for self-realization, mastery, and experiences of the universe. They allow us to know God and become God-realized beings. Source is being really clear to let us know that our spirits travel on these vortices of light. The spiraling vortex process that I am being shown controls how we arrive at particular locations or planes of existence. The vortices provide us the *motion* we need to get from one place to the other. This is more of an *inward* process than an outer one.

You may have heard that chakras break down colors from the sun and disperse them to our various organs. Different organs of the body vibrate to different chakras, and each has its own frequency band of color and sound tone. It isn't only that the chakras provide colors to the organs; it's that the organs anchor the chakras to the physical body.

This perspective sheds new light on the subject of organ removal, doesn't it? We all have a morphogenetic field that duplicates our physical organs on an energetic level. We have an energetic counterpart to each physical organ. Source is saying that these energetic counterparts are still intact, even if we remove the physical organ relating to it. As long as the energetic template is still intact and not damaged, it will still hold its relationship to its associated chakra.

Q. WHERE EXACTLY ARE THE CHAKRAS LOCATED?

A. The chakras are located througout our time-space continuum. I'm hearing sound out at those levels. The chakras *anchor* at different points in the physical body, but they extend quite far out into time-space.

Source is asking us to think of ourselves as a tree where the center trunk is going up through the center of our bodies. When you cut a tree and you see the various rings, it indicates the tree's relationship to its own chakras. Source is giving us the picture of these rings within rings, or wheels within wheels, as a way for us to visualize how the chakra system looks within us. The difference is that the rings are in a spiraling motion and not stationary.

Chakras don't change location, but they do change their *motion* in that they sometimes rotate clockwise and sometimes counterclockwise, depending upon what's going on in the cosmos. In other words, if the big gears or wheels out in the universe move in a certain direction, our own chakras will reverse their spin accordingly to stay in tune with it. These changes in position seem to fluctuate quite frequently. Whether they spin clockwise or counterclockwise or speed up or slow down, is all determined by a bigger rotation happening in the cosmos. Of course, our personal condition can also affect the spin of our chakras, but there is a larger relationship to our solar system that we are bringing to light.

Q. CAN WE GO THROUGH THE CHAKRAS AND DESCRIBE EACH ONE, AND WHERE IT IS ANCHORED IN THE PHYSICAL BODY?

A. Yes. The red chakra is anchored two inches below the navel in the lower pelvic region. The orange chakra is located in the womb/navel area. The yellow chakra is in the stomach/solar plexus area. The green chakra encompasses the heart or upper chest area. The blue chakra covers the throat/thyroid area. The indigo chakra is in the pituitary or third-eye area in the forehead. The violet chakra anchors in the pineal gland within the brain. Each chakra anchors in the body in an area about the size of a half dollar.

When you master a particular chakra, its color becomes a *ray*. Chakras don't remain stationary in a particular location in the body, but actually become vibratory rays that affect the whole individual when they become a purified essence. For example, we are working on the emerald green of the heart chakra, purifying it to be able to move into the blue of the throat. On a small level, we see that green is about love and opening the heart, and blue is about truth and greater communication with all life everywhere. However, the bigger picture shows that we are purifying ourselves and our planet to become *rays of light* that encompass the entire body-mind-spirit system of a person and a planet. This process affects every cell in every part of the body, and every cell needs to be vibrating to this emerald-green love ray in order for that chakra to be incorporated and mastered. When you move into the blue chakra, your whole being is in communication with all life everywhere, not just your voice. Mastering particular chakras involves turning them into rays that *become* your physiology and your very essence. Planetarily, once Earth has harmonized the green ray and moved into the blue ray, its main color will be blue.

The smaller chakra wheels in the body are anchoring points that nourish the body at particular body locations or organ sites. The bigger chakra mastery however, is all encompassing.

When I talk about the emerald green/love that we're working on now, there may be people who do not complete the mastery of this chakra this time around. Keep in mind that we first have to reverse where we place our power from external to internal in the solar-plexus chakra before the emerald-green chakra of the heart can be mastered. We need these two chakras purified and turned into rays within us before we can move into the blue. You can see that this time period that we are in offers us an accelerated opportunity for rapid transformation.

If some of us do not master these opportunities now, Source is telling us not to worry, because there will be many opportunities to cycle through these chakras again and again. Ultimately, we will all make it. Time and attention are only focal points in a lifetime, so don't be hard on yourself if you feel that you still have issues in your lower chakras that you are dealing with. *Do your best.* If it is your desire to work through the purification of these issues, however, this is the time period to do it at a fast pace. We are being given much aid from various sources to help us heal and progress.

Q. WHY DO WE NEED CHAKRAS AT ALL?

A. You need them to become God Man in this dimension. There are energetic templates, or maps, for our biology in this universe. As you come down through the levels, these templates hold certain geometries in place. The chakras are part of the design of our particular solar system. They are our ladder of ascent, so we can be connected and evolve to become God Man. When you get close to God realization, all these things disappear from the light body and the physical body, and you are able to move out of this solar system. You become a flame of Source. While you are in your awakening process, however, your chakra system is your key to becoming whole in this dimension. It holds the geometries that allow expansion to happen. They are part of the ladder the kundalini uses as it spirals up through the body.

Q. WHY ARE THERE SOUND TONES CONNECTED TO THE CHAKRAS?

A. Once again, I see spinning, spiraling cones that extend way, way out into time-space and connect into our physical bodies

Sound is the vibration that is necessary for the making of and dissolution of matter and the ascension into light. It is the vibratory action or motion of creation. Each chakra has a particular sound that matches its plane of existence. It's something that needs to be heard from within. It is an internal *traveling* system. I say internal, but the traveling can occur both internally and externally.

There is the notion in some teachings that each chakra vibrates to a particular note on the harmonic scale, however, the inner transformation that accompanies a particular chakra or plane of existence has its own particular sound tone frequency. The sound can't be described — it can only be experienced. I'm hearing those tones now, but I can't describe them to you, because they are my personal, inner experience. I can hear the chakras hum and sing. Each will be heard internally by the individual when he/she is ready. If you are incorporating a chakra into yourself, you will hear the sound tones, and you'll see the colors and virtuous symbols associated with the particular chakra.

Q. WHY IS IT IMPORTANT FOR US AS HUMANS TO GO THROUGH THESE PARTICULAR CHAKRAS? WHY DO WE HAVE TO MASTER THESE PLANES OF EXISTENCE IN THIS PARTICULAR SPHERE OF REALITY THAT WE'RE IN?

A. Source is saying that it's because we don't get out of a particular system until we master its planes of existence. We can't move into a different universe until we cycle through and master, or incorporate within us, the planes of existence in our particular solar system. It has to do with the frequency we are currently in. Each solar system has its own series of frequency ranges that create the life forms in its varying dimensions. The life forms in a solar system have to evolve through the various frequencies until they are ready to go beyond that system into another set of frequencies. A phrase we will use to describe this process is *mastering the system.* It is part of becoming God realized, because God realization means that you become everything. We continue to reincarnate until we become an ascended master of our particular system. Only then are we free to move out of it. Being an ascended master of a system means that you are an ascended master of *that particular system,* but not of the entire universe. You will have mastered or gained the qualities and abilities inherent in that particular system. This mastering is actually a desire of the individuated spirit/soul as it journeys through the universe and becomes a co-creator with it.

Q. WHAT DO THE CHAKRAS HAVE TO DO WITH OUR BIOLOGY AND ITS RELATIONSHIP TO ENLIGHTENMENT?

A. The chakras were designed to feed us sunlight and colors while we're in a body. Their swirling force fields helped create the body. Human biology was created so we could learn about different dimensions or other systems within a system and be a life contributor to that system. A sun is designed to feed the life forms of a particular system and give them exactly what they need to survive while in that system. We were originally meant to live off of sunlight, as it is a complete menu of colors, sound tones and frequencies for our biology. We began to consume other life forms—meats, plants and fruits—as a result of becoming *externalized* in our consciousness and digressing in our biology through history.

We have been talking about an *inner* journey, and earlier we talked about kundalini, which is also an inner journey that uses the chakra system. Now we are talking about the chakras having dual functions. One function is to break down sunlight and disperse those color rays to the various organs in our bodies to feed us while we're in a physical body. The other function is to expand us in our consciousness and mastery of this system through the different dimensional levels of existence in our solar system so that we may become more God realized.

However, once we became externalized in our consciousness, we forgot our inward journey to God realization and began to focus only on our individualized body or alter ego presence. We got caught up in what was manifesting in our reality externally or in creating new life forms on the planet, so that our focus of attention became material rather than spiritual. We forgot that manifestation occurs from within to without. We forgot how to live off of sunlight, and we began to consume other life forms for energy. When you become a true mystic, or someone who is devoted to their inner path, you move through the various planes of existence and dimensional levels and begin to hear the inner sound tones associated with your chakra system. Soon you lose your interest in consuming outer life forms, and as you move up into higher frequencies, you will *naturally* move once again toward living on sunlight and eventually not even needing that. You can begin to see the change in yourself as you move away from eating denser foods to lighter foods, to more liquids, to sunlight, to becoming a *source* of spiritual sustenance yourself. As you become more God Man, you become a sun that radiates life force rather than takes life force.

In the consumption of foods, we are not saying that eating meat is low consciousness or that becoming a vegetarian or a raw-food vegan is the optimal way to be. You could have a cow whose meat is filled with high-quality color and sound as much as a plant could be filled with environmental toxins. You have to trust and follow your own particular intuition and biological requirements until you *naturally* evolve past consuming other life forms. The word *naturally* is key here because unless it is a natural progression to move to lighter forms of food and then to sunlight, you will become ill or starve. Only when you have reached the frequency of incorporating more spirit will it be safe for you to adjust the way you receive life-force energy.

> I recently got a message from an old yogi who told me to eat only *happy* foods, which, as we mentioned previously, are foods you tune into while grocery shopping that feel happy to you. There were no specific types of foods mentioned, except for consuming more edible flowers. Happy foods could be a particular piece of meat you notice, or a raw food or a canned vegetable. You get the point. Shopping for happy foods is an *intuitive* exercise, and what you are drawn to will change with every shopping adventure.

Coming full circle with this question, we can see that the chakras are designed not only to feed us at the basic levels but also to facilitate our expansion and evolution into God Man.

Q. CAN WE CONSCIOUSLY CONTROL OUR CHAKRAS TO HEAL OUR BODIES?

A. Source is asking us, "What would you do with them?" This is an interesting question because it implies that unless you have a full understanding of a chakra and what it's connected to on every level—physical, mental, emotional and spiritual all the way out into the different dimensional levels and planes of existence, you won't fully understand its qualities or potentials. You can focus all the attention you want on a chakra, thinking that you're clearing and balancing it, but you will be doing so without adequate information. For example, many healers have the idea that a chakra should only be spinning clockwise, and if they see a chakra in their client that is spinning counterclockwise, they will reverse its spin, not realizing that chakras sometimes spin clockwise and sometimes counterclockwise, as part of their alignment with cosmic energies.

Our real job is to meditate on the chakras to gather their information and to *know* them. As you can see from our discussion today, each chakra leads to new worlds and realities yet to be discovered. Source is saying that if you want to work with chakras for healing, the way to do it is to know them on a deeply internal level first, so that it can be integrated fully within your biology, which is what causes true healing and transformation. Certainly though, you can work with colors in a therapeutic way to either add colors to the body where there is a deficiency or take away some color where there is too much. Much healing can be done with the color and sound levels of our biology. Those levels are only a small part of healing in the context of the expansion of ourselves that we are speaking about. However, anything that brings more balance and awareness to us is helpful.

Q. CAN PUTTING REIKI ON A CHAKRA DAILY HELP INCREASE ONE'S FINANCIAL WEALTH?

A. True prosperity is coming to the place where you love yourself and all things, and you know that there is nothing else. You come to the place where you no longer have any judgments or harmful intent toward anything or anyone, which puts you in the flow of life and love, where you are sustained by this in your everyday life. Prosperity has to do with coming into the whole and recognizing you're not a separate entity, but are in a flowing relationship with all life everywhere. The corresponding harmlessness that goes along with this realization naturally provides prosperity. So, I'm not getting a "yes" to this question regarding Reiki and prosperity, because prosperity is not just associated with the chakras. True prosperity is about becoming the abundance of the universe within yourself.

To have prosperity at the level of which you are asking, the task at hand is to undo fear, which is the underlying issue under all experiences of apparent lack. Fear stops the flow of the natural life currents that provide for us. Whether you're in the flow or out of it is really the issue. Fears block the flow of natural good in our lives. This is where Reiki can be of benefit—it supplies people with a higher frequency of life-force energy, enabling them to release fear and heal.

Q. IS THERE A RELATIONSHIP BETWEEN PSYCHIC ABILITY AND THE CHAKRAS?

A. You will gain more of these abilities as you incorporate the qualities and attributes of the chakras and kundalini currents within yourself. As you go into your inner temple and gain more knowledge of yourself and your chakras, the gifts associated with each chakra will become active as part of your natural state. These gifts are built into your biology and are waiting to be activated. These gifts are enormous. They are not limited to psychic abilities, but incorporate tremendous regenerative abilities within them as well as heightening all of your senses. Your *natural* abilities already include bi-location, teleportation, dematerialization, inter-dimensional movement, and meeting other aspects of yourself in other dimensions and planes of existence. The ability to smell and taste someone from miles away is also part of our natural gifts. This ability has a high level of discernment connected to it, allowing us to know the quality and frequency of various life forms before we even come upon them physically. Working with the chakras and kundalini will go a long way toward bringing forth or activating these gifts within us.

Q. WHAT CAN WE DO TO ACTIVATE OR ENHANCE THESE ABILITIES?

A. Besides what we have already mentioned above, you can begin *sun gazing,* which is very centering and regenerative. It will strengthen your inner core and activate higher abilities. You start with 10 seconds in the morning as the sun is rising and again 10 seconds when the sun is setting. You increase to 20 seconds the next day, 30 seconds the next and so on. Information online will show you the rest of the practice and how to safely increase the time spent gazing at the sun.[1]

> *Meditate* on your chakras as previously mentioned, and begin *journaling* and questioning your beliefs, thoughts, feelings and intentions. Change your *diet,* if it is unhealthy, so that your entire system can function better. The quality of your food determines its nutritional value for you. Food affects your energy levels, your moods and even your thoughts. Amino acids, minerals and vitamins and *happy foods* are the basics to a healthy system.

You have a guardian angel who will assist you in your evolution. Your own in-dwelling Holy Spirit will also help you on your journey, if that is your intention. Take some time to explore and focus daily on these parts of you. Even 15 minutes of quiet inner focus and smiling at

---

1. http://tinyurl.com/How2Sungaze

your organs and spirit will begin to awaken and create an inner relationship with your system. When you meditate, call on your own Holy Spirit that is within you and ask it to teach you. Ask it to give you the knowledge that you may need at this time. You can ask it to show you which chakra needs attention or has some virtue or knowledge to impart to you. Be patient with yourself, and wait for an answer. Answers can take many forms—anything from hearing an answer inside yourself or receiving a deep feeling of peace or direct knowing. Your answer may appear in the days to come through a phone call with someone or an event that happens. You may begin to receive impressions of colors that have feelings or information connected to them, or a symbol may appear that you have to look up to discover its meaning. You may come upon a book or document that seems to speak directly to you and answer your question. There are many ways that answers can be delivered. The more practice you give it, the more proficient you will become at discovering your inner self. Make it a daily practice, if at all possible. The more attention you put on focusing within, the more the glands associated with your higher gifts become activated.

Q. ARE HUMANS THE ONLY ONES WITH CHAKRAS, OR DO ANIMALS HAVE THEM ALSO?

A. Humans, animals, plants, even rocks can have chakras. Every life form has a chakra system at the level of its own design. Remember that chakras are the way life forms are connected to the cosmos.

Q. CAN CHAKRAS BE DAMAGED?

A. Yes. For example, if you have a wound or injury in a specific location, it can damage the chakra that's connected to it. Chakras can also be stolen by negative entities. You can have missing chakras. Food can affect the health of the biology and its chakra system. Your environment also plays a part.

The chakras are designed to nourish you, but if your template is disturbed or out of balance in some way, it will affect the health of the chakra and the corresponding organs. So, chakras are affected by many things, including traumas from this life or past lives, as well as biological disturbances. This is another reason why we suggest that you go within and learn about your own chakras and see their condition, so you can make adjustments or healing where necessary. Your Holy Spirit within will show you what to do. You may also find that you are suddenly attracted to a particular healer who may have the tools to provide healing for you.

Q. ARE THERE SPECIFIC DISEASES OR SICKNESSES RELATED TO EACH CHAKRA, AND IF SO, WHAT ARE THEY?

A. I am being guided to address the *feet* chakras first, even though they're not considered one of the main chakras. The feet chakras are located in the middle of the foot and go through from the top of the foot through the bottom. These chakras connect you to the Earth grid. The energy coming up from the Earth grid through these chakra points can either be health producing or sickness producing, depending upon your location. The first thing we want to look at when we are checking chakras is what's coming up from the Earth in your particular area. This is important now because there are so many Earth changes occurring, especially at the level of the electromagnetic field/grids of the Earth. We need to see if we're standing on healthy grids or toxic grids. Grids do fluctuate, but they don't fluctuate to a huge degree minute by minute unless there is earthquake activity or some other catalyst such as solar flares or volcanic activity or methane gas buildup beneath the surface. The exception to these is unnatural stimulation of land areas by fracking, drilling or government/military subsurface programs or projects. Grids can also become toxic from polluted water or compromised vortices or traumas related to historical events.

Living on toxic grids or geopathic stress points will affect your health and balanced perception, because they affect equilibrium on all levels. They affect your mental and emotional state as well as the functioning of your nervous system.

The *root* chakra, which is below the navel, is concerned with what we inherit from our parents. This is the chakra where conception occurs. In the sexual exchange between our mother and father, their genetic ancestry, their gifts and issues get transferred to the newly emerging fetus. They become part of our anatomy. The root chakra also holds our connection to our other lives. This is where we bring forward not only what we've inherited from our parents but also our own soul history from other lives. The information stored in this chakra can affect the organs related to this chakra and can also manifest as issues that would be connected to this chakra. Keep in mind that we may be inheriting fabulous things from our ancestry and other lives, but we may also be inheriting some of our parents' unhealed issues as well as our own from other lifetimes. If we do inherit some negative patterns, it could take the form of illnesses in that area of our body, or we could attract particular experiences or patterns to ourselves that would connect to that area of our body. Or, we may not manifest any aberration in that chakra! Since this chakra connects to sexuality, pleasure, pain, and the creation of life forms, we may want to see how these are evidencing themselves in our own lives.

The *navel* chakra, which is in the area of the belly-button, is the chakra that begins to *anchor* us in the physical world. The root chakra controls what we inherit, and the navel chakra controls the process of anchoring what we inherit into our body and the planet. There is a particular harmonic in the naval chakra that needs to be developed correctly from the beginning. This chakra makes sure that we are anchored correctly in this particular system. Distortions in any of these chakras can manifest as illnesses or issues pertaining to those chakras, but they won't necessarily manifest specifically in those areas.

The *solar plexus* chakra in the stomach area has to do with our relationship to the sun and moon. It is important to look at what the sun and moon were doing when you were born or even when you were conceived. If you are lucky enough to have a mother who is aware of your actual conception, it would be worth having a talk with her about the timing of your conception. It is also possible to remember your conception through rebirthing or past-life regression, which is where astrology can be of good use. The position of the sun and moon and their activities during the time of your birth and conception get anchored inside of your biology. Understanding this can help you get clear on the benefits and influences that could show up as patterns in your life.

The *heart* chakra, located in the area of the heart, ironically holds our fear of death. I find this quite interesting because until we get through the fear of death and overcome death in our consciousness, we cannot know pure love. As long as we have fear, our ability to love and surrender to our oneness with life everywhere will be thwarted. Fear keeps us in a separatist perception concerned only with self-preservation at the expense of the whole. We can see how this relates to what is going on in the world today. It's obvious when we are talking about these chakras that if the distortions we inherit are not cleared or healed it affects us all throughout time on many levels.

I am being shown that the *throat* chakra, located at the throat area, is about manifesting through sound. Long ago we didn't have words as we do now. We emitted specific sound tones from our throat area that were designed to cause deliberate manifestations. The sound-tone frequencies were very pure and would produce instant manifestations. I am seeing mouths that are open and look like they have a circular, open shape as the sound tones are being emitted. These are sound-tone *calls* that are not words. Sound is what brings things into matter but it also disassembles matter. If we could recapture this original ability and emit these sound tones in their pure frequency, we could heal just about anything. We could build up or tear down as required. The ancient time I am tuning into was before we became this dense in matter. We were not solely spirit beings; we did have form, but it wasn't as dense as ours is now. We did not have language, but only sound tones.

The *third eye* chakra, located at the pituitary gland in the center of the forehead, sets our *horizontal* axis and frame of reference. I see a horizontal ray of light coming out of that chakra that affects our linear reality—how and what we see and perceive. Our ability to see and perceive in this dimension is very limited at this point, because this chakra is not fully activated in most of us. If it were, we would see and notice many more things in our field of reality than we do now. We would also be seeing the multidimensional levels that exist right here, right now. In this chakra we are predominantly concerned with *sight* and our horizontal orientation in this dimension. However, there is a point in the evolution of this chakra up the ladder of ascent where our visual orientation changes and disconnects from the physical.

The *crown* chakra at the top of the head, has to do with our *vertical* axis. Energy comes down through the top of the head and down to Earth to set our vertical orientation in time and space. We have a set of geometries within us that need this axis to be able to rotate and spin. The vertical axis allows our sacred geometries to spin so that our core template stays in order. I feel a lot of heat while I'm exploring this chakra from the top to bottom in my body. This chakra puts us in touch with the Christ mind and allows us to anchor this mind and knowledge into the physical world. It can change the body entirely. It can regenerate cells, change the biology of the body, bring in more light and electricals into the system, connect us to cosmic consciousness while being anchored in the physical body and also de-anchor us from the physical body. This chakra is your key to flight.

Chapter 13

The Future

This topic explores the Future itself, not necessarily what's going to happen in the future, but the whole idea of the future itself. Our intention is to explore the concept of the future and how it works.

As I say the opening prayer, I see a beautiful rosy purple color with a line of royal blue with a white line around it. The rosy purple color usually indicates things having to do with karma, or things having to do with hardship or suffering—things that we would have experienced in our lives. So it's an interesting color for today's topic.

Q. WHAT IS SOURCE'S DEFINITION OF THE *FUTURE*?

A. Future is an idea in the mind of God, which means that if God did not intend for life to continue, there would be no possibility of a future. All futures are based on ideas that coalesce, unravel, coalesce again, and unravel again, continuing forever. We are looking at a cause-and-effect scenario. Ideas create the continuation of our future as we perceive it in our dimension. It looks almost like a dreamscape. I'm in moving clouds of color, which seem to be people's ideas, thoughts or concepts that float and become cloudlike. I'm in a horizontally moving frame of reference here, where these clouds are moving forward. They get generated from mind, and they travel together—moving forward. On one hand I'm getting a very fleeting feeling with it, but on the other hand, I'm getting pictures of events manifesing. So the future being an idea in the mind of God seems to suggest that an implied future is inherent in the desire for creation to be—in other words, the future is a continuation that is based on Source's desire for life to be.

Q. WHAT MAKES THE FUTURE? I UNDERSTAND THAT IT IS BUILT
ON IDEAS, OR PERCEPTIONS, SO WHAT MAKES IT CONCRETE?

A. What makes the future happen, or coalesce into an event or manifestation, is simply thought and desire. As long as we have thoughts and
desires, we will have a continuation of the future. Every thought and
desire creates a form of itself on some level. In other words, thought and
desire make things continue.

Thoughts and desires manifest as pictures or imprints, and the more
energy they have, the more they become concrete. We are going back to
the fact that *we are creators*, and because we are creators, we have within
us creative ability, or creative energy. Our thoughts and desires continue
this imaging, or creative process. The power of our creative imagery
coalesces with the elements that are around us and makes things come
into form. Every single thought, and every single desire, takes a form or
shape on some level.

Now, some forms dissipate if they're not very powerful. They may
be ideas that can coalesce into a little cloud and then dissolve, whereas
other ideas, which are heavily energized, may make stronger manifestations. This is because our thoughts and desires create a magnetic field
and begin to cause the elements or substance in the Mind Field to
coalesce around them, creating a plasma field in which the thought or
image begins to take on form.

Source is saying that we create a future because this is how we think.
We are thinking from past to present to future, and many of our
thoughts concern the future. They are about what we are going to do
tomorrow, or in the next hour, or in the next five or ten years in our own
lives, or what's likely to happen on our planet. Our thoughts are creating
the future because we focus on it. If we were not focused on the future,
we would most likely be in a true present moment—we wouldn't be creating future scenarios. It would be quite a different experience.

You may be wondering what happens when you're in a true
moment. Source says that if our thoughts were not future- or past-ori-

ented, we would be eternally in a *presence*. In other words, we'd be in the present moment, which would give us a very different quality of experience, because we would be in direct communication with all life everywhere, in the moment. It would be a blissful existence from moment to moment. Source is saying that this is really where your true power is. Power is in being present, in your presence, in each moment, where you're not directing your thoughts toward creating a particular future or a particular plan. Instead, you are immersed in the life-force energy of the moment, which is the direct connection to God and bliss.

Q. IS OUR FUTURE PREDETERMINED IF WE DO NOT DELIBERATELY FOCUS OUR INTENT ON CREATING IT?

A. Let me qualify "predetermined." Source is saying that the future is predetermined, to an extent. God does intend that life be and continue, but the kinds of futures we create ourselves are predominately continuations of the past—past beliefs, predictions, prophecies, programming, *etc.* The future is predetermined to a point, because we've been thinking so long about it, and there have been many things predicted about the future, and people are expecting a future, so a future continues. In a way, it is predetermined only because there are so many thoughts out there that have been future-directed and are still in a process of coalescing and have yet to become manifest. So, there is a hodgepodge of futures based on people's thoughts in the past—centuries ago, as well as today—that have long been coalescing into the future.

So, when I asked Source if It has predetermined the future for us, It says that Its predetermination has never been about events, but always about bliss. In other words, It has predetermined and set that the experience of life and creation, in terms of Its desire in Its mind, has been for us to experience complete bliss in every moment. So I'm making a distinction here, because Source looks at the future as if it's synonymous with the word eternal. Eternal is being totally present in each moment, in complete bliss.

Now, Source is also telling us that being in the moment would itself be an eternal experience, and the experience would not be static, because the mind of God is full of joy, happiness, and expression. We don't know what that is because our minds are busy thinking about the past and worrying about the future. We are rarely truly in a present moment, and, because we aren't, we don't get to experience what God's eternity is like in that blissful, joyful moment. *God does not have future events planned for us.* That is something that we do with our own consciousness by thinking linearly.

What Source does is hold that eternal future of bliss for us whenever we redirect our consciousness to the present moment rather than to the past or the future. If a person is not consciously directing their future, it will unfold according to their beliefs, thoughts and programming, and it will also evolve astrologically, according to their birth charts, if no conscious changes are made. In this sense, their future would be predetermined.

Q. ARE THE PAST, PRESENT AND FUTURE ALL THE SAME THING?

A. Only in the sense that they are all based on thoughts that we're thinking. Say you're using your present moment to think about your past. What you're doing is bringing that event into all of your present moments and, in this way into all your future moments. So, in this regard, past, present and future are the same thing. It all depends upon where our consciousness is focused, or what we continually think about. So, it isn't that the past *is* the present or the future, it's that we recreate it to be one continuous event. You could say that your past is in your present, and that your future is assured because of what you're thinking. In other words, you will re-create past events to re-appear in the present, which then re-appear again in the future. This is because that's where your consciousness is. It is a function of where your perception is oriented, and what you energize with your thoughts and desires.

Here is another example: Let's say that something traumatic or blissful happened to you when you were a child. If your consciousness is built around those events and has a strong memory of them, it will keep repeating the same patterns, or the same type of experience. In that way your past, present and future are all the same, because you're focused on a particular type of event or experience. Your experience might express itself a little differently, but the underlying pattern will still be the same.

Q. CAN WE TRAVEL INTO THE FUTURE, AND IF SO, DOES THAT MEAN THAT IT HAS ALREADY HAPPENED?

A. That's a good question. Well, it has already happened on a particular level because of what we're talking about today. In other words, because we've already focused on the future, an event has already been created from our thoughts, and we may not encounter the experience until its expression or manifestation happens in 3-D. If you continually think about the future, all those thoughts and desires go out into the Mind Field and become expressed in some form at some time, depending on the kind of energy they carry. So, if you travel into your future—which you can do in meditation—where you look at yourself in the future, you can see the effects of your thoughts. You can see how your thoughts are coalescing into the future. In this way, some parts of your future have already happened, but they may not have manifested in this particular density yet. When you go traveling into the future, you're at a different dimensional frequency than you are when you're in 3-D.

It is the same thing that happens in a *déjà vu* experience—a part of us wanders off into the future while we're sleeping and has experiences. When we wake up, we forget where we have been, but when our 3-D reality finally catches up to that journey, all of a sudden we "re-experience" it—we feel that we have already done this, or been there, which we have.

Q. HOW CAN WE CHANGE THE FUTURE?

A. That's another good question in relation to the answers we're getting. There are levels to this. If you travel to the future in a meditation and you see a particular scenario unfolding as a future, you can actually redirect the forces or the elements to manifest a different outcome. You have to tell it to rearrange itself into a different outcome. So, yes you can change futures. So, this is interesting because we're looking at the part of us that is truly a magician, but only if you are conscious of it. If you do move into the future, and you're watching something unfold in a future event that you don't particularly like, you can say, "This is not the outcome that I desire." You can define whatever alternate outcome you desire, and you can redirect the elements to manifest that just by your conscious intent alone. So, yes, you can change the future, but only if you're consciously in the dimension where it's manifesting.

When you see the results of past thoughts manifesting in your everyday life, you can redirect that manifestation as well, but it has to be done consciously in the present moment, as it is happening.

Q. HAS EVERYTHING ALREADY HAPPENED?

A. Source is saying no, not everything has already happened, because people are still thinking—thoughts are still being thought, and desires are still being generated. So, It's saying no, absolutely not. Actually, I'm a bit surprised at that answer, because some people believe that everything that could happen has already happened, but I'm not getting that. Source is saying no, because consciousness is unlimited, and the ability to imagine is both unlimited and ongoing. It may look as if there is nothing new under the sun, but that is the result of perceptions that haven't truly changed for centuries. However, if we had the ability to truly be in presence, in the present moment, we would be in an eternal and unlimited experience of blissful expressions. Unlimited because God is still thinking! God's mind still has thoughts.

Q. DOES THE FUTURE ONLY HAPPEN BECAUSE OF TIME?

A. Source is saying no, because time is only the result of our thinking. It is there because we are perceiving past, present and future. If we were not thinking past, present and future, there would be no time. Time is a concept that we create by thinking linearly, *i.e.,* horizontally. It's very different than being in the present, which is a vertical or moment-by-moment orientation. If you were truly there, you would not have thoughts of past or future, therefore time would not exist for you.

Q. WHAT IS A MOMENT?

A. Source is giving me an image of a droplet of water. I'm having an experience of it. It's hard to describe, because I feel great amount of energy rushing toward me and surrounding me when I ask this question. This feeling is indescribable and hard to express in a one- or two-word answer, but Source is defining such a moment as pure pleasure, which seems to be the effect of the moment, while the moment itself is an energetic experience. I feel it, but it is hard to explain it. If I start to put an explanation to it, I am not in it anymore, but I will do my best.

It's like being totally and completely aware of yourself. This tremendous energy is coming toward me from all sides, surrounding me, and it feels as if it keeps moving inward toward a center in me. It is concentrated and focused into a center point, where there is a huge awareness not only of self, but also of everything else at the same time. So, the present moment does have a motion to it, because I feel as if I'm moving in, and instead of an outer focus, I am going more inside, which brings me feelings of complete pleasure and bliss. You have to experience it yourself, which you can do just by concentrating on "what is a moment?" which is the question I asked of Source.

There's huge power in this—huge energy and peace. It is as if you're more alive than you've ever been, with an awareness of your existence that is completely internal, but yet you are aware of everything. Because of what I am feeling, I can understand what Source is saying now about how, if you are truly able to be in that presence, the experiences you would have would be completely different. I can see how our focus from past to present to future is a whole other reality system that we've created with our minds, based on a linear view that precludes an experience of a true moment. It is like a camouflage on reality that we create with our minds. I am realizing that the energy coming towards me from every direction is my own energy and personal power returning to me, as I take my focus off the past-present-future!

Q. WILL THERE ALWAYS BE A FUTURE? WILL HUMANITY ALWAYS THINK IN THIS HORIZONTAL WAY, THEREBY CREATING FUTURES?

A. Source is saying that the futures we create may last for a very long time. People like to use their minds in that way. Until we have more people shifting their focus to the present moment, you will see futures created from the past. As we can see, hardly anybody is in the present moment that Source describes, so, you will see our version of futures continue until all people shift their minds to the moment.

When you asked this question, Source was smiling from ear to ear—It thinks it's all grand. If you use your mind to conceptualize a false reality, and you are thinking about the past, present and the future, you are creating scenarios that manifest as those futures. You can create beautiful experiences, or you can create horrible experiences. It's all about the quality of your fears, beliefs, perceptions, consciousness, and all of that collectively as well. This also relates to world events. What we all collectively use our consciousness for does manifest as world events.

Source is still smiling, because It knows it is all one big dream. What we're doing with our consciousness, in terms of the linear way that we do things, is a dream. We create illusions. We create ideas and images, which manifest as events that we call reality. The illusion is that it isn't the reality that Source is describing when we're in the moment. Source's moment is a true reality—a blissful, eternal, pleasurable intention from the mind of God. There is incredible power in it, which we would be experiencing if we were in the moment. In other words, we would be experiencing true creation as Source laid it down.

We don't experience true creation because we have all these concepts that are built on false ideas of reality and God and what we think is important. We teach our children whatever we believe, so that pattern will continue, so long as we continue to use our minds that way. It could end at any moment, if everyone suddenly decided to turn inward to the moment. It could end our dreamscape futures. Think about all the people who are having and raising children with their own beliefs, telling them what reality is, how the world works, how they have to believe in this religion or that, and how a good education is required so they can make money. Such ideas have been handed down for millennia.

The ancients worshipped the sun as God, then they worshipped Nature as God, then they believed that all the Anunnaki gods were the real Gods, and then they worshipped Yahweh, and Jehovah, and on and on it goes. Every time parents teach their children a religious or scientific belief or a military perspective of conquering or protecting a boundary, they are teaching them to co-create the future the same way that they did, so the past repeats itself.

Q. WHAT ABOUT THE FUTURE OF THE EARTH?

A. Source is smiling at this question too, because It's saying, "Now isn't that an interesting game that you've made for yourselves? You can actually destroy this Earth or turn it into a paradise." This is where everything that we've been talking about comes into play. This question might put the whole idea of time in a different view for everybody. Again, our thoughts coalesce into physical events in our world because of centuries of past thoughts, and that takes time. Densification of a thought or manifestation starts with the thought itself. We see cartoons of someone thinking in a little cloud over their head. Think of thoughts and desires as those little clouds—thoughts about anybody or anything. Each little cloud or thought could get energized over and over. If our mass consciousness keeps focusing our attention on particular thoughts or scenarios, the cloud gets bigger and stronger and at some point starts to materialize and coalesce in our 3-D reality. Eventually, it is an event. There is usually what we consider a time lag between what people think and the event that manifests as a result. Because that's the way it is here, something could become a future event in our time frame because of collective past thoughts from a century ago.

This is why we're interjecting the idea of becoming conscious. When you become conscious, you understand that you can de-energize some old thoughts so that their potential manifestation collapses. You collapse time when you do that. You collapse it so you can create a new future through your conscious awareness. But you see, when we are not conscious of our own thoughts, and we're not conscious of ourselves as creators, we will all manifest according to the quality of our collective mass thoughts for positive or negative outcomes on this linear track that could continue far into the future. Now I understand even better what the whole waking-up process really is—it allows us to be keenly aware of our thoughts and change them in the moment. We realize that our thinking will manifest a future in its likeness, which is why there's so much emphasis on examining our beliefs and judgments, what we fear, what we think about, what we worry about, *etc*. We donate those thoughts to the collective consciousness as well as to our own personal futures. Of course, our positive beautiful thoughts get donated too, so do that a lot!

It takes a lot of people changing their mind to truly collapse a mass future event, but then again, I'm hearing that if one person was truly conscious of their power as a creator, they alone could collapse events by changing their thoughts around it. God smiles at our perceptions about the future of the Earth, because it is really determined by what we've been thinking about, which is why it's unfortunate that so many people are focusing on the end of the world—storms, plagues, destruction, bad weather, and Armageddon.

We are witnessing such disasters now, but how long have people been predicting this? You can go back into the 1800s, 1700s, and even well before, and you can find many ancient predictions about what we are experiencing now. When did those fearful thoughts start in people's minds? For how many centuries have people been believing the same sorts of scenarios? People to this day still energize these scenarios from their religious traditions and books, but then it cycles around, the consciousness changes its mind and declares that we don't want the world to end. You can see how people in the past have helped manifest what we are experiencing now, but we can still undo these negative prophecies in our present.

If we are conscious, and we stand up and are aware of this now, we can say "No, no, this is *not* going to be the way it will be." We can use our power to say, "*We are creators*, and this image is *not* the unfolding of events that we would like to see on Earth. We choose this vision instead."

On the first Sunday of every month, I conduct a free group Akashic Records sessions, in which we do a meditative journey to Paradise Earth. We consciously interrupt the mass-consciousness past and present ideas of the end of the world and put our attention on the Paradise Earth that is already in existence on another timeline. Our intention is to merge with that timeline and bring it into our 3-D timeline.

If we are directing or redirecting this new picture that the Earth is a blissful, beautiful place, we are consciously, deliberately interrupting the old paradigm of war and suffering. We can all do things like this. You can do this in your own life as well, but remember that all this is still within the context of the dream. Even creating a positive Earth future is still within the context of our dreaming linearly the past, present and future, whereas, if we were truly in the moment, we would be experiencing something totally different—we'd be in this blissful moment, which would automatically be creating more bliss as the continuing result of our being in the true moment.

A lesson in *A Course in Miracles* says, "My salvation comes from me." In that lesson Source declares that the healed mind does not plan, which is representative of what we're talking about today. We plan because we're afraid of the future, which is why we try to cover ourselves—we're afraid of our future. We don't truly believe that, by being in the moment, we would be continually sustained by the love of God Itself and Its power. In my experience today of being in the moment, I was astonished at the power and peace that rushed toward me, which is a very different view of what we're doing here, and what reality is.

Q. WILL THE U.S. STOCK MARKET CRASH? WHAT'S GOING TO HAPPEN? WILL IT GO UP OR DOWN, AND WHAT'S THE INDICATION FOR STOCK MARKETS IN 2014?

A. You are going to see a rise and a fall, because that is the game. No, I don't see the whole stock market crashing at all. Right now people want improvement, so they will manifest improvement in the stock values. Then you're going to have a group of people who want to manipulate a fall, so they will cause stocks to go down, so it will still be a roller coaster ride. You will see the same ups and downs, but with more "ups."

Q. WILL THERE BE MORE DISEASE, STORMS, OR WARS IN THE U.S.?

A. The way our consciousness is moving, people really don't want any more big wars, as was evidenced by what our consciousness did with Syria. You saw most people saying that they didn't want a war, and by declaring that, war was avoided. I think we're going to see more avoidance of war. As for diseases, it looks to me as if the mass consciousness still has much self-educating to do, because it still believes in things like vaccines and pharmaceuticals. We will keep creating diseases because we have not cleared our consciousness about it, which is really an imbalance within the self. So our consciousness regarding disease still has not changed much, so diseases will persist. The masses are still turning their power over to pharmaceutical propaganda. Consciousness is changing slowly, but as I see the momentum of this change, I still see much ignorance out there about disease.

We take disease too seriously. For example, when a person comes back from the doctor with a diagnosis of cancer, the collective energy around cancer is that it equals death. Most think that someone with cancer will soon die, when the truth is that cancer is toxicity—an imbalance in the system. There are many components to it, but it can be unraveled with self-care, detoxification, and nutritional diligence. There are many alternative therapies, and many people survive.

With regards to storms, we are watching the Armageddon scenario play itself out in the collective mind, but we don't have to. Source has been saying that we don't have to experience more Earth changes—we could immediately see a pristine Earth. We're all creating climate change because of old beliefs that go back hundreds of years. We've all heard that the Earth goes through cycles—a dark age, then a golden age. People say that at the end of 2012 the end of the Mayan calendar was showing the end of the cycle where we have been in our darkest dip. We went to the bottom of the barrel, and now we're moving into this new cycle called The New Golden Age, or the 5th World. We are watching this purification process happen as the old darkness lightens up. These cycles have been going on, up and down like this, for millions of years. What it would be like if we all stopped believing in cycles? What would happen if we all used our consciousness to be in true moments instead? If we were all truly present, there would not be any of these ups and downs, light to darkness and then back again.

There is a correlation between the way we think, what we believe, and what happens historically. Our repeat consciousness is why history repeats itself.

Let's take Nature as an example. We believe that animals killing one another in the wild is just Nature, and that our consuming food is just Nature. Is it fundamentally true that we have to keep killing and consuming, that this is the way Nature is, the way animals are, and the way Nature keeps the balance? Nobody really knows what a mass consciousness living in a true moment would produce for animals and people. Certainly the animal that is being brought down by another and killed is not in a state of bliss—it feels pure fear and is not in God's bliss. So, we have a lot to think about with this. We have a lot to ponder about how we use our consciousness.

Our consciousness creates the future, so as long as we think the above is normal, and this is just the way it is—tides rise and tides fall, people live and die and we accept this as a normal—we will keep creating futures like this.

Going back to the topic about Source and Original Creation, Source was trying to get across to us that we have no idea of the true love power of creation. We don't know what Source's creations of love are. There's an expansive experience that is very different than what we've been doing linearly.

Q. WILL ALIENS MAKE THEMSELVES MORE KNOWN IN THE FUTURE AND IF SO, WHO ARE THEY, AND HOW WILL IT BE MADE KNOWN TO THE MAINSTREAM?

A. Many species of aliens have already been making themselves known. I do think there will be a point in time when more of them will actually come down and interact with us. It is certainly set up that way in our consciousness—we want that. We are gathering momentum from many people who want that. They want the physical appearance of the ETs to interact with them. What the masses want is to be ultimately interacting with beings from other worlds on a daily basis. We are creating that for our future.

You will see more sightings and landings, and they won't be so covert in the sense of the military getting to them first. ETs themselves will be making more appearances to people in the future, and that feels by 2024. I'm not always great with time because remember, we are all creating it as we go along. It could be sooner or later, but it is inevitable, because our consciousness wants it. In terms of governments coming out and revealing that the ETs are real, that's already happening. Disclosure has already begun. People think that the U.S. government is the final authority—if they come out and say it, then we can all believe it—but that's just nonsense. The U.S. will be the last to come out with it because they have the most secrets about it. Other governments have already disclosed information.

Q. CAN WE VISIT THE FUTURE THROUGH MEDITATION OR OTHER MEANS LIKE DREAMS?

A. Yes, you can definitely travel into the future in dreams. One way is to use CDs that teach you how to become a lucid dreamer. This process helps you be awake in the dream state and mold the outcome of the dream while you are in it. Another way is meditation, with the intention of taking a look at your future. Even a psychic reading will give you a heads-up on what kind of future you are manifesting.

Q. WILL WE BE CLEANING UP THE GMO MESS AND ITS ASSOCIATED VIRUSES?

A. There will be improvement. As I see the collective consciousness right now, more people are choosing non-GMO food and taking their food production into their own hands, which is fantastic. But think of how so many people in the world have no awareness that their food has been genetically modified. So many people in this world are just worried about surviving, and they will eat anything, no matter what it is. Many people are on tight budgets, without much income, and, if they have a big family to feed with a low income, they're going to buy cheap food—anything to keep their children's bellies full. So, we still have a big problem around food.

The bigger problem is food distribution in general, which is why Source is talking to us so much about being more community oriented, and starting community gardens, where all participants of the community have access to food—good food, conscious food, non-GMO food. More and more communities are popping up like that, but it's still the minority. It will take time, and it will take more people becoming more responsible and contributing to the health of all of us. As long as we maintain a separatist view, where we're only concerned about our own hunger and our own family, we will not solve the world food problem or the GMO-food issue. We have been making progress, and more people are becoming aware of it, and as long as we keep putting pressure on companies to stop using GMOs, we will continue to succeed.

All that is fantastic. We are making headway, but we still have a long way to go.

Q. CAN WE AFFECT THE OUTCOME OF A MAJOR ILLNESS BY AFFECTING THE PRESENT WITH MORE POSITIVE THOUGHTS?

A. Any time you donate a blessing to a person, you donate more energy, love and power to them that they can use to heal, so you can affect sick people, if they want to be healed. Again we're dealing with another person's consciousness, and some people sicken themselves through their own thoughts, because they want the sickness, or because it's teaching them something. Many factors affect why people get ill. Some people want to get well but just don't have the energy, so whenever you send healing energy to someone, you are donating energy for them to use as they choose. So the answer is yes, you can help people.

Q. In the Future, Will We Have More Activated DNA Strands, and Can We Affect That Now?

A. The more you take time to be in the moment, the more all of that actually happens in the moment. So, again I am going to talk to you from two completely different reality perceptions. To answer your question in the linear perception where we keep our consciousness on past, present and future and we think of our DNA as an evolving process, yes, you can activate more DNA as you change your consciousness and your emotions. They have proven that emotion changes DNA, so, clearing up issues that you know are binding, limiting or confining you will activate other parts of you. Once you free yourself from limiting perceptions, you will create cells and chemicals that reflect your state of mind. Keep in mind that the body responds to your ideas and beliefs, and what you think is possible. We also have help on the linear side in the sense that there are things going on in the cosmos that are stimulating DNA evolution, which is evidenced in the Indigo, Crystal, Golden, and Rainbow children. With their extraordinary gifts and intelligence, these children have more DNA strands active, and this evolution is happening in our linear level of reality.

The next reality perception is when you go into the moment that most of us have not truly experienced—something that may seem unreachable, but only because we haven't focused our attention there yet. If you focus on the moment, and have a experience like what I had today, I can tell you that it will erase the evolution idea and replace it with a timelessness that is eternally creative in likeness to the Divine Will of Source. In linear evolution, you are in time, because it's a perception that we believe in. In contrast, when you're in the moment, you're not in time, so other rules apply.

Conclusion

We began our journey exploring God and Its Creation. Immediately we found that God and love are one and the same and we have nothing to fear. We caught a glimpse of the vastness of Creation and its ever expanding potential. We found that we each have an intimate place in it and that we are all valuable beyond imagination. As we moved down the levels, we explored the process of consciousness and how to become self-aware. We discovered the levels of consciousness and how they can be expressed. We found the role higher beings play in our lives, and we gained an understanding of love. We saw that miracles happen by love and through love.

We extended this understanding into time-space and began to see how the template of original creation patterns Itself through all levels from the spiritual dimensions to the densification into form. It looks after us in our dreams and sustains us while we perceive ourselves so far from Home. At every level there is a ladder taking us up, out and in, ensuring our safety on our journey. The same light and love that is Source coalesces into an array of colors and music to form our bodies as we shape ourselves with our consciousness. Its life impulses beat our hearts, Its breath is our rhythm, Its aliveness carries on our body functions while we play with creation.

And then one day we come to it. We wake up and remember we are It, the I AM. The memory was there all along, through every lifetime and dimension, waiting to be discovered. It was everywhere. In our hearts and minds, in our bodies as the sleeping flame of kundalini waiting to be awakened, waiting to ascend the ladder leading Home. Spiraling through the chakra wheels, dancing in celebration, arriving, purifying, becoming... alive.

About the Author

AINGEAL ROSE O'GRADY

Aingeal (Ann-gail) Rose O'Grady was born on November 11th, 1953 in Plattsburg, New York. Her given name was Gail Anne, which was changed to Aingeal in 2006. Her heart's desire when she was young was to marry and raise children.

She has fulfilled that dream with her three beautiful children, Clayton, Brooke, and Janai and her delightful granddaughter, Grace Rose.

Aingeal's spiritual journey began when she was just 19 after the tragic death of her first husband three months after their wedding. She dedicated herself to finding the answers to the deepest spiritual questions by journeying into the mysteries of the spirit world, while exploring consciousness and its expansive potential. She spent years meditating and being taught by Archangel Raphael, who took her on many journeys into other worlds and planes of existence. She went on to study the works of J. Krisnamurti, Sondra Ray, the Science of Mind and *A Course in Miracles*.

During the past 40 years she has acquired certifications in numerous healing modalities including Reiki (all levels to Master Teacher), Psychic Laser Therapy (a form of psychic surgery), Hypnotherapy including past life regression, Rebirthing, Kathara Healing, the Christopher Method Sound Healing and Cellular Re-patterning. She had a thriving healing practice in Illinois for 12 years and taught her skills to many teachers and students alike. Today Aingeal teaches The Authenticity Workshop, How To Read the Akashic Records, Transformational Writing, the Tarot, Beginning,

Intermediate and Advanced as well as Healing with the Tarot. She holds spiritually focused Akashic Group sessions online from San Diego, California and Ireland. She has been a reader of the Akashic Records privately for over 20 years and has been interviewed on radio shows worldwide including Coast-to-Coast AM with George Noory.

As a seasoned spiritual teacher, Aingeal delights in facilitating the awakening of consciousness in her clients and students. Personal freedom, realizing the God within, loving and respecting all life everywhere is the goal.

Aingeal is the author of the Honest-To-God Series of books, which includes *A Time of Change* and *The Nature of Reality*. She is author of *Tarot for Beginners* and numerous spiritual eBooks based on spiritual topics. The recordings of her Group Akashic sessions can be purchased from her website: http://worldofempowerment.com

Address all inquiries to

Wild Flower Press
Post Office Box 1429
Columbus, NC 28756
or visit
http://Granite-Planet.net

GRANITE PUBLISHING, POB 1429 COLUMBUS NC 28722 828-894-8444	**SOLID GROUND IN A SHIFTING WORLD**
WILD FLOWER PRESS:	**DOCUMENTING THE UNEXPECTED**

A Time of Change: Akashic Guidance for Spiritual Transformation	Vol. I of the Honest to God Series by Aingeal Rose O'Grady		

SWAN-RAVEN & CO.:	**ANCIENT WISDOM IN MODERN TIMES**

So, We're Still Here. Now What? Spiritual Evolution and Personal Empowerment in a New Era	by Gwilda Wiyaka, Galactic Shamanism Practitioner		

NOT MADE BY HANDS.COM:	**COSMIC ENERGY ESSENCES**

Not Made By Hands: Energy Water from out of this world	Collected by Barbara Lamb Decoded by Aingeal Rose O'Grady via the Akashic Records		

GRANITE PUBLISHING:	**HTTP://GRANITEPUBLISHING.US**

Common Sense in Uncommon Times: Survival in a Changing World	Brian L. Crissey and Pamela Meyer Crissey		
Aingeal Rose O'Grady http:// aingeal-rose.com		Join our mailing list for updates and more information:	

Made in the USA
Charleston, SC
30 May 2014